The Always Present

Present

To Muriel and Leonard
from
T and Renée
Weiss

Theodore & Renée Weiss

Letters – Poems
The Always Present Present

QUARTERLY REVIEW OF LITERATURE
& SHEEP MEADOW BOOK

All inquiries and permission requests should be addressed to:
  The Sheep Meadow Press
  P. O. Box 1345
  Riverdale-on-Hudson, NY 10471

Designed and typeset by The Sheep Meadow Press.
Distributed by The University Press of New England.

Printed on acid-free paper in the United States. This book
meets the guidelines for permanence and durability of the
Committee on Production Guidelines for Book Longevity of
the Council on Library Resources.
Library of Congress Cataloging-in-Publication Data

Weiss, Theodore Russell, 1916-2003
  The always present present : letters, poems / Theodore &
Renée Weiss.
    p. cm.
  ISBN 1-888545-45-3 (hardcover alk. paper)
  ISBN 1-931-375-18-8 (pbk. alk. paper)
  1. Weiss, Theodore Russell, 1916---Correspondence. 2.
Poets, American--20th century--Correspondence. 3. Editors-
-United States--Correspondence. 4. Marriage--Poetry. I.
Weiss, Renée Karol. II. Title.
  PS3545.E4735Z48 2005
  811'.54--dc22
                              2005003786

T & R
THE PRESENT

*R: Our anniversary deserves a special
present?*

*T: Rather than a trinket beaded out
of flashy stones, something lively
we'll create together, unique
and wholly living.*

R: A gift that will grow out of us?

*T: Yes, a present, out of all our past,
to keep us constant memory.*

*R: But you
haven't said what that should be.*

*T: Bee's the word. Or words like bees
ever in-tense. Plucking them out
of air, we'll string them—*

*R: words
or bees?—*

*T: together, each ahum,
into one melody.*

*R: Humm. A composition.
Sounds appealing. But how, beyond
their buzz, did bees get into this?*

*T: Words, much airier than bees,
but like them thrumming side by side,*

also contrive a honey-brimming hive.

R: A cluster of ambrosial words!
Still if they're as airy as you say,
how long can they cling fast to us?

T: As long as we depend on breath.

R: But how long before they sting?

T: As long as we agree to agree.

R: A risky delicacy!

T: While it lasts, this present lasts
forever. Roused by a breath—

R: Sleeping
Beauty waking to a kiss?—

T: in turn
inspiring the breather, such present
presents an always present present.

R: Isn't that a bit too lumbersome
for winged things?

T: Such weightiness,
such wittiness, must also be stamped
by winter bedding down, by earthquakes,
wars, by holocausts.

R: But most of all,
by friends and family storming through?

T: *Yet loving too. So flavored, words*
spread, a preserve, over everything.

R: *The earth one heaped up, savory dish!*

T: *I give you what,*
honeycombed by your lips, you give me:
a present celebrating our sixty years.

R: *A present, fraught in the past, made*
not only of the said,

R: *but the unsaid,*

T: *as well as the unsayable.*

CONTENTS

PRELUDE

After more than a half century of jointly editing the Quarterly Review of Literature, it seemed to us inevitable that we should move on to composing poems together. The present collection celebrates Ted's long life of letters and poetry, and celebrates more than sixty years of our marriage.

The poetry is accounted for. Opportunely, the letters accompanying the poetry, I think, justify themselves. Ted had written them to me at our beginning. Although the letters are Ted's, they reveal us both more intimately than any portrait could. The letters offer a poetic record of the first stages of a love affair that began in the 1940's. At the same time, they give an intimate view of the joys and terrors of the war years, and of love over a lifetime.

I have happy memories of our giving joint readings in various cities and countries—a night in Princeton, where we encountered flashing lights, helicopters overhead, sirens screaming—it seemed for joy—in the midst of a bank robbery next door, which I now remember as farce amid our joyous, lucky and tragic lives.

Renée Weiss

~ 1 ~

October 17, 1939

Liebling,

Only after you left did I realize how wrong it was for me to agree to your speaking to my parents about us; there was no reason in the world for your assuming any risk of humiliation. It was as though we had been guilty of some mean or criminal deed!

My parents, sorry to say, refused to swallow the smallest fraction of our story. Carefully in a letter I received this morning Mother plotted the career of our "ignoble" actions. Who knows what she means by "ignoble"? Your age? You're too young! You're the girl. The next-door girl? The money? If you were rich, would you be "noble"? She wrote to let me know they are aware of "all that is going on." But I assure you, Renee dear, there is nothing in this to disturb you. In a way it is for the best that the whole matter is out; at least no further suspicions exist. They know that you are visiting me in New York. In addition, Mother promises to bother me no more (!) with such business. Strangely enough, my dear, their letter troubled me much less than I had thought it would; perhaps subconsciously I had been preparing myself for it.

Since they have given you no sign of resentment, you, I need not tell you, had best simulate ignorance of their true sentiments & continue your relationship as before. But enough of such distasteful trivialities.

Saturday was a period of listening to the echoes of the day before. One of the most memorable moments living has given me was the seemingly simple one in the railroad station when you rested your head upon my shoulder, as graceful & complete a moment as I have experienced in a long time. So it has imprisoned within the web of my memory all that the light of that moment saw fit to fall upon: the little boy with the Catholic chances, the young girl on the bench across the way watching us furtively, the Jewish woman with the Hershey Bar, the little girl who first had water & no cup & then the cup but no water. Since then, save for recollection, my feelings & thoughts have been at lowest ebb. I've neither cup nor water. And no Hershey Bar that would do.

And here I am, locked away in this Columbia cubby-hole, soliloquizing!

~

T & R
ROOM

This room fits so tightly
not any stratagem—no, not
if a rain let down its ladder
or the sun, its Rapunzel stream—
can get him out of it.
               Welcome
a roach, a rat, a swooping bat
to breach the solid, silent,
screaming space?
             The mirror
lours emptiness.
             Once swept
along, a tidy sea, this book,
now in a dead calm rebellious,
is jabbering away.

And air
box-like nailed together, this
room turns its window inside
out.
    Try the door?
                       It screaks
open onto another, another,
endless, deadend corridors.

But see.
      Through the slot
a letter slips.
           He rips it
open.
      Breath, knotted to a hair,
puffs out.
        Her fingers pressing
hard against the words,
her voice sounds through.

At once the room fills up
with room. He is, is everywhere.

~

October 24, 1939

    Your letter, Liebchen, came just in time. Despite my
questioning the advisability of our corresponding, I've chafed
at your no-word. O, I know it's unreasonable, but— I was all
ready to send you a note saturated with the anger-pique
brewing in my brain since Saturday. Even though your dear
letter relieves the situation entirely, I am still writing you
some of the thoughts that formed then.

    Look, Love, I understand how hard it is: so little happens: the routine of daily existence is so unimportant: you don't know what to write: these matters wouldn't interest him, etc. Or am I doing you an injustice again? If there is one truth I want to impress upon you this year it's this—I am not interested in you, My Dear, as a profundity; nor do I want you as a philosophy or a vocabulary. These I can get galore in books. Such is only my parents' idea of what a "woman" should mean to me. For god's (& mine too!) sake, send me you! Show me you are living; give me some crumbs of your life: brush your teeth, eat breakfast, read books, walk to school, practice the violin in letters—anything, only write to me.

Frankly I do not care what you say & how you say it as long as YOU say it. I would even gladly receive plain gossip! As you realize, there is never a dearth of material, only a dearth of you or me: the world, the earth, the sky, people are just as rich today as in Shakespeare's time. Only you & I are poor in seeing them, feeling them, thinking them. Your life is not dull—I assure you, it's the most exciting thing you'll ever know—& every day, every hour, every moment is altogether different from the next. If, as you do, you admit the validity of this platitude, then there must be something wrong with you (& me). We are not wholly awake to the world flowing around us. My Dear, prove to me that I am correct & at the same time underestimating you.

You see, Dear, this feeling I have for you is something like art: when I've grown intimately fond of some poet, Hopkins or Stevens say, I'm not so much concerned with the ideas they're expressing as that I'm hearing their inimitable voices once more. If these voices are saying words filled with a thought that pleases me in its novelty or striking truth, I take this as an additional delight, but one not essential to my initial pleasure. So, my Love, tell me about high school, your violin lessons, your brother, your sister, Allentown's Town Hall meetings, tell me about your reading, but tell me!

Like a delighted idiot, my face is aglow with the fact that my parents invited you to supper. You may even have to make a fine violinist out of my sister with those special coaching lessons you're giving her before my parents will be convinced of your sincerity—& virtue!

My life here moves slowly. I know I should be studying for my exams but other things come first! The pile of rejection slips grows. Last week I received a "lovely" letter from *The New Yorker* telling me what an "impressive batch" of poems I had sent them, but none was really "right for us." It doesn't dishearten me very much—especially when I receive a letter from you. Immediately on the heels of that rejection I sent them another poem. O, we'll break through the magic circle yet! Never fear. And here's one of the rejectees, which, despite *The New Yorker*, "impresses" me still.

Imagine it: a timeless summer day,
Leda playing with the willing water,
her thoughts as vague and easy as the waves.
Desire, spying her, having no mouth
with which to kiss, seizes
the nearest thing and softest to sidle
up to Leda with: the swan, vague, white
and billowy as her thoughts: she
might accept it casually as a dream,
the whiteness of the bed
she spends night in: and then
it is upon her like a wave;
she shrieks with joy and passion
awakened by the ecstatic blow,
but only then she knows
by desire she's been deeply laved,
wave that eventually would wreck
an entire nation's pride and glow
and ring a resounding golden bell

through time's eternal flow.

My Hopkins M.A. thesis progresses by leaps & bounds or, more accurately, starts & stutters. I've passed the 200 page mark in it; fortunately I'm rapidly approaching the end. I do hope to have it finished soon.

October 27, 1939

Liebchen, may I tell you to be proud, ask you to share the pride your letter produced in me? Lovely letter! It brings you nearer in the rain now than any thought I've had of you since I came back to Columbia. It strings a singing garland of birds around my head—or is it the joyful blood drumming in my ears? That it should be able to slip you, even a fraction of you, through the sentinels of distance! Dearest, I kiss its every word as I would kiss your fingers, your eyes, your lips, your every inch of body, & finally your you.

The Garden you describe? Liebchen, we've already begun to get whiffs of its flowers! So strong is your image, in my mind, almost involuntarily my arms come round to embrace you & my lips form the contours of a kiss.

You cannot have known how many mornings this summer when I was home I imagined walking with you to school, & then sat waiting hours impatiently on the porch for your return. The price of living—& loving—next door!

Your studies, particularly the drudgery-end of them, let me say from long & wearing experience, are irrelevant, most of them, save as you find inner passion for them, a desire to steep your whole person in them. No study means anything in itself, except as you are willing to give yourself, yes, yield yourself, to it. Then that study, no matter what it may be: railroads, recipes, or the variety of whistle-sounds, becomes wholly important, helping you to hints of your own personal truth. Study, as you have discerned, is really self-discovery: getting to & exploring yourself for yourself. Or, as you say, finding the Garden.

Your words on Poe please me immensely, start the weaving of several patterns in my brain. Poe, though in himself not a very attractive personality, except for those characteristics which make him seem child-pathetic, has much significance. Perhaps not in himself, but as the impotent papa of a large sector of modern poetry. Baudelaire—one of the great 19th-century poets—declared, after his first perusal of Poe, that, to his happiness & horror too, Poe had in many ways anticipated him, often to the exact word, & that reading him was like talking to himself if, one would have to say, at a more mature, more articulate stage. (Baudelaire of course soon surpassed the heights—& depths—of Poe.) In short, Poe—both in theory & practice—is partly responsible for symbolism. (You remember I tried to define it for you, lamely enough, last summer in one of our "innocent" discussions on the porch.) Thus, paradoxically, though not too much in himself, the ripples & currents Poe started are in some particulars of paramount significance. It is interesting: a fairly minor figure (Pater was another such) initiating a major change, if not a revolution.

Baudelaire translated Poe so superbly his translations are generally considered superior to the originals. I sometimes think what we need are translations of the French translations of Poe by Baudelaire, Mallarmé, & others back into English so that we might get some better sense of what these great poets found in Poe.

Ironically enough, Poe's direct influence in America has been negligible; on the continent, however, poets fed on Poe's theories & works; so, via Pound, Eliot, MacLeish, & other students of these French poets, Poe has seeped into modern American poetry.—Forgive this lecture, Dear. It seems as though the very thought of teaching has already catapulted me into pedagogy!

You SHOULD dislike Poe's stories or at least be disturbed by them: that was, as you say, precisely the effect he desired. You tell me you wish to grow out of fear. I reply, it is only by growing into it that we overcome it. Not so much Poe, but the men who followed him, understanding this, deliberately entered into the very heart of horror. They realized that only by becoming intimate with it would horror cease to be horrible. But what a strenuous assignment that is! In the main even Baudelaire failed here.

(The rain is talking louder now; huge bold drops jump through my open window onto this page as though eager to read & read aloud what I'm writing. I find myself writing faster & faster to keep up with the rain's cadence & its prompting curiosity as well.)

But a later German poet much influenced by Baudelaire, Rainer Maria Rilke, had the spirit-strength & fortitude to endure horror's most severe weather & so gradually to relish its most oppressive conditions. Dearest, anything life can do to us has in it some roots of joy. O I know I've not believed this in my actions: that is the weakness of the clay, my manifestation of it.

Can I still say this, you may well ask, with all the daily monstrosities going on in the world at large. Because of them, I insist, we should wring every drop of sweetness out of the pleasures of being alive; & then take on pain & terror too. In those moments when our emotions—pleasant & unpleasant, physical & mental—involve us most are we most alive. The cowardice of fear hinders growth. These last few weeks I have even come to understand a little more thoroughly, & therefore honor, death.

Dear, you & Rilke led me through the desert of my first few weeks here, gave me strength to confront full-panoplied solitude & the wolves of my mind. Please continue to do so.

I'm glad you're beginning psychology. Freud belongs to those few who have remarked for us the infinite worlds of the mind & the heart & have made us a little more aware of the wonder of the human being. By increasing the wonder, the knowledge of it, they have reduced the horror.

I'm pounding the mags all right, but they're pretty stubborn. I've received another personal letter from *The New Yorker*. Please! please! send us MORE poems. I have several out right now. Every rejection seems to spur me on to new poems. What an adorable muse! At this rate I'm bound to be prodigiously productive! And a poem just for you:

OF
What color do I think of
when I think of you? Orchid?
Chestnut, leafy green? as you
pirouette out of that little park
toward me.
        A lyric air soars
through the tangled underbrush:
a cheering, most emphatical, of you.

Streets, with dawns mirroring,
nights shimmering the stippler
rain, what do they come to
but enabling me to follow you,
like hollyhocks bent toward
a secret radiance.
        O smart
they are, and every thing,
of you, the clambering smoke
so telling, squinty windows
goggle-eyed.

Yet this room wobbles on the brink
of a whirling chaos.
        Still strength

the winsomeness of you commands,
I know by how much of that chasm
I have—for sundry colors,
every sound, declaring you—
so far, survived.

November 7, 1939

A gray cold morning—the kind that smoothes down its robes & prepares itself to receive the visitor snow. A gray cold morning, My Love, inside as well. Eight o'clock & a holiday (Election Day), breakfast eaten, & thousands of insistent pages waiting to be read & memorized, & I here with not the slightest desire to read any of them. The thesis waiting to be revised & recopied & I distinctly finished with it weeks ago.

A propos de rien, my professor liked the section I gave him. As he put it, "I'm very enthusiastic about it." More, he suggested I write it in book rather than thesis form. But that was a week ago & so too distant to warm me. I sit here in this morning—happily, intimations of the sun, coming around the corner, begin to gild the weatherbeaten rustcoated watertanks squatting like blankfaced statues on the roofs across the street—hoping to pluck some meaning out of it for you & me.

I've actually begun to study, Liebling; right now I'm plowing through the poetry of Tennyson. Reason enough for being depressed! Such a superb technician & such a sloppy intellect! He's brought home to me more convincingly than ever how very far I still have to go in craftsmanship; but much more important, he's made me realize how absurd it is for the poet to meddle in matters (problems, etc.) & write about them pontifically & prophetically if he refuses to familiarize himself with them thoroughly.

Because of such failings, there's little stability in his

verse; almost never does he make me feel at home, of being at one with a root truth as Rilke does or Browning. Possessed of no real sense of proportion, he was a victim now & again of halfbaked thoughts, commonplace sentiments & ideals. Now that I've expressed myself on Tennyson & delivered myself of the necessary bit of lecture, perhaps I can go on to write to YOU.

You speak of your Music Club &, even better, of faces. But why didn't you collect & send a couple to me? I'm much interested in them too. Let me give you a little of Rilke on faces.

"...it has never occurred to me before how many different faces there are. There are quantities of people, but there are even more faces, for each person has several. (The reverse could also be said: There are only a few basic faces, passed on from person to person, one generation to the next.) There are some who wear the same face for years: naturally it wears out; it gets dirty, it splits at the folds, it stretches, like gloves one has worn on a journey. These are thrifty, simple folk; they do not change their face; they never even have it cleaned.... The others? Since they have several faces, what do they do with the others? They keep them. Their children will wear them. But sometimes, too, it happens that their dogs go out with them on. And why not? Faces are faces. There are others who change their faces in uncannily rapid succession, and wear them out.... Scarcely have they reached forty when behold, they have come to the last of them...worn through in a week, [it] has holes in it...and then gradually the lining—the no-face—comes through, and they go about with that."

And here we are face to face with our problems! You ask when I'll be coming home for Thanksgiving. With you the only real reason & my parents there like the wall that separates our two houses, why come home at all? To cause you-me (& them too) unhappiness & pain? Seeing you a little will only hurt a lot & make Columbia a little more impossible.

O, but I want to see you & I will! It's not that I'm unhappy;
it's just that I'm not as happy as I might be, as happy as I have
been. So the bittersweets of our summer.

~

T & R
A COMPANY

Glancing in the mirror, you catch
glimpses of
      "My self? Her self?
Him self? All those other Them selves?"

Most, long dead, yet avid after pieces
of your dreams, jostle one another.

There she is, "Mother." Just behind
her, intently overseeing, "Father,"
strong-willed aunts, docile uncles,
and great-grandparents,
              "reeling me
back to a runty, scruffy ancient,
his rages hopping up and down."

Like wrangling winds let loose,
they clamor at your ears. Pulling
on a sweater,
      "Mother's gnarled
fingers warming in it still,
Father's concern cross-stitching it,
I throw my arms around them all."

This body of yours a gobetween,
your heart a highway many-laned,
you steer them to the garden,
basking in the sun.
                    "The maple
mother bought substantial now,
its young leaves—an easy breath
among them—sway together,"
                              as they,
joining mother, father, and the rest,
encompass you with murmurings.

"Together we host the morning,
host this early spring," gossiping
the same old, new-as-ever news.

With squawky triplets and a mate,
tenants of your guesthouse flowerpot,
a wren
        "is it the one we welcomed
years ago?"
            in a rage of singing
bobbles on a brandnew twig.

~

November 10, 1939

My Lovely, there's nothing wrong. Simply this, I had
no envelopes & no money to buy them. So there your letter
lay on my desk waiting for its proper reader. But the thought
did occur to me that, long as she takes to answer, here, acci-
dentally & not because I wish it, she'll have a dose of her
own medicine. And you didn't like it. Neither do I. Let this
be a lesson to both of us.

If I'm incoherent it's because I slept at the Schuberts last night which means I didn't sleep at all. Talk about creative debauchery! I couldn't feel more shaky & ecstatically exhausted than I do after a verbal todo with David. I wish-wish-wish you could meet David & Judy. I wish-wish-wish you were here.

And here I have hundreds of ruthless books clamoring to be read & thousands of miles of sleep to climb over before I can get to the awakeness necessary to read them. And what are we going to do about Thanksgiving? (At least, thanksgivingly, Roosevelt has won!)

November 16, 1939

Me too, Renee Dear. When you come to me in your letters I seem to drop the dross of me, & my spirit, possessed of wings, soars easily & gaily toward the sun. But gradually, as I travel farther & farther away from the time of your letter's arrival, I grow heavier & duller, a wretched burden to myself. Moroseness becomes the prevailing mood.

You speak of the multiplicity of your emotions; with me it's not so much emotions as moods; they come fast & furious these days—some rainbow-hued, light & frolicsome as wind, but others envelop me like tar; sticky & foul-tasting, they smother all spirit out of me. Why the latter? Because your letters are so many days away from me, the miles & miles involved in your receiving this, answering it, & sending your answer off; more, because I know YOU are so many days away. And even when I come home I think of the pain I may cause you. Thus the tar-mood masters me.

But, Liebchen, I've just about reached the point where I no longer consider, with such great compunction, the possibility of my engendering pain for others. If I augment the fund of feelings in my loved ones, I do not think I am committing a great wrong. As I suggested some letters ago, all emotions, even unpleasant ones, enlarge (or should) the person entertaining them. But perhaps this is one big rationalization. Please do not understand me to say that I intend to set out to produce as much pain as possible in those I love. This I DO say: it is our duty to act as stage to as profound feelings as we are capable of—our duty & our joy. The writers I've been reading keep insisting on pulling the curtains back all the way. And at any price, at least to their characters.

When you tell me of your violin lesson & suggest I have had a hand in it, you please me vastly. If only you can learn to play with your heart, rather than your hands. Once you have fully found your heart I believe you will do so. If you sing out your violin will have to also.

I'm no longer shipping poems out, not because I'm discouraged. On the contrary, it's because I realize I have many things to learn. The more work I do the more I discover I have to do, & O so rapidly the time grows shorter. Locking my mind to such thoughts as best I can, I plug away.

But I've hogged a whole letter. Please write right away & send me as much of you as you can spare. Fortunately feelings have no dimensions. Send as much as you like & no one will notice a shortage in you. Rather, paradoxically, the more you dispatch to me, the more, you'll learn to your surprise, you have left.

This Chinese stationery I'm writing on I received from my good friend, Yun Hsia. Even the envelop, you see, becomes a landscape of one big tree ready to deliver its leaf—& fruit—of a letter,

But, Liebchen, Carlyle is waiting & I've exposed you to enough stupid musings. I will see you soon.

Dec. 14, 1939

Just back from a mellifluous breakfast of orange juice. I've been on the trail of oranges for some time. I've a growing conviction they & their fellow fruits have more to tell than anyone has yet realized—even Rilke who enjoins us to "dance the oranges." So I come to you straight from a lovely grove of orange trees: most appropriately the Florida in me.

But I've another emotion to report. When I returned to Columbia, & the days immediately after, I found, to my wonder & worry, that my Renee-feeling was pursuing a career quite unique for it. I, a person of ups & downs, discovered that the emotion had become most equable & even, I then thought, slack. Was my old fickleness— which I had warned you of—& my tendency to spread my feelings rather than concentrate them setting in? O not that I didn't think of you: all the time, but the frame around you was cool & steady rather than heated & frenzied.

But for days you didn't write; & silence began to do its work, till lo! one morning I woke all excited & perturbed once more. The explanation? Up to the time of the letter-worry a certainty had set in. But the no-writing, growing more & more positive, disconcerted this certainty.

Christmas has troubled me considerably. My first impulse, strengthened by your letter's paragraph about your going to Newark with your parents, was to remain in N.Y.— largely to give my parents the dose of discipline they expect of me. But I can't be that cruel, much as I mean to them & they to me. Please try your best to dissuade your parents from going to Newark.

Your "Democracy in Poetry" paper much interests me. Perhaps, if you wish, we can discuss it. I've a well-established stock of notions, not to say some original clichés, on the subject. And even though you decide to use none of them, they may provide you with clues to your own position.

If I come to Allentown, we'll see each other, of course, but I fear in a roundabout way. I hate to resort to subterfuges, especially in something as near & dear to me as this; but I raise my hands helplessly.

~

T & R
ROUNDABOUT

A wall away. Shall he,
mustachioed like the milkman,
come to deliver his stuff?
Or a burglar sneaking in
ready to steal the goods?

Maybe she could scale
down a string of notes
and make her escape
into his arms.

What's this roundabout about?
The thief of love making off
with the queen of hearts?
All this, just a wall,
a world, away.

~

January 14, 1940

A Lovely Sunday Morning Rain...

Remember, Dear One, ever since I returned to Columbia in October & before I had been a seething mess: dejection continuously combating my more positive, cheerful nature; it seemed as though I had lost my grip on my lifeline & at times were fighting for dear (& not so dear) life. Reasons? Of course the obvious ones, those I've enumerated to you many times: you, the uncertainty of my position— getting a job & writing well enough even to satisfy myself. And then the world's uncertainties, with the horrors loose in it.

What do I mean by "you"? My appreciation of the fickleness of feelings, my anguish at leaving you, & the impossible attitude of my parents expecting me to be absolutely concentrated on my studies and nothing else. These reasons, believe me, were strong enough to paralyze most of my actions & thoughts. This led me to the brink of the greatest of negations: suppose I achieve everything I wish? What then? I, such a vociferous yea-sayer, was of a sudden confronted by the worst of scepticisms: the shallowness of life & denial of its value. Everything—certainly this fly-speck of a life—crumbles, & one, with his proud emotions & mighty thoughts, in a second's blink will like a mist have been blown away.

A most unhealthy outlook, you say, My Dear? By all means! But the reasons I offer you above & offered myself then are very superficial ones. Briefly, I was full of fears &, worst of all, terribly soft. I had reached the point where I was content to characterize myself a romantic; at the least provocation I would launch a most prodigious defense of romanticism, especially what I called the good variety.

In truth, Dear, most of us are too small & too weak to enjoy the fruits our times have to offer. Our day, no worse, I suspect, than many others, also holds out to us unusual emancipation, are we but strong enough to accept it—release from superstitions & everything that acts as a barrier between us & real living. Your father believes this. That speech he gave his friends on Bertrand Russell makes it clear. What does our age ask of us & what does it offer? In a word, strength! This is the end-all & be-all of existence.

Forgive me, Dearest, for being so long-winded—the only kind of wind I seem to know! But I feel this to be of utmost importance to me & to you too. But I stop abruptly. My exams are due the 24th & 25th; there's nothing I could desire more than to see you before then—to reassure me. This after all the above huffing & puffing about strength!

~

T & R
HUNGER

He lectured guests—
on Bertrand Russell, Einstein,
Norman Thomas:—
his business crowd,
the neighbors, family, friends.
Or struck the happy chords
accompanying
his children, strangers,
a promising young talent.

Insatiable, he feted guests
with cold cuts, cakes and wine,
and with his jokes dispelled
their astonished looks:
"I'll match you two to your every one."

Rehearsed, he headed for a bigger
stage: to make a juster world.
A capital socialist, a pugnacious
pacifist, a consecrated non-believer,
he fought for workers and good wages,
against the terrible cost of war,
against the bloodiness of faiths.

~

February 8, 1940

I just take off ten minutes, Liebling, from the endless application blanks for a job to tell you how much I miss you. Seems, Sweets, you've become an indispensable ingredient in my happiness. I go around looking for a comfortable corner in Columbia, but all I discover is jagged edges monotony, & misery. Odd that the so-called calm & contemplative (academic) life can so readily mask a seething inside. But I find plenty of company for my misery: I can't think of a single instance of real happiness here. No wonder I envy my Allentown being (parents & all!) with you. Returning to N.Y. this way becomes more & more distasteful every time. But I'm certain (I hope!) that in a short while, what with letters rolling in from you (?) & my memory functioning in orderly fashion, I'll adjust myself once more. But how are you?

The morning I left I lived in the window waiting for you. At last at 8:10 you came out. I tapped on the glass. You must have heard something, for you hesitated, looked about, then took yourself out of my sight. Windows can make wonderful frames to pictures thereafter among memory's fondest & most vivid. And poems!...

MY ABSENT YOU

Someway desperately
out of a lopsided desk and chair,
a wobbly chest of drawers,
some old-friend books,
a letter laden with looks
and repeated fingerings,
four/five tattered memories,
bent and dirty as a pack
of busy playing cards,
and this gray day,
doing itself in rain,
its mood and gesture blue,
I must make my absent you.
And maybe presently
some snow will come along
to help, and an idea or two.

~

February 10, 1940

Another fine morning, rain falling in sprays of silver dust. Wonderful what one can do with a letter. Take this last one I received from you; I remove it from my mailbox in a glow of anticipation, admire it in its neat white little jacket, pat it on its fat little white belly (the fatter it is the better I like it), & take it in to dinner with me. For the moment I put it aside, thinking to keep it for dessert, but no it yammers to be read. All fresh in my hand like a just-picked orange, it waits for the hungry mouth to suck out its feeling & meaning. The rattle of dinner utensils, the clatter of plates, the mumble of male voices, the accents of recorded jazz swimming around me, I open the letter &, for a moment, instead of removing it, slip into the envelope, like walking through the looking glass. I open the sheets, become the sides of a tent, I deep inside, shielded from all sight & sound; I live in these thin pages, these inked words, these recorded feelings & thoughts—for the present my whole & only world. So whenever I feel blue (or any color you like), I take that letter out &, living in it, begin to feel much better.

But your lines were the kind to write answers to endlessly. You hear a noise that sounds like a tap or a telephone ring? I go around looking for a wall to tap on, a telephone to ring! Tapping on a wall, like the one between us in Allentown, inevitably reminds me of Shakespeare. Do you suppose that evening we read the parts of Romeo and Juliet at your house, your father assigning the main roles to us, started our whole affair? So we (my parents!) could say your father! was behind it all? Did he appreciate then what the consequences might be? And does he now?!

As for "the attitude I don't want," there too I must qualify. Such an attitude, stressing as it does our natures as natural, I cannot consider the whole truth: though I said man needs no more reasons for living than, say, a tree, nowhere did I say that we were not human beings or of the human race. And as such, in the usual relationship of person to person, there is no better, saner, more salutary attitude than the one you mention. Most people (fortunately) do, should, & must live in the human world. So you & I. And this is a world, I suppose, made justifiable in the main only when we live with reason, as you say, & the reason each other. And not at gun point.

You speak of a philosophy; being as content as possible, accepting life as it is, are as much the fundamentals of a philosophy as those entertained by many intelligent & sophisticated thinkers. But, it's true, such a life is not enough for me: I too retain a touch of the reformer—as you, with a socialist father behind you, do even more. Loving this life as much as I do, I want to help make it lovelier & for all.

Major philosophies, like religions, ARE attractive for the wholeness, the coherence, they propose. In them all things are accounted for & so become meaningful beyond themselves. The trouble is that in its very containment such a philosophy can become a prison. It tells us what things are but only as it sees, so limits, them in its larger context. Beyond itself what does a lark mean, a much fissured rock, a waterfall, however scribbled? Being what they are IS their meaning.

No, I had not finished my thesis, & I still haven't, but—with a little less "philosophy"—will (praise de Lord!) in a few days.

~

T & R
A LITTLE WOOD

Our old neighbor,
the ornithologist, kept
that little wood, last
stand of sycamore and
locust, from the forest
which once fulfilled
this land.
        Kept here mid-
town to ensure the birds,
opossums, flocks of deer
their browsing rights,
unharried tenantry.

And kept for our sakes,
a modest sampling
of this country's past,
each dawn accompanied,
each feathery dusk,
with trills echoing
among the wood-winds
every breeze inspired.
The old man dying,
tree-and-grassy kin
attended to this wood,
the elements, and—some
warble luring—the two
of us.
          Then one early dawn
screeches tore the sky.
Before the day was done
the wood had disappeared.

Now, while winds hiss
through, as of tongues
plucked out, a lone blue
jay, fixed on a stump
like a moment's monument,
looks and looks on all
the toppled, empty scene.

As little as it chirrups
or complains, bewildered
it must be, bewildered
past extremities of pain.

~

February 18, 1940

I hope, My Dearest, you have forgiven (even better, forgotten) my crazy phonecall. The Weisses, seeing me at my brooding best, insisted I call. I started at 9:30 & continued at half-hour intervals, accumulating all sorts of fantastic fears. Thus, when you did finally answer, all I could do was stutter incoherently. Given three minutes & I ask over & over "how are you"!

But let me tell you a little more about my friends the Weisses. Imagine meeting another Weiss, unrelated except as his father is also a Hungarian, with a wife called Renee! And one continuing to work on a thesis on Thomas Wolfe, something I had originally thought to do till I wearied of him. Paul is an honest-to-god, quick & free-tongued fellow: realistic, with a warm, embracing laughter & a most comfortable personality. Few people I can be at home in as well as I can with him.

Renee is an innocent, gentle, kind little person, with one major passion—her husband. Like a number of Jewish women I have known (& other kinds too!), she gives me the feeling she lives wholly-solely for him. And they are happy.

They have been excessively kind to me, implore me to visit them everyday & stay the day; they cram me with food & affection & concern for us. You see, they also have experienced family opposition, but even worse, on both sides. Paul's mother uncompromisingly rejected Renee. Also, they want me to go into the book business with Paul, he providing most of the money. It's a comforting thought, should all my teaching chances evaporate.

February 28, 1940

Feeling that it may hinder you more than it helps, I had promised myself, My Dear, not to write this way to you again. But once again my selfishness insists &, against my better judgment, I surrender to my impulse. Forgive me.

Dearest, I still feel that in your letters, & sometimes even when we are together, you do not yield to your desire. In your letters, for instance, it seems to me you are hiding; shyly you put words up before you like so many painted screens. I find little real freedom, except for a few sentences you have permitted yourself or that have unwittingly slipt through. I do not feel your fingers, warm & eager, reaching through your words. Your voice in the main merely whispers.

What do I want? I want YOU to talk through your lines, walk through your words straight to me, proudly & nakedly. I want—! Oh, Dearest, now probably I have driven you deeper into yourself & lost you a little more. But tell me, tell me. Is it I who imprison you?

Again I beg you, Liebling, to forgive me, if you can, & to realize it is my hunger for you that makes me write so, & my growing dissatisfaction with words & writing generally.

Have you wondered why I have not written sooner? Do you know how long a time elapsed before you answered my last letter? Can you possibly know what fantastic images crowd through my head? What have I done? How have I offended her? Have my parents spoken to her? Do her parents object? Is she ill? Etc., etc., into the night.

March 5, 1940

We'll do it, Dearest! This latest letter of yours, it seems to me, is the first big step you've taken either in words or feeling. But why this fear, this diffidence before words? They, you know, are YOUR servants, not your masters. All you have to do is have something you want to say & in obedience they'll say it. Also, like Aladdin's lamp, the more your feeling's fingers rub them the more they glow, speak, & do. And though, My Dear, it's as if you're an engine just learning to walk, fearfully taking your first step, in this letter—read 17 times, if read once—I really do feel YOU. Soon confidently you'll stride & then, Dear, run.

But speaking of lamenting your absence, I think now of those times when I want you most. The want, though everpresent underneath, surfaces unexpectedly like a time-bomb that, flickering all the while unconsciously inside me, flame eating the fuse away, suddenly goes off. I'm walking, say, in last night, night my only companion, living in that limbo between old thoughts & no thoughts when abruptly the hunger erupts.

So I wish you were here to help me see the rime-clad trees & the water frozen inside. Here to run with me to catch a bus, to share the midnight moon, to do the wind & stars, to watch a morning in its tentative, first-bird-chirped waking the sun spreading its benison of light. Here to wake in my arms, our dreams so entwined we cannot tell one from the other, so that my hands, reaching out, find the right fingers to grasp, & my lips— An unshared world, My Dear, is an unlived, unloved one.

You speak of understanding people, me. As I've repeated countless times, it's not so much a matter of understanding as it is of growing in wonder & love, an opportunity for you to get to know yourself a little better through exploring others. Everything that happens gives you a chance to express a part of you, a thought or emotion, you had never used or suspected yourself of having before. Each face you look into, each book you read, is a little pool in which you see a face of you you may have never seen before yet recognize instantly with astonished delight or fear. It's as though each event—whether it be person or passion—is a little drama that permits you to call into action an actor inside you hitherto unemployed. Unfortunately, for most of us, there is not strength-money enough to employ new actors; so we make old ones play all the roles, limit ourselves to very small customary plots, & blind ourselves to all the other dramas.

Could you possibly come to N.Y. soon: the ballet is on. Wouldn't you like to see Martha Graham? You know how important she's been to me. One of America's true originals. She was one of my happiest experiences, a profound eye-opener, on my arriving in NY. She is as close to being the total artist—dance, music, theater, even words—as anyone I know, the kind of poetic drama I wish I could work in.

~

T & R
TERRA INCOGNITA

You enjoy it, this bumbling
into foreign speech, like entering
a wilderness so crammed with life
everything you meet dumbfounds.

Enjoy the sense of starting
over, a world to be discovered,
yet despite its sounds—lacquered,
hook-beaked bird cries, voices
hard to say it's not the landscape
speaking silent, wholly sight.

But then, your tongue blind
in its voluble wagging, you lose
touch, not only with this world
around you, but with yourself.

                              Still,
eyes fixing you with indifference's
contempt, you feel yourself always
more exposed.
                    O, you are here,
but just enough to be an absence.

                         ~

March 14, 1940

    You can hardly know how glad I am you've discov-
ered the violin once more. As I said to you long ago, the arts
are some of the few keys that let us into the boundless store
of life & the world.

    So for me yesterday was a magnificent, a cataclysmic
day: all day I wrote & wrote & wrote. What do I have at the
end? Twelve—count 'em—pretty little poems. Oh, Dearest, if
I'm anything I'm a person who must write & if I'm not that
I'm nothing!

    But tell me, what countries are you visiting on your
violin? Has it gondola-wise wafted you through some Venice
air or are you climbing as by the alpen-stock of your bow the
arduous alps of some mighty master? You know, I was going
to listen to music faithfully every morning. Well, for this
writing-spree I've been on the last few weeks most of my
noble plans have collapsed. So I've listened just once. Guess
music is too good for one person alone; you should be here
to share it. My piano lessons? They too have gone the way of
too ambitious ambitions—but for almost purely financial
reasons. I can't afford to rent a practice piano.

    This afternoon I'm lunching with a professor who
the other day sent me a very pleasing letter anent my
Hopkins thesis. "I have recently had the pleasure of reading
your study... and wish very sincerely to congratulate you on

an unusually discerning account of an important and not easily interpreted poet in whom I, too, am much interested. I have rarely read a more forceful piece of criticism. It would be a further pleasure for me to talk with you... to consider the very hopeful future of such study." etc., etc. Once more, Dearest, pardon this parade of ego; if you can't take it, who will?

You count the days? I plot the schemes to see you. When will we be free to see each other when & as often as we wish? But why complain? How lucky that I'm not an athlete! That fact saved me. At that (I pipe boastfully) I came pretty close, you remember, to being a Rhodes Scholar. When I met with the final examining board several members congratulated me on being the first Muhlenberg student chosen to appear before them. During the questioning one asked, "What do you think of Lamb?" My "In a word, lambent" elicited a surprised "Is that Your epithet?" After the exam several assured me I'd find whatever I needed wherever I went to school. And I have—YOU! But imagine me mooning for you over many, many, moist miles, my seeping deepening them. O the tears of things! And the cost of postage alone!!

March, 28, 1940

A day away, My Only One, & still I do not miss you, certainly not as much as I thought I would, not as much as I did moments after I left you. For as yet you are most close to me, fresh in my fingers, your eyes my sight, your body pressed tight to mine, my arms & my lips curved to your being. Ah, men hug nothing so near to them as their dreams, & what more dream than the dream reality can be? So much are you with me now that even thoughts of tomorrow cannot worry me, thoughts of the things that will do their best to rub out the deeprooted image of you.

I have your lovely love-note, Dearest, the first you've ever really written to me. At last you stand before me naked & direct; more than ever you have taught me to hate the hypocrisy, the cruel deceit of clothes & conventions. Such a letter at my lips & you become the laughter springing from my throat.

Mr. Charkow, my Father's business partner, drove me back to N.Y. Amid all his pompousness, bluster and bluff what a rich character he is! Like a great bolt of cloth, slowly he unfolded himself, exposing all kinds of surprises. Many people, though you have just a tiny sample of them, like a swatch of goods in a tailor's catalogue, exhibit the whole of them at once, so much of a piece are they. Charkow may also be cut of one cloth, but what splendid variety of patterns it contains—gentleness, great sympathy, even in that bulky, heavy body a kind of delicate poetry!

If I write chaotically, it's because I am terribly tired—up at 5, now it's 1 a.m. The Weisses wouldn't let me go till a little while ago. Then I hurried home to talk to you. Know, Dearest, I am speaking with people & suddenly you walk into the room. You seem to carry walls with you; for immediately we are cut off from all others like so many strangers. People can never enter this sanctum, this new existence we have made between us—this refuge that is a release.

April 1, 1940

Ach, it's wrong, terribly wrong, I feel, that such a big lout of a fellow should be so brain-&-heart-dependent on such a spice-mite of a girl. "Spring is beginning, gradually throwing off the grip of winter, but I am frozen over with fears: She, My Little Spring, has not written." So I began my letter to you this morning when I did not hear from you. My Dear, why must you wait so long to answer me? You tell Rowie about fears & you are right: think of the fear you can make for me & what it does to me. A hundred huge miles stand between us; you do not write, & immediately my enemy of a mind insists on plunging into that mazy hell of possibilities, from "Is she ill?" to "Is her love for me waning?"

You see, I'm the sort that must be reassured almost every day. And you permit to open up before me the bottomless abyss of no-answer! Even if it be a paragraph, three lines, three words, please write to me more often. The you of the past I have firmly tucked away inside me: she can never escape. But unfortunately I know too well how quickly the you of now—& the you I cannot see save through the little windows, the sunshine glints, of letters—how quickly this you is changing. This very change can prove a pure delight, but only of course when I know it.

You may not believe it, Dearest, but my largest fear— all the others by comparison are mere infants, even the fear I may not write as well as I wish—with all its myriad facts, concerns you. So many times I sit in my room, arguing with myself, many times nearly writing to you, telling you to forget about me, to find someone else who will be able to take better care of you. I understand such feelings imply a very big love. But if this be so, I have an even greater love, one which prevents me from writing such stuff (& nonsense)!

You cannot know how often & deeply, how many ways I think of you. That such a little girl should cause me so much thought! Thus I think of you & the something you have made between yourself & your friends, the something you experience between yourself & your mother, the relationship in its most subtle unseennesses you enjoy between yourself & your dad, your sister, & your brother & even those accidental ones between yourself & my mother, say. How I envy them this experience your being permits them. And then I wonder if our love subsumes all these relationships, if the feelings you have for me include your father & your Rowie feelings. You see, Sweets, what crazy tortuosities my thinking undergoes because of you.

A list of books? Dearest, the books I want you most to read I want to read with you. Frankly, what I wish you most to read—& not just because I try to write it—is poetry of course. Nothing I know in words can teach you so speedily to see, to feel, to understand. But this, & especially this, we must do together. Try Dickinson, Frost, Shelley (since you like him), Keats, Browning, Blake, even Edna St. Vincent Millay (who, though by no means a major poet, in her very accessibility will help to lead you in.), Whitman, Yeats, etc.

As for your college, first words that come to my mind: go to the college where I'll be. (But who knows where—if any—that'll be.) First you must decide how far away from home, all-girl or coed, small school or large, one with a long old tradition & reputation or a new one with modern ideas of education, etc., etc. But I'll write more about this later. You still have another year to think about it.

April 5, 1940

Really, I couldn't write any sooner; not that I didn't want to. But do you remember the books I was supposed to read & the reports to write? Well, after I left you & returned to N.Y. I took them out. There they were, a heaping pile (five) to read & review in five little days. So I roll up my sleeves &, deciding it's really time to get to work, really get to work. Two days roll by (how the guy who shifts the scenery can push our days away!), I'm in the middle of just the second book & miles deep in despondency when, Glory be! your letter comes. Dearest, it is exactly what I need to pull me out of the dumps & to supply me with the power to keep me going, enough sunshine inside now to endure the winter of my work; and I walk around, my whole body loping-lithe.

Back again & I plunge into the books once more. What desert-pages! Every now & then, dying of starvation & thirst, I turn to the oasis of your words, drink deep, pacifying draughts. Sounds melodramatic? sensational? Well, it was. On & on, literally into the night & your letter traveling with me—my comfort & light-leading companion.

The last night speedily comes along; with tremendous mental might I've elbowed my way through all these stubborn (like jammed subway-passengers) books, wrung the last reluctant drop out of them before I let them go. 10:30 & I take to bed. 4 o'clock I rise, & in my pajamas I, still crumpled with dream, get to work. On & on I write. WRITE, WRITE, WRITE!! 6 o'clock, 8 o'clock, 10 o'clock. Three reviews to do. 11 o'clock & the two last & most difficult to compose. Will I make it? Give it my last surge of energy &, Dearest, it's done! Just in time. I dash it over to the Prof. feeling O so free & relieved. But as he takes it I wish he had already returned it, so that I might read it. Only my pen & paper, & only those dim hours, know what I wrote. Forty pages, Dear, from 4 to 2.

Once more the world opens up endlessly; I lean back on my thoughts of you, relax in the sweet comfort of my fatigue. Actually, I enjoyed the work, every bitter bit of it, the exhilaration of progress, the end in sight & the end itself. Eagerly now I look forward to returning to my own reading & writing & the world of you—all made dearer, more delightful, by this enforced vacation, this journey into a forbidding, foreign land.

And here I sit at the Weisses: Friday afternoon & evening the special set time I spend with them. Writing this, I listen to Honegger over the radio, incapable of any real thought, my mind a lamp turned off, & mildly, like an old man, I sit in the pleasant darkness of myself & the room of you.

But, Dearest, your letter, your letter! You have definitely arrived; with almost unbelieving joy I bask in its freedom & certainty. At last you are beginning to possess yourself. Strange, but in the moments I lose myself, you not only find you but me too. Believe me, yours is the most grownup letter I have ever received, the openest & the dearest.

April 13, 1940

Here it is Saturday night, you in Allentown & I in N.Y. with a bit of casual hell in my head. Renee Dear, I'm feeling pretty low right now & for rather legitimate reasons—not the vagaries that have so often prompted my tantrums in the past. I have all I can do to prevent myself from writing even you a sulphurous, take-her-severely-to-task letter.

You see, Dearest, my castle of cards has (at least for the moment) collapsed. First, my Ph.D. thesis topic falls through (I wanted to enlarge my M.A. Hopkins paper); second, I miss the poetry prize; third, I'm informed that not only are there no job-vacancies at Penn State this year, but two men have been fired; &, finally, as far as a renewal of my scholarship is concerned, I'm an alternate. My scholarship is meant for people just beginning graduate work, not those in-between like myself. If however one of those awarded the scholarship should die or refuse it, then I might get it again!

What am I doing to get over my melancholy? I'm going to type out a batch of poems & lay siege to the magazines once more; then, I'm going to rewrite my Hopkins paper & dump it on the Oxford University Press.

Dearest, what depresses me most is the thought of next year. Can you imagine, remembering what my Dad thinks of teaching, he who expected his son to be a doctor, a lawyer, a powerful presence in the world (as he said in dismay, "You mean to spend your whole life with children?!" &,

given his notion of independence, "You're willing to depend on others for your livelihood?!"), & what your Dad said about "glory" (though he DOES respect learning & my interests) & "He can't even support a wife," what it would be like were I to return home with you right next door?

Sweetling, do not take this whining too seriously: I'll get over it; fortunately I always do. I guess writers & would-be writers, like everyone else, have to go through a certain amount of trials. And word-mongers that writers are, they have to make the most of them.

Take it easy with your dancing. After all, you can carry this once a week business too far. I just now reread your lovely little dancing letter.

~

T & R
ARIADNE

He, the exultant swimmer
of change, has taken
to the sea.
        I, I stamp
into stone. And through it
I grope
        for the fire
that baked it. Quarrying
the promise,
            shapes
begin to stir: out of this
ghost of me

                    I reap
a dower rivaling the sea's,
a dower the body hoards,
the world
                the body
                        builds.

~

April 21, 1940

        Now that you put it so, Sweetling, & begin to under-
stand, I'll try to get to the truth of me in this matter. As you
say, "Such a feeling of depression is too narrow. . . unless you
can enjoy & make the most of it." But you do not seem to
realize how horribly deep—& wide too—depression can be.
Here you touch one of my taproots & I must warn you
against it to preclude confusion & your undue hurt.

        As I mentioned long ago & as you intimate here,
sometimes I overplay my moods (not that you & I haven't
ample encouragements to moodiness!). But aren't we all,
caught in the moment's grip, especially if we have a well-
developed sense of the theatrical, tempted to do so?

        My tendency to melodrama (I can hear you mutter-
ing, Who does he think he is? A junior Hamlet?!) does not
exclude my exhibiting it before those I love or, for that mat-
ter, myself. Occasionally, in fact, I detain & coddle long a
feeling that may be passing by. Why—you no doubt won-
der—is he telling me this? To caution you not to be over-
whelmed by such play-acting. NOT that all my feelings are
makebelieve or exaggerated! And if I do submit to such a
mood, for me at least it can be powerful. Imaginary ills, you
know, can equal authentic ones in pain. But soon enough,
I'm confident, shrewd as you are, you'll know what moods
of mine are to be taken seriously and what not.

        But, Liebkin, your little live skeleton of a letter
prompts all manner of questions. Why don't you flesh out

your letters a little more so that I needn't guess so much? You confess, "You arouse so many different feelings in me," then, beyond remarking our reciprocal holding of heads, do not bother to describe your feelings. Yet you do speak of souring. Haven't I a right to know why?

Don't let ANYthing I say or do embitter you. Holding a head or having one's head held is not as different as you seem to believe. The person holding is as dependent as the one whose head is being held. As you said a letter ago, it takes two to make one.

April 28, 1940 (Monday Morning)

Do you remember, Loveling, our talking about the dislocation most thinking people have experienced in our time (&, I've been learning, most of the distinguished Victorian worthies as well), their misery-making belief that meaning has passed out of their world? So they wander through life, ghosts to themselves.

Well, such is my feeling this morning. The sun is at its brawniest; the birds shower their gold-&-silver much as ever, embroidering with little sparkling stitches the hugeness of the early day. But I am altogether out of it. When the train pulled out, I rushed home, gladly taking refuge in my fatigue.

You cannot know, Sweetling, how thankful I was for my exhaustion; so, though I felt heart-weariness, I could not think it. Even walking with you in the almost-too-much fullness of the day, lapping up tremendous draughts of sheer delight, I felt unhappiness insist on sitting on my shoulder. It is usually this way: in the midst of ecstasy I can't help thinking of its transiency. The greater the pleasure the shorter its term.

Yet surely, lamenting the happiness your being here gave me yesterday, was the fool's & ingrate's part. Aside from the added spice of poignancy, tomorrow when, time applying its divers ointments, the wound has healed a little, I will once more joy in our together, savor it over & over slow moment by moment. What are all my weaknesses beside this love?

May 3, 1940

Of course, I'm sorry that your Dad told my sister of your visit, & she in turn, my parents. (I only hope you can make a friend & confidant of her.) But, in a sense, I'm almost glad: I've grown very tired of deceit, of forcing you into a duplicity for which there is no earthly reason. We've done nothing to be ashamed of. Somehow I have to convince my parents of this. You see, Dearest, I want you to learn to love them & they you. Impossible though it may seem now, eventually I think it can be brought about. Slowly, with effort, intelligence, sympathy, love & tact, all qualities I know you have, we will make it happen.

The manner we must pursue at this time is extreme discretion. They love me. Despite their superstitions & limited mores, they do respect what mind I have & ultimately, I believe, my wishes.

Because of the turn of events, I think it best I stay away from home for the present. Arguments might rise & aggravate the situation beyond later healing; & there is nothing I would hate more. In fact, I may not even come home this summer. I've already begun to hunt around for a city job.

May 8, 1940

For a moment, Dearest Mine, hell seemed to be pouring over. The world insisted on shaking itself like a giant dog & throwing me—one of its minor fleas—off. My folks not only learned of your N.Y. visit but also got wind of my telephone call inviting you in. Infuriated, I suppose, by the "deceit" (again!) we were practicing and by jealousy—I had telephoned you, not them, Poppa sits down in whitehot rage &, like an exacerbated volcano, spills all his lava into a letter. Dearest, that was probably the most sulfurious piece of writing I have received. Have I ever told you what magnificent rage my Pop can summon up? He storms like an element, as though he were Aeolus and his belly the cave where he keeps all the winds. In such moods he is a spectacle awesome to behold. But your father also has not a little of the elemental in him.

Well, the letter caught me totally unprepared. Dumbfounded, I felt the ground tremble under my feet. All I had to hold on to was the hope of you. I thought: nothing for it but go hoboing, join the army, go off to the war, etc. All day I wandered aimlessly, lost in the hellish labyrinth of my thoughts. One takes ones parents' love for granted & of a sudden it explodes into something akin to hate.

Then in the evening (around the very time, I believe, your folks were visiting them) they telephone me, implore tearful forgiveness, & beg me to come home this weekend, bringing the Weisses with me. Early this day, about the time his letter arrived, Poppa had called the Weisses, told them of the "terrible" letter he had written, & importuned Paul to watch me. Perhaps they're wrong, Poppa admitted; I may do as I like, etc., etc., just come home.

All of which means, Dearest, that this Friday the Weisses (if his poor witch of a mother lets go of them for a day or so) & I will be in Allentown. But, Sweetest Mine, prepare yourself for anything. Know that whatever occurs, if you still want it, you have my heart. In the meantime, for my sake, Dear, keep mum about the whole thing. As I've said before, however, Shirley is our most likely wedge into my parents' irrationality. From what I hear, to some degree at least she's on our side. Win her, Dearest, win her.

May 16, 1940

Now that you have remarked it, I shall not hesitate to dilate on it at my usual professorial length. My Sweets, I am fairly certain that "new experiences & feelings" do not respect or, for that matter, recognize age. They, sensitive as they are, visit us largely on the strength of our alertness—the welcome we give them. People do not stop feeling because they are old; they are old because they stop feeling. You know, Dearest, the daily man & woman, after a certain amount of struggle (what we call adjustment), settle down to a well-defined, minimal set of feelings that satisfy all occasions. This corresponds to their vocabularies & their ways of thinking. If you closely observe a so-called run-of-the mill human being you must realize that he makes a limited number of words serve all his intellectual (etc.) needs. Of course, to some degree this is true of all of us. And I suppose for most people it is inevitable. Such a streamlined personal vocabulary & roster of feelings do make for a kind of efficiency, particularly when, as now, the cash register keeps the accounts.

Paul's mother, for example, has the most fixed (therefore most elastic, since she stretches her words to fit a variety of occasions) vocabulary I have encountered. Her feelings too have hardened; now she forces each one along rigid little superficial personality-ruts. "Elegant" for her means all degrees of virtue, goodness, superiority. "Fine atmosphere" is the highest compliment she can possibly pay a place & connotes for her all manner of grandeur & delight. When she describes a person as "full of character," almost invariably meaning that he or she has given her a gift or shown her some kindness, she is bestowing her brightest accolade. These are, obviously, key words to HER character.

But as I said, most people gladly surrender to a small number of words & feelings. This is much the easiest way: knowing the boundaries of their little personal world, they can curl up comfortably as in old clothes or pipes & get about with a minimum of effort or surprise. Most people fear novelty, shudder at the thought there may be another stranger world outside their own. Building walls around themselves, they pretend the outer world does not exist.

The reason I have written so laboriously about this is because I must constantly struggle with it myself, particularly in my writing. It's much easier, takes infinitely less energy, to give oneself to a carefully-routined, two-by-four life. In my poetry I'm often tempted to lapse into commonplaces that, to put it mildly, do the writing little good; on the contrary. Certain subjects recur with dismaying frequency: rain, birds, trees, sky, morning, day, light, night, stars, love, you, I, etc.

The explanation is plain enough: even as these items are the staples of lyric poetry, I've become comfortable in this verbal world I've made my own, I have no difficulty, & need exert almost no energy, in translating these objects into poetic images. In fact, that's the trouble: they ARE poetic images to begin with. But if I intend to write poetry at all worthwhile, just as if I intend to live a life at all worthwhile, I MUST reach beyond my customary boundaries, & come to grips with other things.

This morning I begin a poem to you in my usual vein, entitled something like "Thoughts on a Morning Waiting Dismally for its Visitor Rain" or "Sun Called on Account of Rain." A small amount of such stuff goes a long way; relied on frequently, it becomes a vice &, worse, a bore. Poets are as prone as anyone to verbal obsessions, by their focus on writing probably more than most people.

But I'm working on a poem about your walls; in project it's most ambitious—it involves Pygmalion, the Sleeping Beauty, Open Sesame, Richard I's walls, etc. In execution? Let's hope for the best.

Odd, isn't it, how little of war & "our times" occupies my writing? I fear my feelings, our personal situation, & the tears of it sweep all the rest away. All except the walls.

May 21, 1940

My Dearest, your last letter has pleased &, at the same time, perplexed me probably more than any other you've sent me. Your determination delights me; yet the apparent conflict, the self-struggle, worries me more. For this reason I've taken so long before attempting an answer. All day yesterday I sat at my desk, fairly breaking my brain, looking for the "correct" words to write to you.

Frankly, your confusion does not trouble me too much: any thinking, sensitive being must, I suppose, pass through such periods of self-examination. But, Dearest, you make me feel sometimes that I'm harming you more than I'm helping, that I'm rushing you. My Dear, there is no hurry. In due time the walls will give way. Never have I accused you of your age. Such walls must crumble slowly; they cannot fall at once. Don't take yourself too seriously; let me do that!

What I am afraid of is that you are making an idee fixe out of the walls. Ignore them; forget them; & turning around one day, I assure you, you'll see them lying in bits around you. Walls such as these, I fear, fatten on attention. Actually it is not wall at all but hypersensitivity, fear, & the desire (as you imply) to make a good impression. I've experienced the same thing. I suppose, if examined closely, it reveals itself as nothing other than an inverted superiority complex. We know how good we are & we want the other person to realize it too. In my case, I hurriedly hunt around in myself for the scintillating remark. By the time I locate it the person's interest has moved on; this disconcerts me & I blurt out some inane (or offcolor or wholly inapposite) phrase that astonishes me as much as the person hearing it. After experiencing something like this several times, some of us (you?) decide we better not talk at all.

Love, believe me, you'll get over it. Just take it easy. I assure you I had no intention of making an issue of it. I mentioned Renee's remark to you simply out of personal hurt. Naturally it irked me that you should shut yourself up before her. So with my Parents. As you surely realize, their margin of age is hardly reason sufficient to make you feel inferior. Just take people as they are, examine them, enjoy them, & so forget all about yourself. I beg you once & for all let us drop the walls forever.

But this matter of "belief," "exactly what I am" (whatever that is), & "afraid to be myself" poses another big problem. Because you may not "believe" later what you "believe" now is no reason for NOT "believing" now; nor does it in any way mean that what you "believe" today will be "wrong" tomorrow or what you "believe" tomorrow nearer the truth than today. All it means is that you "believe" DIFFERENTLY since YOU ARE different. Age, as I suggested earlier, doesn't automatically bring wisdom & "truth": it brings change &—usually—more caution. Age seems wiser because youth is usually rasher, doesn't take the time to think. Age, however, hurt so often because of its younger rashness, & much fatigued, DOES take all the thought necessary—& more!

Dearest, if only we could accept thinking & feeling as they come without questioning their "right" or "wrong," their "good" or "bad." As I said ages (days) ago, we must ACCEPT all & BELIEVE nothing. Our duty is to the truth of ourselves & the truth we owe each other: this involves giving ourselves to the feeling we are enjoying (or is enjoying us!) as much as possible. Learn to read your feelings & emotions correctly, then show them the fidelity befitting them. Your doubts about what you are, what you feel, & what you think, I assure you, are shared by the oldest, wisest, & most learned human beings living today. One need merely look at the world & its condition to appreciate this.

I could go on & consider some more the matter of your "people as patterns," but I've foolosophised far too much already. You're probably bored or asleep (& rightly so). Yet I've continued because I realize too well what a lonely world we live in. Whom (including yourself) can you say you really, thoroughly know? Love, however, such as ours is the one supreme possibility for the exchange of & sharing in each other. Pray all the above doesn't frighten you away.

May 27, 1940

I've just now come out of a first rate cataclysm with Renee & Paul. Of all the unmitigated madnesses Paul's mother is one of the best. With a mind of bile & a mouth like a cesspool, she's as close as I've come to a monster in the dis-guise of a "human" being.

At the moment, at least beside her, all our troubles seem childish indeed. You know the radio-commentators who've just come from the front? Well, I've sat at the front of the Weisses' dinnertable & experienced the tremendous explosion of Paul's mother—a human bomb, but a careful, conscious one. Day after day she snipes away at them, bayo-nets them; then, at the moment she considers most appropri-ate, off she blows. This is a battle for which there is no truce, it seems; certainly no peace. You must forgive me for exhibit-ing her in such detail. She was a window I shuddered to look through for fear of beholding chaos itself.

But to turn from that hell to my private heaven, how shall I tell you the pleasure I feel at your growing confidence & therefore ease with the violin? Now all you need do is extend it to the world & the people around you. And you needn't worry about my "worry" at your self-explanations:

I'm big enough, I hope, to understand them. Just please continue sending them.

Meantime, affairs here have been moving along. I've not heard any more about the English teaching. And I have to clear out of my Columbia room by June 4. If all goes well I should return to Allentown by then, but whether I can stay—!

Much as I'd love to be with you & my Folks, that seems impossible. If we can raise the necessary capital, Paul & I are contemplating going out on the road selling large electric fans. Then, Paul's mother having left, I might remain with them in N.Y. & attend summer school. You would visit. Meanwhile keep your fingers crossed.

June 3, 1940

I will, after all, be coming home for the summer. Need I say any more?

~ 2 ~

September 25, 1940

A whole summer gone, & since returning I'm still head & heart deep in the expected pea soup of my feelings. I sit here with Paul & Renee, horribly lonely—even lost & lonesome with myself. It's as though I'm going through an emotional shortcircuit: the world & I, for the time being (I hope!), have lost contact. As in the comic books, I've stept out of this world's dimensions, but, alas, there's nothing there & I hang by my non-existent necktie. It's little fun being a ghost-man flapping his empty sleeves. It seems I missed you so much in the thought of leaving that, having left, I've no strength to miss you more.

Yet this numbness is a kind of blessing; it shields me from the otherwise truculent importunities of my heart. Already vaguely I hear sundry thoughts peddling their wares, clamoring at my feelings' doors for admission. And all of them carry somewhere a banner with your picture on it. But there will be time for further tears & despairs. Now just a simple word—I love you & love you & love you. WRITE!!!

~

T & R
BECAUSE

I wake, morning clouded
over, the tea misty, the jam
stuck on its sugar, bread
turning into mold.

"And you,
the trains and trucks still
rumbling out of your sleep,
squint away after goods
you'll never recover."
                    Well,
is it so bad being shadowed
by breakers far off?
                    "You know
the rumbling is some sort
of language you'd comprehend
even less if it drew near."

Such fortuitous meetings,
suddenly flared, are they not
signaling more than promises
or threats, of themselves
fulfillment?

~

September 26, 1940
        The longest, the neatest, the dearest, the sweetest let-
ter yet. And I'm studying its face again as it lies stretched out
before me on the Schubert desk. Coming to the Schuberts
was the least noisome of my N.Y. experiences thus far—the
last block to their apartment I literally ran; & in the warm
ambience of their room & the ember-glow of David and
Judy's greeting, I almost attained delight once more. But the
ruthlessness of my mood brooked no such frivolity; the let-
down proved all the larger for the anticipation. Actually the
only thing that holds me together, the fragments of me, is
memory or habit. Even the push & the reaching to write this
to you takes on the requirements of genius.

Yet I know this jag of mine must settle down; my emotions must accommodate themselves to living. By the sheerest chance I did manage to reach my one class in time—but there was no class; it was the Prof. who was absent!

My Dear, till you blew my being wide open, extravagance (of feeling, expression, etc.) seemed extravagant, but now it's merely undertone looking for fuller, more adequate expression. And the superlatives, woefully naked though they may be, I see now the reason for their invention. You know what I'd like to do? Collect all the finest love poems ever written (& will be or ought to be), lump them together & distil the essence out of them. This done, I'd send the result to you, then hop a plane &, beating it to you, prove once more the superiority of person & experience to expression. You remember the hyperbole of Wolfe's verbalisms? Well, that's a little the status of my passion.

But I'm tired of looking for a word meet to this boundless feeling: just think of a sky-big tempestuous sea & a seashell caught in the central mighty sweep of it: that's me.

Please, please put the blocks to your Pop so that he crumbles into a YES! & you'll be here by the 11th.

September 27, 1940

Better & better, My Sweetest, you frighten me: if your letters continue to evince growth at the rate the past two have set I don't see how I can keep up. But for your starting out with such a bang, how shall we ward off a whimperish conclusion?

You say my letter is not physical enough. That rather accurately, if mildly, describes my present state: I'm hardly physical without you. Succumbing to my emotion as I have, I've taken on its peculiar contours; & emotions, you know, are generalizations. Chrysalis that I've become again, the future alone knows what winged affair, a moth monster probably, is developing in here.

And writing becomes as clumsy & stubborn as the telephone (almost). I sit looking at this page, its blank face staring brightly, indifferently, back at me. So befuddled am I, instead of it submitting to the contagion of my thoughts, I seem to adopt its vacuous qualities.

To redeem myself a little from my paper-hypnosis, I retail a few incidents that might interest you. At last I'm in full possession of my college room, my books all recovered & partially shelved, & I somewhat orientated physically.

I've spoken with Professor Van Doren & arranged to see him soon to discuss our personal problems. What a resolute charm of a man he is! Another teacher friend of mine, whose new book on American poetry I read at his request, has acknowledged his appreciation of my suggestions in his preface.

September 29, 1940

It's no use fretting or regretting, Dear; two days away from a you-letter, yet my being insists on living & loving. The night insists on being enjoyed. Were you here how together we'd luxuriate in its company. Yet I know that right now you are breathing & living in, enjoying this selfsame night. So it acts as ambassador love between us.

Are you reading, practicing, & writing—a letter to me? I feel, as I sit at David's desk, writing on this David poetry paper, that for the moment at least I've revived a good bit of my best self. David's stopped coming to classes so I have to come here oftener. You sit gracefully, firmly, inside me. And my writing (Old Faithful!) starts to geyser again.

But, Dearest, there are still those sharply jagged moments in which I seem to be thrust off a precipice. Last night a few doors away some fellow turns his radio on full-blast. And as the classical music enters my room, it ruthlessly plucks at the old strings, looses copious tears. Seems I'm several kinds of gushers!

September 30, 1940

God Damn it! Dearest, come! Our life is too unsettled, what with oncoming conscription, war, & what have you, to give too much attention to parent-alienation & the long-time view. Selfishly I say, I want to see you, I've been planning to see you, fixing my feelings that way, & I don't care to alter them for parents or anyone (bating you, of course) else. Eventually, I'm sure they'll come around. If they don't, it's too bad— But tell me, are you suggesting I not see you the entire year?!

I can't help feeling that your Grandma frowned on a threeday visit for "moral," rather than parental, reasons. Those, of course, are even less tolerable than the latter ones. So, if you know what's good for both of us, you'd better come. What do you want me to do? Visit Allentown? Join the Army? (I may have to do that soon enough anyway.) Or take up with somebody else, a blonde maybe?

Busy as they will keep you, it pleases me that your dancing & violin lessons begin again. Aside from what they do for you, they must surely reduce your amount of possible flirtation time!

My work? Oh, I'm just about ready to take it on, but the plenitude of things to be done not only disheartens but almost defeats me. Exams in French, German, Latin, Anglo-Saxon, History of the Language; preparation for my orals, locating & working on a dissertation subject; attending classes; writing a novel, essays, poetry—not to forget revision!

P. S. Sweetest, don't misunderstand me; I more than appreciate your desire to win my parents. In easier times I would probably accept your suggestion; our age crushes my little philosophy & magnanimity completely.

October 1, 1940

Days, My Sweet, seem to exist just to provide me with material to write to you. But by the time night rolls round I feel as if the day has trampled me day long. This life of ours is such a chaos, my hours, even the gayest, riddled by worm-toothed worries, about you-me, my parents, my work (& the nebulous likelihood of my getting a job), all steadily chorused by world worry. So the day is a barrier that must be jumped to night, & night a barrier to day. Naturally then writing such as this becomes an immense ordeal: how, out of the vast world of my muddy emotions and the roiled things round me, seize some few letter-sized thoughts bodied in words crystal-clear! And me with my long vaunted reverence for writing! But in the end it does compel me to collect my thoughts that had been pasturing, so many prodigal sheep (no doubt gathering wool!), who knows where, & to corral them in the pen of a page.

And despite the despondency my world's become, I still continue to write, wellnigh automatically, I suppose. The nearest I can come to you, Dearest, is in poems. But without you even this becomes a prodigious chore, & drear. O how shall I (when shall I) ever revise? How return to the past, when, like a mountaineer climbing a steepest Alp (you know my powerful fear of heights!), I can hardly retain my foothold & clutch the rock-cold, slippery side of the present? On the other hand, those moments when joy is my portion, how possibly revisit poems past? To do so is to compromise & lose a present pleasure. Nothing for it but to write on & on & on.

When you are near, as you blot my worries, so you make of love a benign, easy master. So no matter at all, but serving me. But with you away at once I turn into a lackey of love whose ruthless commands I cannot possibly execute. A beaten slave, I drag this stubborn, burdensome body wherever I go.

Your cummings joydom joydoms me. He has, as you see, that innocence & fraternity of things I love so much, that easy oneness with the world: the world in his hands is a sauntering along, a song, a gaiety as of a late spring rain (at least in poems like "Chanson Innocent").

In our mephitic times the Weisses & the Schuberts are as well as can be expected. As for your muddle, Dearest, never mind. As you can see by this letter, I'm also muddling. All we can do is muddle together, partners in the present, caretakers of each other's joys & tears.

October 2, 1940

I'm standing in the elevator, reading your letter. A fellow next to me butts into my world, asks the date. Contorting my face into the mask of a smile, with all my will I hide behind it the writhing snakes my emotions have become as a result of your words. Will you kindly, gently, sweetly tell your Grandparents & your Dad to go to hell? My work! My career! (Conscription & possibly war?) But pray tell what do these Nestors advise? No more letter-writing? No more seeing? Feelings neatly folded & put away inside a locked drawer, filed for future reference? My anger is so huge this minute it spits & sputters from my pen.

And yet out of a multiplicity of reasons I can understand them. But you, My Dearest, you? Don't you realize how easy it was for my parents to persuade your grandparents, much as they think alike, of our "wrongdoing"? Of course they're wrong, as wrong as their lives & opinions are.

I spend my thoughts on you, instead of writing? Don't you yet know that my thoughts on you are the very stuff of writing, that our love is one of the few fruitful experiences in our life, one of the most precious (if not the most), & they want to take that from us!

But I can't understand you. First, that their words should shake you so. Perhaps you want to call our love off—on account of the battering rain & their recriminations? If you do, say the word. "...they are not wrong,...they are not right"!!! More of such uncertainty & I fear we're through. I've never promised you anything; certainly not a nice easy domestic life. All I have to give you (& I'm not singing popular love songs!) is my love. Take it or leave it. But make up your mind now while the leaving's still easy (apparently!). If you feel you've taken on more than you bargained for, O.K.

Then you add the insult of ignorance (don't you know me yet?) to the earlier injury. "Would I really want a position in some minor college! Would it afford me the advancement I wish for!" Jesus! Don't you know all I want, now & forever, is some job that will give me enough dough to marry & support you & some time to write.

And in a footnote, the sort professors write when they're not sure of their position or are afraid they might offend someone if they didn't acknowledge them: I love you!!!

October 3, 1940

Just fresh from bathing to write you a nice, clean (I hope! & for a change) letter. The anger, most of it, has ebbed, though plenty of befuddlement is still keeping me company. My Dearest, I simply can't understand. You think you know a person & whoops! he slips through your fingers just like that. It's your Pop I mean. After all, for a long time we had been very close &, I thought, understanding friends. He did take me along to those Dell concerts and gardens and museums. One might even say it was that friendship which first brought you & me together.

As I recall, your Pop was the foremost exponent of probity; remember his indignation at our backdoor tactics?

54

His front door was open to everyone. Now suddenly not only does he applaud but he suggests further duplicity! Nor, Renee, do I fully know what to make of your attitude. Because of my "parents' feelings" you say you had better come in only for one day; Sunday my parents won't be home. Then you say I should decide which day since they're all the same to you. I don't see how you can come to N.Y. any day without my folks finding out. But as I've told you umpty times, I don't care if they do. Seems to me the sooner they realize how definitive my feelings toward you are the sooner they're bound to accept them.

Forgive me if I seem snappish. But here we have this tremendous, endless boggling as though it were a matter of major significance. A tiny visit & it involves my parents, your parents, your grandparents, not to mention you & me! Must we spend weeks of thought, decisions & revisions, on a one day visit?

Again, Dearest, forgive me. It may well be that I'm not able to endure the thought of not having everything my own way. But I'm sure you are large enough to accept my smallness. And I had at the start held out the hope that this would be a "nice, clean letter"!

October 4, 1940

All day an icy paralysis, the frost intensifying as the hours pass: the winter of me blowing its wildest, freezing my brain & fixing my feelings as only the rigors of winter can. Then slowly, My Lovely, throwing myself into the heart of Shakespeare & the thought of you, I begin to thaw. And at this moment warming myself before the royal flame your letter is, I'm grateful almost for the winter. Once more you've broken into & blossomed the island of my loneliness. But O what intimate neighbors, how hand-holding, heaven & hell are in me these days.

Well, now let's settle down to a long, comfortable chat. First off, penitence is in order: I'm sorry for my rashness, my arraignments, & my inconsiderateness of you. I suppose this was as close as I could come in writing to leaving you alone suddenly & dashing off to the park, say, as I did this summer. But remember—& this is my only alibi—my anger sprang from my love. Because I felt that you were, perhaps unwittingly, introducing via Grandparents & Pop the first wedge of difference between us, I blew up so. You wrote as you did because you feared for the future, I because I feared for the present (so the future too!).

But you know, don't you, that my anger was further underlined by my unhappy realization of the truth of what you might be intimating? We've talked about these things before: the unpromise of our future, etc. Naturally I'm hypersensitive about it. Thus, whether you intended to or not, when you put your finger on the sorespot, there was nothing I could do but jump. Though the future at this moment may seem remote to you, you have every right to be concerned about it.

But how in the hell are you impeding my work? Believe me, you have had very little to do with the formation of my present attitude, which I consider the sense at last of approaching maturity (I think!), a result of the desires of an artistic, rather than scholarly, temperament. Whether I had fallen in love with you or not, I am certain this would be the same. But even if you had been the one most responsible for promoting this point of view, pray tell what would you suggest as a remedy? That I disregard you for a year? Better, that I rip out the roots of you in me & discard the whole thing? Do you believe that would give me peace & make me work more industriously? Haven't you learned that feelings are hardly as docile as that?

You are wrong; our love is not entirely my writing.
But it IS the necessary background, without which the writing loses a great deal of its source, its place, and its raison d'être. And a poem:

TARDY TRUTH
I knocked on the beggar
I knocked on the thief
I peeked through the keyhole
of Indian chief

I rapped on the rich man
I struck at the boor
but no one O no one
would open the door

I bent to the flower
I rose to the wind
I battered the tree
turned a leaf as a key

I sat on the stairs
of the star and the rainbow
I pommeled the door
of the dream and the shadow

Then I fled to despair
and yielded to grief

Lo your heart so unheeded
unlocked soft its doors
and fed me relief relief

October 6, 1940

My Dearest, Nearest, Hereest You, sometimes walking with my loneliness, I hear my heart tick tock, & I know it's a timebomb ready to go off. At such moments my reason nearly persuades me that you should accept that scholarship to Miami University for next year & go off to live with your grandparents, as you did a couple of years ago. I remember what wonders that year did for you (and for me!). It was then that I really saw you for the first time. And, of course, the new visit would give you a chance to re-evaluate our relationship.

Fortunately or not, such moments of Olympian selflessness on my part do not last very long. What would I do if you were to leave & there were no opportunities yearlong to see you! God knows how miserable the situation is already!

But why do your grandparents object to us so? Because they believe you are arresting my work? Or do they fear for your future? And I had thought they rather liked me!

Dearest, I'm grateful to you for being grateful to me about *Sons and Lovers*. Your reading of it is something I feel we've done together. You a Miriam? You are not less spiritual than she, rather more because more natural. The last hours have been hectic indeed. Last evening the Schuberts visited the Weisses'. We spent a mild & pleasant time, though a little after the evening began, again the better part of me departed & left the ghost my body behind. (This often happens, as though I break away from the tether of me to meet you some- where.) Though I smiled & exchanged pleasantries, everything about me seemed embalmed in sleep or dream.

About 1 o'clock the Schuberts & I were ready to leave. A chance statement kindled a mammoth argument (friendly) between David & me on how the artist should conduct himself today. David advocated art for art's sake or, as he put it, art for my sake. I preserved remnants of my old political leanings. At three David admitted I had won, & we left, but the Schuberts refused to let me go home. So off to Brooklyn we went where we talked feverishly till five. They retired, I stayed up to see a Brooklyn dawn rise—& think of you—so slept almost not at all.

October 7, 1940

Is anything the matter? All day I trudge along like some weary traveler crossing Siberia's endless ice & flailing snow. However, encouraged by the thought that at the end of the day stands the log cabin of your letter I somehow survive. But today no letter! Saturday's letter will have to serve as snow-shoes another day. See how all-purposeful your letters are!

I think as I sit at the dinner table, why am I not stronger than I am? Why can't I extricate myself from the morass of emotion I so easily, & often, sink into? Do I coddle my feelings? I try to scorn myself out of my depression by contrasting my, after all, exceedingly comfortable position with others I have known: here you are almost 24 & you've never had to work; you have nearly a whole free year before you; the girl you love loves (doesn't she?) you; nor is she ever really far away. But, Dearest, despite my rationalizing, my feelings insist I nurse them with every bit of my strength; like leeches they suck my spirit dry.

I spoke to Professor Van Doren today. What a gem of a person he is! He took my problem to him as though I had been his own son. Dear, I love this man—as some one who has earned the spiritual right to be my father. Someday perhaps I can be as fine as he. He feels I am unduly pessimistic about teaching; despite the racial question, he insists there is still room in the teaching profession for capable people. Then he proposed I leave my Hopkins paper with him & immediately get in touch with one Laughlin who is putting out a series of such critical works, write him with Van Doren's recommendation. I'm to see him again on Wednesday.

May something come of this! As yet, however, I cannot feel too elated. It seems to me that Van Doren had never bumped into the Jewish problem before. I told him about my letter from Lewisohn & his troubles with academia. But he maintained it was the man, his arrogance, etc., & not his race that stood in his way. And when I mentioned the difficulties Zeitlin had had (you remember at your father's urging I wrote to him about the situation), Van Doren countered "Well, he did get a job, didn't he?" So, Dearest, let's keep our fingers & our hearts crossed.

Each day I love you it seems as much as heart can bear; but next day somehow heart's sinews stretch a little more.

October 8, 1940

It's raining here, each drop beaming as it slides along my window, each framing the picture of you. I take one drop aside, whisper that I love you; he relays it to the next drop & so on like a telephone till it must surely reach you. Do you hear it? As for your visit, feeling as I do this moment, I'll gladly accept just a day of you.

You find discrepancies in Miriam? You are nearest the truth, it seems to me, when you suggest that perhaps it is "the evident contradiction in every one." Yet if you examine her a little more closely, I think you'll see that what you indicate is really not a contradiction. Miriam's mother was a prude & at the same time a zealous lover of nature. This certainly conditioned Miriam. Then too she indulged herself, unwittingly, in what a Freudian would call sublimation—one of the more pat terms of Freudian jargon—that is, she translated her fund of love & feeling (excessively large in her, since she was so alive) into objects that did not possess the odium—for her—the "dirtiness," of sex. Her passion having to find some channel, she deflected it to her brother, to flowers & to "spiritual" things. Recall how emphatically this love expressed itself? Largely because of her restraining (inhibiting) its normal expression. In short, she deemed love's functioning ugly & "animal"; things like flowers, however, for their robe of beauty, their purely vegetal nature (she never heard apparently of man-eating blossoms!), she felt no compunction about lavishing all the richness of her sensuous (& sensual) nature on. She was just a younger example of Paul's mother. If Miriam had had a child, she would, I suspect, have repeated the performance; relieved of her squeamishness, her conviction that man-&-woman love is lust, she would have dumped her passion on the child & nearly smothered it. Miriam had not learned, certainly not felt, that the flesh & the spirit are an indissoluble one & that there can be no spirit without flesh.

Obviously, as you say, a huge difference separates Steinbeck & Lawrence. Of course Steinbeck was trying to project a whole mass, almost a panorama, of people. Lawrence concentrates on a few. More, Lawrence's are intellectualized, "cultured" people whose lives are chiefly introspective ones, most active but in the head, heart, & feelings. Steinbeck's people feel too, & deeply; but their feelings are not so well articulated. Don't forget that feelings are actions also. All in all, I should adjudge Lawrence's exploration of the inner life of individuals as much more profound.

October 9, 1940

I've just returned from Van Doren. What a conversation! For the first time since I've known him I saw feeling come to the surface of the man. He prescribed heroism, nothing less. He's after the biggest things & little interested in trivial desires (except as they are enmeshed in and serve larger matters). That's what comes of reading (& believing) the Big Shots of Literature! What comes of associating mainly with Dante, Shakespeare, Homer, Milton, Thoreau. Van Doren not only loves what they say, but believes in living it.

He suggested I'm too much worried about myself & my future & would do myself the greatest favor by forgetting "the problem" & getting down to work on my Hopkins paper. But I asked whether he really considered that wise, since it meant neglecting so many other things. Whereupon he fired back, "Are you doing anything now?" I replied just as fast, "Writing poems!" That stopped him for a moment & he grinned. "But, apparently you'd better stop writing poems." "Why?" "Because you're not happy at it." "I am, but there's such a thing as eating." "If you're more interested in eating than poetry, stop writing. Anyway, you could still rewrite your thesis & find time for poetry." When I declared that I didn't believe I am cast in such a heroic mold, he countered, "I'm interested only in heroes." A pretty exclusive diet!

So there you have it! But Jesus! am I—are we!—big enough to do it? Ideally I agree with him; I always have. In fact, had I thought it through I must have realized he would respond in this fashion. And I suppose for him there was nothing else that he could honestly say. But what do YOU say, Dearest? I love you & I want to marry you—soon. Under his terms, pray tell, how do I do that? And yet, Loved One, I feel as though I MUST do what he proposes. As he put it, "Wells [another professor] thinks your Hopkins paper is very fine; I think so, & so do you. Revise it, & I can't see why it shouldn't be published. Do that first & put everything else aside." Immediately, with your permission, I proceed to do so.

John Eisenhart writes me that he & Antoinette are marrying in a week or so. Would we were doing the same! I never thought, My Mighty Diminutive (see what you've done to me!), that I would envy John. And I have not till now, not in high school when he was Miss Gerheart's obvious favorite, not when he published an essay on Frost in *Scholastic Magazine*, not even when the scholarship he won was to Colgate & mine to Muhlenberg. He sends you his blessing.

October 12, 1940

I stand in this chaos called my head, watching the train's red lights balefully wink at me. Then in one big lurch the train is off; with all the powerful sinews of my heart I try to hold the train back; the sinews grow taut, strain & strain till putt! they snap hauling my heart with them. Mockingly the lights gesture to me from the distance.

I take the ferry, watch the lights & dock approaching, wonder frantically why we must be apart. As I wrap my eyes in the folds of water & light blending into a black velvet that shines almost light-white, I muse on the past's hordes of human beings reflected here, & the emotions working in them. Why cannot these waves be tears? The lights from a passing ferry are spilling jewels on the water, & their zigzags of colored lights become nervous rainbows.

The man beside me rubs his face as though to answer the steady watery wind nibbling at it, a man I'll never see again, but ever dear because caught in the tangled skein of my feeling. And suddenly I understand: the earth, tiring of its inertness, grew birds & threw them ball-like high into the air, bloomed crops of eyes & harvests aspiring of hands. Man is earth's restlessness, earth as will-of-the-wisp & wanderlust. But in the end all must come back to old earth's solid self again.

As I stumble down the streets I lick my lips to get a last taste, squeeze my fingers & wring my brain to garner the crumbs of you, store for the lean days to come. In the subway I see a party of noisy young boys with their happy young girls & wonder why we must be apart. I turn myself inside out like a glove to study the geography of my head.

But at once I'm FORCED to return my eyes & myself to the outside: a huge flock of motley leaves are clamoring for my senses. As if knowing they are soon to die, they've expended themselves in one desperate venture, one brilliant gesture of red, yellow, & green—their defiant swan song. A huge yet birdy woman nests behind them. Nearby a man, drunk but affable, seeing my seeing, turns to me & with exaggerated politeness suggests: "Flowers for My Lady?" Flowers indeed! I walk to my room, wafted on the acrid scent of leaves dying, riding the air.

I sit down to my desk, write this. At once a fat, rattling buzz of a fly, crackling like fired dry stubble, throws himself frenetically around my room, assails my lamp, dashes himself against my desk as though eager to escape himself, eager to escape oncoming winter, his earth—& death—boundness. And I am swept up with him in a wild whirligig.

Thank your parents for the gift of you, thank your father for his beneficence in letting you visit me in N.Y. I mean it, Mine, from the bottom of my bottom-lost heart.

~

T & R
ATTACHMENT

A matter
mostly
of skittery legs,
a speck
of a spider
skips

across the back
of his hand.

There
on a knuckle
it takes a stand.

Shaking his fist,
he makes
what surely
must be
an earthquake
for the likes
of it.

At once
reeling out
a thread
too thin
to see,
mid-air
it
spins.

Then,
as if intent
on angling
supplies enough
for it
and all its kin
a lifetime,
it winds in.

Or can
this hanging on,
  this reeling,
  simply be
a fellow feeling,
  delicate
  yet resolute
  attachment?

October 15, 1940

I come home from the Schuberts (I slept there overnight: what wondrous, harried dears they are), grab for your letter as one might clutch a lifesaver, & Pop! all my resolutions about bringing to an end my emotion-nurturing go plump to hell! I come home, the entire way my heart a jagged lump of ice. Your letter's warmth focuses on it; immediately it melts to flood my eyes. What can I say except that cold hostile night had held on tenaciously to my day till your letter came & brought crisp April-singing morning.

I knew my parents would come around; even if they should suffer a relapse, eventually they will accept us & love you too. How can they help it? But how did YOUR parents take it? Haven't I mentioned several times what a fine person Shirl is? In the mail with your letter I received one from Laughlin. He says, "Thank you, I should be happy to look over your essay on Hopkins."

October 16, 1940

Close? Any closer & you'd push me out of myself entirely; as it is, you've deposed me, most eagerly obedient to every thought of you. Even when I harbor ideas not made directly of the experience of you, even then you are the obliggato, the atmosphere, the weather of each. Just imagine being the framework to my just now reading about the parentage of Rimbaud! But you are.

Finally, my Dearest, the Weisses have come around; finally, they admit your loveliness! It pleases me to think how "right" I was so long ago. My primary worry these days is, in fact, a growing fear that I'm not worthy of you. I had had hints of this long years; now everything—your letters, your you, serves to confirm that early fear. All along I've known what a fineness you are & what greater fineness you'll become. Believe me, I'm not trying to flatter. Rather than customary love-myopia, this is a detached observation. And eventually, I fear, you will not be able to put up with my childish petulance & easy pique.

But how dare we despair? I've just met a handsome, brilliant young Indian who can stay here only three months. A disciple of Gandhi, he must return, to imprisonment probably & possibly death. He tells this casually, punctuated by his radiant smile.

October 17, 1940

Of course I intended to write to Mother & Shirl. But I decided to defer doing so till I heard from them. In the same mail with your letter I received one from Mother. Not a word about your visit, not a word about what transpired on your return. So, emboldened by your advice, I've taken the bull by the horns & just now written candidly to each separately. May nothing I've written serve to revive the it-would-seem dying fires.

I wish I could say something a little more pointed about your violin lessons. I understand your hesitancy. I know how much time your homework & your dancing, not to forget your letter-to-me-a-day, eat up. Yet I cannot help disliking the thought (forgive my presumptuousness about YOUR work) of your coming under the tutelage of some inferior Allentown teacher, especially after your years of study with such an excellent teacher in Philadelphia. It pains me to think that, maturing as you are, you may not have the best guide for that maturing. And yet, Dearest, you will do what you deem soundest. Only remember that I insist—yes, insist!—on music from you. I'll try to supply the poetry.

~

T & R
SUNDAY EXERCISES

This October morning
one cacaphony intones all
past racketty Sundays:

Father, hunched
over the piano, practicing;
upstairs the violins

scraping away, she
intent, brother reading
comics as he fiddled scales.

The house a bedlam,
Mother hovers near, longing
for a moment's harmony.

Over and over
relentlessly Father strikes
those obstinate notes

to make them listen,
to exorcise his grating
business week: rows on rows

of sofas, tables,
beds and bureaus, ads to be
prepared, rigid as his

Pennsylvania Dutch
customers, his salesmen,
bills piled up, unbudgeable.

Devout before his
outrage at a wrathful,
arbitrary God, religiously

he's hammering
at keys that, precisely hit,
unlock the gates

to magnificent
concords swelling up within him.
Then rows on rows

will graciously
resound, the windrowed crops,
the bulging barns,

the cloud-light
hills, hosanna to the heavens
every brook reviews.

He batters away.
No bird, ravenous for spaces,
open, glorious

spaces just beyond,
beats more stubbornly at bars,
its feathers flying.

~

October 18, 1940

Just out of bed & sleep, but hardly fresh. Even my dreams dog me & hound you too, My Dearest, as you penetrate to the very inners of my sleep. I suppose, were I wise, I wouldn't repeat this dream; but it's still tugging at its leash, & since I promised to report to you as much of what happens in me as possible, here goes. Dreams are rare with me (used up in writing poems?). Furthermore, several times I've mentioned my pettinesses to you: here's a chance to show one to you in the flesh, though this one, I think, you're pretty familiar with by now. I love you too much to try to show myself to you in disguises. I'm given to inveterate suspicion & jealousy. Somehow we'll have to uproot this. But the dream!

I'm walking down the road, scuffling my feet & tired, probably returning from a long hike to the mailbox. Piano-puling bars of "Love's Old Sweet Song" engulf me. Infuriated, I dash to the side of the road. And as though to oblige my anger, a connected series of one-story rooms grows up before me, all clad in shaggy fur. I knock on all the doors, but there's no answer, as "Love's Old Sweet Song" idiots away, nearly driving me mad. Finally, I batter the last door to the right & it opens. There is your brother sitting at the head of a long table, surrounded by friends. Apparently he's presiding at some special meeting of a secret (your civics paper?!) organization. They're also dressed in shaggy fur, wearing orange around their throats. "Where's your sister?" I insist, my voice mottled with rage. Bobby evades, then, "She's busy." The piano, meantime, is still playing away. And I know

now somehow that its song & you are synonymous. At this juncture I begin to see a rage of rainbows. "Where is she?" I hoarsely demand. "She's with somebody else," someone pipes up. "Give another guy a chance; you've had yours," chimes in a third. I can endure it no longer; so I shatter my dream & myself in the dream, shatter my sleep, jump right through its fire-papered hoop. And the dream drops in tatters around me. What a field-day this dream would make for a Freudian—especially an amateur!

Just returned from Van Doren's Shakespeare class, the wind whooping it up something fierce. See how cramped this writing is? The wind's still blowing through my fingers. But I have your letter (& your rose!) well in hand; they will thaw it out.

My excessively high thought of you? Balderdash! Just last evening I was retailing your excellence to David (it was his birthday) in those matters in which women are supposed to be "catty." Deeply impressed, he congratulated me on my good fortune. (I know this sounds a little puerile, but with my temperament I sometimes just can't help showing you off. If I flaunt some of my pretty bad poems in people's faces, what must I do with you!)

David, by the way, read me a light little poem he had written—delightful is hardly the word for it; he's a master of words & atmosphere. I trudge along my at least ten so-called poems a day, but not too well. I've come under a very injurious influence, it seems. Myself! Living alone as I do, way up on the 14th floor, except for my classes & books & occasional sorties to the Schuberts & the Weisses, & of course you & your letters, I'm forced to look to myself for nearly all ideas, settings, etc., etc. It turns out not very satisfying. But before I die of self-pity & unrequited self-love, I better ask myself how much more—if indeed as much—David has.

October 20, 1940

Sleep-laved & showered, the Sunday morning streets also sun-washed & clear like the cool ringing of bells, I come to you, My Dearest. As I dressed I couldn't help thinking how much our letters are, in our most desperate moments, like notes enclosed in bottles entrusted to the questionable care of the sea. At more pacific (!) times, however, I become a doge casting, on the holy day, a ring into the wave-hands, merciful, of sea. He does this calmly, secure in his faith in God; I do it intensely, strong in the sacrament of love & my belief in you. So, My Lovely, accept this little prayer. May it arrow-swiftly hit its target.

You recall my telling you about the scramble-jumble I had slipped into with the Weisses & Schuberts? Moments this week I felt nearly certain the Weisses & I had ship-wrecked. During our dinner I experienced a certain distance in them. Paul, seeing me telephone, immediately surmised it to be to the Schuberts. However, roaming in the landscape of my thoughts about you, I brushed it away. The next day without you & terribly alone, I could not thrust off this feel-ing of possible alienation. Telephoning, I visited them in the afternoon. They were cordial but cool. Piqued, more so by the remarks they passed concerning you & me, I left, resolved to leave the future of our friendship in their hands.

Nothing happened. I neither saw nor heard from them. Annoyed by our mutual infantility, I decided to try again. I called Friday late noon. Renee, very contrite, said they were invited out for dinner, but that I must come over Saturday afternoon. I did so. If our friendship had to end, at least I wished to know why.

Time passed pleasantly enough, they as affable (& affectionate) as ever. They insisted I stay for dinner. Then the entire business blurted itself out. Their roster of grievances were these: I coddle you too much; I monopolize you & everything around us as though to shield you from everything & everyone & so do not give you the opportunity to get to others.

To a considerable degree, My Dearest, this charge is too valid. In all my selfishness I've wanted to keep you totally to myself. So I take over. This is surely terribly wrong & hardly helpful for you. What I'm doing is continuing the regime of your father, the very thing I've criticized him for to you.

My motives are too plain. I'm the kind who has to impress HIMself continuously (must be an inferiority complex!). If I don't write at least ten poems a day, so enjoy a seeming victory over myself & time, I'm despondent. Since you're the person dearest to me, I feel—usually unconsciously I maintain—that every minute I must impress you with my brilliance, my wit, etc. Apparently I think I must rewin your love everyday. (To some extent it IS necessary.) Consequently, when someone else, especially a male, comes into your ken I try to keep you entirely apart & then to prove to you by my scintillance how intolerably dull he is. The same thing happened with the Weisses. It's almost as though I stood over you with a huge club, glowering at all comers, daring them to approach.

That's not all. Paul persuaded Renee that she mothers me too much, that I'm a free agent & should be permitted to determine the course of my life by myself.

After all this, I was irritated. Despite their extreme goodness, I pointed out to them, in the end they had proved inconsiderate. Certainly I hogged you, but isn't that usual enough in young lovers? I had, it appears, I continued, taken their friendship too much for granted. Had they been less close to me, I'd not have acted as I did, disregarding them. Moreover, they seemed to forget I had you for just a few hours.

Though they do not realize it, the heart of the matter is that they were jealous. I do not think I overestimate myself or their affection for me. This was palpably clear in the Schubert tangle. As the Schuberts told me some time ago (not realizing that they were presenting a partial portrait of themselves: we almost always do ourselves to some degree when we describe others), when they were alone with the Weisses one time this summer, they were deeply struck by the jealousy (unconscious) the Weisses revealed in speaking of you & me. So like hurt children they drew away from me.

Yet I'm not angry with them; on the contrary. How can one be when, as Renee put it, "You've become a necessary part of the family." But what's much more important, a pleasing evidence of their after all essential bigness & goodness, they like you, & very much. They arraigned me, never you. In many ways they consider you (as I always have) more "grown up" than I am.

Excuse, please, this steamroller of a letter; in all its plodding I think it right you should know all this. Furthermore, an occasional (if very occasional) boring Sunday sermon, especially with a happy ending, may not be amiss.

October 21, 1940

Just received your letter, My Own, & it starts morning out on the right foot. The only objection I have to receiving a morning letter is that there's none to look forward to at noon; I have to make the early one stretch & work overtime till tomorrow. But a letter such as this is sturdy enough to last the day & more. Reading your words, I've been walking back & forth in my room to give my love & delight elbowroom. For feelings large & numerous as these one should have at least several bodies and a huge estate.

Off to Van Doren's Shakespeare. See you after dinner. . . It's happened! Two letters in one day. I casually look into my mail-box & there you are!

74

You needn't play the piano, Lovest; it's enough that you are associated in my mind with music. As for the "give another guy a chance" from my dream, that has not so much to do with you as with me—the excessive strength of my fear. But how do you account for the fur & the orange?

My Pop's employing you as a paragon of girlhood surprises me even less. All the time, Dearest, believe it, my parents have been compelled, if begrudgingly, to think highly of you & your conduct. Before you & I became lovers they were often most profuse in praise of you. Only when they realized how much I was yours did they begin to ferret out ulterior motives for your actions. Even during this summer, when my Pop's fury was at high tide & overflowing its banks, even then he resorted to you as an object lesson & model for Shirl. They do not know it, but early they helped to awaken me to what you are.

Your Philadelphia decision pleases me very much. But will your lessons fall out on a Sunday & will you be driving all the way to Philly & back again, particularly in winter weather?

October 23, 1940

I thought so, Dearest. Affairs are hardly as hunkydory as you believed & I hoped—though doubted. Why the devil can't your dad keep his mouth shut?! Instead of explaining what I mean, I'll just quote a passage from Mom's latest letter:

"Sorry you have so much work, but according to Mr. Karol's complaint you certainly must have lots of time, writing Renee a letter every day, which, I'm sure, he very much resents (the liar) so he says. I am again reminding you to please take your work seriously." And then her last sentence: "Please don't write Renee everything I tell you."

Why must your father blab as much as he does? Was

it your father's remark that angered you? Did he chide you for writing every day, did he say that I was wasting your time, not allowing you to practice, etc. as much as you ought? Or does he dislike the fact that writing daily costs money? Forgive me, Mine; he IS your father. Attribute what I have written here to my anger, not to me (though I AM anger this moment). And remember that I take the tone I do because someone has tried to come between us. Let us somehow keep our love clean of all the to-doing and dirtying of our parents.

However, if letter-writing IS interfering with your practicing, perhaps we'd better settle down to letters twice a week? You yourself write: "I haven't been practicing regularly." Does your dad blame your growing interest in dancing also on me?!

Already, Loveling, the anger's beginning to subside. It's fortunate indeed that such passions cannot last longer than they do. By the very strength of their fire they burn themselves out quickly. In any case, your dad & I have been too close friends for me to hold a grudge against him more than briefly.

October 24, 1940

Ah, Sweetest, in this day of almost excessive sun most things seem fantastic; but upon the inrush of thought nothing is more fantastic than the sun itself. What a dolt nature can be! how insensitive to the world's suffering! and how fortunately. If nature cried with us there'd be nothing to hold on to, nothing to shake us out of ourselves.

You are right; the situation is indeed untenable. Mother has sent me a long private letter telling me of your dad's most recent exploits. They apparently are more than willing to make peace, but equally apparently he is not.

Upon reception of Mother's letter I was primed to

write him a fire-&-brimstone note informing him of my exact & complete contempt &, finally, to take the next train home. Fortunately prudence took the reins. What could we gain by any of these actions? Further, I can little afford to estrange him more. He supports you & so somewhat (!) determines your conduct. Suppose he were to decide that you cannot [visit] N.Y. anymore? We must bide our time.

I'm afraid, Dearest, to give us some stability in this business, we'll simply have to marry soon. At the moment I feel that would be an answer to everything. What do you think?

October 28, 1940

Of course I realize Mom sent me a bare third-hand version of the situation. Do you think I could for a moment forget her hates, prejudices, rage? Her statement alone I'd not have given any credence. But it happens your Mother substantially confirmed everything my Pop reported to my Mom. And with your letter I receive one from Shirl suggesting: "Perhaps if Mr. Karol would keep his mouth shut everything would be nice & quiet." Mother's letter was really a cry of desperation, not anger or hate, this time. Apparently she had been working long & hard on my Pop; now she finds all the good work crumbling about her head.

Were we not so immersed, I could easily find material for rich humor in this situation. Your Pop—who is, of course, a much more subtle person than my parents—was, I should say, taking human, if not sharply humorous, advantage of them. As you said, he was making my father "eat his own cooking." Maybe for a Hungarian that's not all bad?

Thinking about the whole affair, I must confess I can't quarrel with Abe's point of view. He knows what I want to do & be in the world. Theoretically I'm sure he applauds it, but practically he's doubtless uneasy. After all, he IS interested in your future welfare. He realizes what a hopelessly hard time I may have of it, & you too, tied up with me. With the entire Karol family already in his furniture store, he doesn't look forward to the burden of yet another family. As his friend I was fine, but as a son-in-law? And as a dealer in furniture!?

October 29, 1940

The Weisses & the Schuberts go along lickety split. The Schuberts are especially mature in this matter & terribly dear to me. Seeing how miserably much I miss you, they insist I stay with them more often. But low as I usually am, so more susceptible, David is not too good an atmosphere: he's much too infectious. Only when I'm at my healthiest are we fine together; then I bolster him. The other day he went to Van Doren's class with me. He sat (as he is wont to do) with his luminous eyes staring inward till I thought any moment they would swallow him up entirely. He struggles so with such a plethora of problems.

No, My Sweetest, I've not been working on the poems. New ones won't allow it. David, however, has insisted it's high time I call a halt. And he proposed that, as soon as he gets a grip on himself (Whenever that will be! Poor fellow, he still enjoys the happy illusion he's always just on the verge of recovery.), he will go through all my poems with me. That should prove an exceptional help. First, because I would have to consider them again; second, because David could give me the fruits of his unusually fine (instinctive) critical faculties. Almost at sight he knows a good poem from a bad. I did, however, already read a few poems to David & Judy that they claimed they liked very much.

What do you mean, "Dad had decided to wash his hands of the entire affair?" Is it in disgust or anger? Or had he returned to his original position, that parents shouldn't interfere?

October 30, 1940

My Lyric Mine, who's the poet in THIS family, you or I? Look here, I'm getting tired of praising you. Do you think I want to spend the rest of my (our) life hurling superlatives at you? Seriously, Dearest, from a purely artistic point of view (whatever that may be!) your letter charmed me head to foot. How far you've travelled from the hidden little rabbit-girl I first knew! Your words are just the nosegay (nosegay, hell! heartgay) I need in this drizzle-day. Morning started with a bang, poems buzzing in my head like honey-sucking bumble-bees. But now (1 o'clock) my energy has ebbed. If you don't mind, I'll take your letter again as tonic.

I Yes your analysis of love: there are times when I want you to share the world with me, others when I want you to shield me from its cares. But I'm still too deep in the smoke & flames of love to be able to remark the essential features of it. Whatever's up, good feelings or bad, joy or sad, I require you, require, require. In the former I want to take you for a ride in my delight; in the latter I want you to save me from being ridden over by depression.

Though I envy it just the biggest bit, I'm glad you're dancing. Keep up the good footwork. And make sure every step brings you closer to me.

~

T & R
THROUGH OUR HANDS

I see an intentness in you
as of one gazing out a window
to the far distance for something
gathering there, a face perhaps
strange as it's familiar.

At once I sense you too
are watching someone watching
in your head, like mirrors clear-
eyed in a veritable Versailles
of watching.
                    In turn I peer
through you to the next onlooker,
the next and next until I feel
I've mined them all.
                                This spot,
small as it is, but one blink
brief, the whole world wings
to through our hands clinging
to each other.
                        Stars may borrow
light more readily from remotest
kin. And waves lunge far above us,
far beyond, yet, of a single water,
cannot make a sea as uniform
as ours.

And because we've been
so intricately interknitted,
the lines between us drawn out
long yet taut, we're free.

Wherever the waves have ended
and the sun has set, the starlight
fettered in some far-gone time
and place,
                    or in a time
and place not yet named or met,
already I, my hand through yours
outstretched, can spy those faces
blending, intent, in your face.

                            ~

October 31, 1940

Whoops! She's coming in! She's coming in! Give my undying gratitude, my joy, my library, my stamp collection, my best suit, my gold medal, my whatyouwill to Bobby for offering to look after Rowie. I've been a dog, a rat, a snake, a mere head, a snob, a wordmonger, et. al. to have said you're too much concerned about him. I embrace him, a splendid violinist, a good sport, a real comic, & dub him Sir Robert Karolahad.

Last night, returning from the Schuberts in the autumn-fragrance, spurred by the rain, deep inside me I pick you miles, miles up in terrible love & hurting, killing joy. I love you so frantically often I'm ecstatically afraid of it. What's to prevent the flame from burning me to a cinder? If someone had told me about such a fellow & such a case before, had described his "exaggerated" feelings & language, I'd have scoffed at him as a maudlin, sentimental, incorrigible romantic. Yet here I come along & do the very same thing! But am I sorry? Hell, no!

How is it you spent the afternoon & evening with my Folks? Just a friendly visit? I don't know my draft number, Sweet; I'd have to send to Allentown for it. But, as I see it, it doesn't matter very much whether I know it or not: if the government wants me to appear, it'll send me its questionnaire soon enough. Anyway, THEY know where to find me, if they want me.

~

T & R
May Commotions - for bob

As the gingko
   twirls
through a symphony
   of leaves

   a solo ou
      bobs
on the string-
   taut twig
of its tweet
   while a rain,
      drowsing
in a puddle,
      dreams
its long flight

   and from Boston
      to Hawaii
the high-wire
   violist
still plucks
heart's strings.

~

November 1, 1940

Once more, Dearest, the old ball of love (not a snow-ball either!) has started rolling. I've tried to prevent myself from becoming so head-over-heels excited at the thought of your visit. But slowly, inexorably, the frenzy accumulates. Sometimes I think I'm just a huge pot of consciousness & some invisible witch is madly stirring all kinds of steaming-hot juices inside me.

As for my Parents, since you offered to keep them informed of your visits, I suppose you better tell them. This you can do boldly. If they approve, fine. If not, well. . . .

I hope I haven't burdened you too much with all my talk about growing up. I stress it so because I've known right along that already you're much more mature in many respects than I could ever be. Seems to me in certain regards some people are just born grownup, something in the essential fiber of the person. Or, as you more practically might say, a result of the responsibilities thrust upon you: a baby sister & a mischievous, unpredictable younger brother. Charges of yours because you did not altogether trust your pretty passive mother. Now, exceeding all three in the need to be looked after—me!

November 4, 1940

Nature in her cruelty is often exceedingly considerate. Thus the blessed numbness still prevails. Morning-long I wrote, little more than finger exercises: the hands moved & spoke but hardly knew what they said. Then at eleven I went to Van Doren's class. There, by sheer strength of his gentlemanly brilliance, for a moment he pulled me out of my stupor. He was talking about the verbal splendor of Shakespeare's lines & one in particular, "The uncertain glory of an April day." The line, set as it is in love sentiments, coupled with the fact that Van Doren's remarks here & his eyes were addressed to me, momentarily kindled me. And for the first time since I've been attending the class I volunteered (quite involuntarily) some observations of my own. Fortunately this exchange let out (& in) thought, but no feeling.

The day itself, Loveling, is a splendor, one of the sun-brooding variety Autumn prominently carries in her repertory. I know this even though I do not feel it. Seems you are the violinist necessary to tune me so that the music can play. Without you I'm jangled, turning everything I touch into discordancy. Remember some of the phrases I muttered yesterday? Here's the outcome:

Eden Is Where We Touch
So we New York this day away
on the sixteenth floor;
& all razzledazzle Broadway,
but humanly, is here:
Eden wrapt up in a room,
paradise disguised as walls,
a myopic, astigmatic window,
a bed, a docile radio, a bible.
While the radio floods
the room with rainbows
we go first to the concert
of our looks, from this
to the brightlights
crackling of our fingers,
then a play, one of lips,
a Shakespeare of a kiss:
from this to rise
to one of Christ—
O Christ! kiss as crucifix—
how did Christ get into this?

84

& last the night spots,
the hot, the cabarets,
the binges,

        till I'm not.

November 5, 1940

    Last night, running from myself as I always do when you've left, I fled to the Schuberts, slept there & stayed (since it's Election Day) till late afternoon. All morning I spent alone on the Schubert roof—Judy was at school, David had an appointment. The roof-hours I divided among you, Rilke's *Wartime Letters*, & the view: the sun, a bold, fullfaced, naked sky & tugboats dragging the distant busy water.

November 8, 1940

    Gosh, I'm lucky! A Sweetness like you loving me, a leaven even through my loneliness. My luck? Having such three in a row: you, David (he spent yesterday with me at Columbia; we talked till our words reached sheer releasing laughter), & writers like Rilke. I've just finished his letters. It is amazing how much of a fool such a wise poet was, & wisely had to be, to be wise. I read him page after page with the feeling that he was merely writing, caught in the snare of his own technique, when suddenly I collide with a thought, a phrase, an image that shoots off sparks everywhere. Then I come away thinking that probably all these abortive attempts were needed to produce the final bouquet of flames: one must strike the flint & tinder together many, many times before fire starts. Or maybe it's spontaneous combustion: a lot of old rag-phrases, greased with living, crammed into dark closet-lines; & presto! conflagration. Anyway, it makes me happy just to think that this man should have lived—one of the few who attract & intrigue life so that the child of it, the innocent, completely freed, at breathless moments steps out in all its vibrant loveliness.

As I go out into the beginning of the day, you three make the morning a gaiety, my blood a light, a lightness, a laughter, O so rich. I cross the street to take my alarm clock for repair. Coming out, I see a little carriage-seated child looking about with piercing question-mark eyes. I send you, Dearest, a snippet, a snapshot, of the child's unblinking astonishment.

You hate the thought of a two-week wait no more than I. In some manner we must learn to employ the time between visits so that it intensifies rather than damages the visit. Till now for me, as you know, each day has acted as a chisel chipping away at the pleasure I reach when you are here. Then not only do I have the past to contend with but the future also, thoughts of how soon you must leave & how much more accentuated my loneliness will be because of this brief taste of you. So between them the past & future diminish our present. This must change. Hereafter we must come to each other, full to overflowing with the fruits we have plucked from our days apart. Day after day, My Lovely, I will strive to gather these fruits to deposit joyously into your lap when we are one once more. I (we) must learn what Rilke so sagely says of himself:

"I long ago accustomed myself to take given things according to their intensity, without, so far as that is humanly achievable, worrying about duration; that is perhaps the best and discreetest way of expecting EVERYTHING from them—even duration. If one begins with THAT demand, one spoils and falsifies every experience, indeed, one hinders it in its own inmost inventiveness and fruitfulness."

This can only happen if we make our days apart ones of constant effort, culminating in the climax of our being together. So too we must desist from laments of love. Too much leaning on this one feeling can become stifling. Then love, desiring to be an absolute, reaches an impasse & gradually declines. By leaving love to discuss other matters we will give it an opportunity to grow, unhindered; & we will return to it renewed & deeper in love than ever.

Before I close I'd like to repeat a little more Rilke: "I call fate all external events (illnesses, for example, included) which can inevitably step in to interrupt and annihilate a disposition of mind and training that is by nature solitary. Cézanne must have understood this when during the last years of his life he removed himself from everything that, as he expressed it, might 'hook him tight,' and when religious and given to traditions as he was, he yet gave up going to his mother's funeral in order not to lose a working day. That went through me like an arrow, when I learned it, but like a flaming arrow that, while it pierced my heart through, left it in a conflagration of clear sight. There are few artists in our day who grasp this stubbornness, this vehement obstinacy. But I believe without it one remains always at the periphery of art, which is rich enough as it is to allow us pleasant discoveries, but at which, nevertheless, we halt only as a player at the green table who, while he now and again succeeds with a coup, remains none the less at the mercy of change, which is nothing but the docile and dexterous ape of law.

You, Dearest, must help me achieve such stubbornness, such consecration. You realize well enough that art like life must be courted religiously, not casually like the sundry flirtations of a philanderer. Art demands fullhearted, fulltime devotion such as I feel for you. You must give me your hands to find similar dedication in my writing & to help fortify me against the multiple insidious distractions of our days. You must help me to push deeper & deeper into myself, rather than losing myself in momentarily attractive surfaces.

And yet such dedication—"Leave thy father & thy mother & follow me."—can have its worrisome side as well. Its rigor suggests the ruthlessness of a god or the indifference of a self-absorbed beast. How can one be sure one is one rather than the other? And would Rilke, however much I left my father & my mother, condone my all-out love for you? His comportment with his wife & their child would certainly suggest the reverse.

~

T & R
A MODESTY

I

This carving, like the cat
minus half an ear, not yet done
with stalking mice, abides here,
taking every day and every night
as the night and day most apt.

II

Soil the carving's maker
ploughed, fruits he gathered,
cows he milked, the cat admiring,
taught him his seeing hands,

deepened by the woman working
at his side, as by the child
passed through them.
                              And passed

beyond their reach. Carefully
they wrapped him, then put him
back into the ground.
                    The cat,
slinking in and out, helped
to keep things going.

            III
Innocent of designs on us,
this carving's true as any scrap
of lumber worked by rain, wind,
snow.
        Its parent maple inspiring
still, it reaches out, the sun
direct on it.
                Like a brown study,
its fissures—fresh ones scoring
old—appear as telling as the cat's
half ear, strokes cut in the face
of him who would make a something
lasting.

                    ~

November 10, 1940
        My Dearest, You must write, write much more, poet-
ry I mean—not simply to gratify my pride in you so that I
can go around (like my Pop) spouting your poems to peo-
ple. I urge it primarily to sharpen your senses & to cultivate
your articulation. Writing poems means that you will have to
observe more & more, so live more fully. Read the poets,
your heart, & your senses. And WRITE.
        Your letter was all that (& more than) I dared to
hope. How you've come through for me. That's another rea-

son I need you: you make me examine myself constantly & try my hardest to "improve". Whereas you might have become righteously (& legitimately) angry, you reply with utmost consideration & love. I wasn't wrong, if anything, fairly conservative, in my estimate of you. Forgive me for gloating, for telling myself, I told you so!

But I feel a wee bit shabby taking you up as quickly as I am going to do now, holding you to your "Any place you are is my happiness." I want to marry you as soon as possible; the thought of waiting two years, three, maybe four seems utterly absurd. And soon you'll be quite old enough—the past is full of brides considerably less than 18.

But doing what I'm doing now, the prospects of our marrying soon are meager indeed. Even armed with a Ph.D. in, say, two more years, I MIGHT—just might—get a job at $1400 or $1500 a year. Is that a livelihood? Thus far the best (really the only) proposition that has presented itself is the bookstore in Minneapolis with the Weisses. The past week they have become increasingly enthusiastic & urgent about it. Despite my previous dubiety, the idea has begun to take root.

Two bookstores on Broadway deal in publishers' remainders. These stores are usually packed—with buying customers, not only books. Paul & Renee insist such a shop must go like a house on fire in Minneapolis (a city they praise most highly for its landscapes & its man- & woman-scapes). Not only is there no such shop in Minneapolis but, despite the large, literate population, no half decent bookstore of any kind. Paul & Renee are tired of cold—in people, not temperature—New York, so enthusiastic to leave at once.

There are other inducements. If the store worked, we could marry when you graduate in June. You could attend the University of Minnesota, many heads above Miami U. or Allentown's Cedar Crest.

During the summer the Weisses scoured Minneapolis. They claim they hit on the best spot for a bookstore; they've even won the enthusiastic support of several successful business men. So where's the catch? We'd need $1000 each to establish the store. Normally my Pop would sign a note & monthly I'd pay him back. But Pop, I'm convinced, (if I could talk to him at all!) would scoff at the idea: a "little bookseller!"; then he'd attack it with "You're doing it just to get married" (& he'd be right!). That leaves YOUR Pop! How do you think he would take it, if I told him I intend to marry you & laid out the proposition? Two proposals at once! Surely more persuasive than one!?

November 11, 1940

I have to prepare an oral report for tomorrow, have to push my way through at least ten books. Still I have to keep you up to date on my reactions to the bookstore. Despite its attractiveness, thinking it over more calmly, I've less & less stomach for it. Yesterday I spoke to the Schuberts about it: they, particularly Judy, voiced my deepest sentiments. In the best part of me I despise the idea. Were I man enough—Judy agrees—I'd hunt down a job in this city, try to make enough for the two of us to live on, if need be in one room.

The thought of going to Minneapolis appealed to me, for a moment: to wit, escaping both our families. But there's the risk of our falling under the heels of Renee's large &, I gather, oppressive relations. More, there's the possessiveness of Renee & Paul. I'm exaggerating undoubtedly, but I can't help feeling that they'd immediately start to swallow us up. O I know this must sound ludicrous. But, Dearest, it's our future I'm thinking of: rather the pinch of poverty than imperious people. Or do you say I'm talking nonsense?

November 13, 1940

You are, of course, as ever, right, Sweetest: I must decide & then do it. But decision in this matter (Minneapolis vs. N.Y.) is, as they say in the movies, veiled in mists & fraught with perils. O, I know one must take a chance; that comes with being born. But I hate like hell gambling with your future. What are my plans for N.Y. now? Taking up the teaching job hunt again; then, going around to all the employment agencies.

You make one prodigious error; you insist that I must decide, first of all, without considering you. Don't you realize that's no longer possible? Where do I end in me & where do you begin? I know that work I dislike will probably take all my resistance to prevent my blaming some of my resentment on you. Any work that takes me away from writing is bound to nettle me. Thus there's nothing to do but steel myself to whatever job comes along.

At this time I can consider the Minneapolis proposition more calmly. Surely we are intelligent, strong, & in love enough to cope with its problems? Were the Weisses to become too domineering, I'm confident of your resourcefulness. Would it be foolhardy for me to pose the situation in a letter to your Dad?

November 15, 1940

Liebling, we're in a tough spot truly; the decision we make now will leave its mark on the entire character of our future. You propose that I hunt a N.Y. job; I will. But you know that, no matter what I do, most of my time will be taken up; my writing will have to play second fiddle; I'm afraid there are no casual jobs. In addition, the pay is bound to be miserable. If I were to make $18 a week I'd be fortunate. Of course I've not abandoned teaching; I AM scouring the agencies. But I cannot help feeling very pessimistic. It's not a matter of finding anything I like, it's a matter of find-ing SOMEthing. As for the Weisses, I believe my open talk with them has dispelled most of the possibilities of trouble.

In any case, if you are as fixed in your heart about me as I am about you, it's time I had a thorough talk with your Dad. He & I have never spoken about us. I want to know precisely what he thinks. Would he frown upon (perhaps even oppose) our marriage? Furthermore, I'd like to put the business end of it before his larger experience. He also had to decide whether to marry & go into the furniture business or to con-tinue with schooling. And he did decide on business. Was he sorry? Or do you think I ought to find work somewhere, make money enough to support us, without approaching him at all?

What worries me in this is that there may not be time enough: the draft's upon us; we may be just days away from war. Loving you as I do, I can't afford to wait that long. As you can gather from the little paper I'm including, Roosevelt is clearly war-minded. And although marriage would hardly keep me out of the draft without at least one dependent (& war would destroy even that), leastwise we'd be one, united as much as is possible today.

No, I've not finished the thesis. I've had an unexpect-ed paper to do; & my own writing has been too engrossing to give the remaining time to a dull M.A. subject. But with a few weeks of concentrated effort I can easily clear it out of the way.

~

T & R
THE TIME REMAINING

Suddenly he who had, it seemed,
time more than enough, and room,
to welcome every lively thought,
is
    (after several men, identical
in business suits, storm through
his books and papers)
                swarmed
over by a mob which, gobbling
his last crusts, hacking furniture
into fire-wood,
             assures him
jeeringly that, any moment now,
for crimes even his dreams could
not dream up, a jet-black limousine
will bustle him off
              to a last
resort in which eternity waits,
its choice accommodations fitting
to a T.

~

November 17, 1940
>   "Birds of sorrow may pass over your head
>   but they don't have to make nests in your hair!"
>   —said by Judy

Leaning on the Schubert-desk with the amber light embracing it, I listen a moment to the talking of my thoughts, thinking what words you would most like to receive from me. (David, lying on the bed in the opposite corner, mumbles to himself—whispering to God, then says to me: "The words are sure coming out fast, Teddy Bear," hearing the hurried scratching of my pen.) I listen a moment & all I hear for the moment is the hummingbird radiator, twittering its bright promise of heat.

I shared this Saturday night with the Schuberts. Late afternoon now. I'm so bewildered. You feel certain you've made some progress in understanding people, telling kinds & characters apart, etc.; then something happens, a snow avalanche, & you land at the foot again, aware of how high, how unattainable the top of the mountain is.

You see, My Sweets, I'm forced to believe we're all made of the same stuff, but differently distributed & in varying amounts. Why this geyser of generalization? I rose about an hour or so earlier than David & Judy; so I went up on their roof. After seeing birds exercise the morning snow-sky & feeling sufficiently aired, I came down. Judy & David had slept off sleep. We talked. A chance word set David off. As though huge piles of dry brush had been lying about, a most bitter fire broke out between Judy & David: they went at each other hammer & tongue. Though just a witness, near as they are to me, I felt terribly involved & even guilty. (Surely I had a finger in the fight.) An hour-eternity they harangued each other, I acting the feeble umpire, Judy shouting from the kitchen, David flaming back from the other room. Suddenly David stood up, said almost in glee, "I'll have to subdue her" (I expected some love-expression), dashed into the kitchen, grabbed Judy, smacked her, pushed her to the floor. So quickly it happened, so stunned & horrified was I, I hadn't time to utter one word of protest.

Must such things happen to people cultivated even as the Schuberts? Are we all & always savages? Why all this effort then? Why all this schooling, this art, this music? I'm shaken by fear.

What if I were David & you, Judy? The thought of such happenings makes me ask, Maybe people oughtn't marry? If I truly love Renee maybe I shouldn't expose her to the ugliness in me (as in us all)?

Yet there are women, David later said, who require (enjoy?) such treatment. I knew one girl who boasted about her collection of black-&-blue marks given her in great love of anger (!) by her lover. Even Lawrence maintained (I believe) that beating the woman you love is merely the consummation of love & the love act. Jesus Christ! Dearest, what kind of madness is this? Perhaps it's that I'm a coward, so soft? Perhaps these facts of living mean nothing at all & are to be accepted quite casually? But what is the significance then of our vaunted human beingness & dignity?

Paul & Renee fight too, often, & fiercely, & with joy: Renee, it seems, relishes it (the fierceness of love?). Though it offends me, I accept it in them. But in David & Judy? It implies such a bankruptcy of spirit, such an accumulation of hate, such a defeat of heart & head & such a triumph of brutality. (For David to raise his hand!) It indicates such utter confusion, such belittling of being, such chipping away at self. Liebling, we'll quarrel & truculently too, but I pray there'll never come the time when we violate the boundaries of each other's being, when love lets go & hate tramples the other person.

I can blame neither David nor Judy (blame!): we are all such godforsaken victims, it seems; but surely there exists SOME dignity & understanding in love? Why do we so often turn our weaknesses, our shortcomings, the hates we gather from the world around us, on the ones we love best? Judy tells me the fight didn't mean anything. Just now David kisses her, makes a paper dunce-hat for her & puts her in the corner. She says something & immediately he begins to shout again.

Though we (& the world too) have agreed on the close kinship between pleasure & pain, & though I can understand why a woman might momentarily thrill to the expression of caveman superiority in her man, it seems to me the blow it must be to her sense of equality (or partnership) & dignity must ever thereafter seriously impair her own self-respect & foster an ever-growing resentment.

But the role of the shrew (a woman endowed with a barbed tongue, one that as though by magic hits on her man's most sensitive spots—as I've often seen my mother unerringly do with my father) persisted in, sometimes leaves him feeling helpless, furious, with no mind but his hand.

Judy, I assure you, hardly liked that moment (no more than David did). Both attempted to joke it away, but.... The act in itself is, of course, like most acts of violence unimportant; but the set of circumstances which produced it, the impasse it implies (mentally & emotionally), is of the utmost discouraging significance. Yet somehow, romantically I suppose, I go on believing that WE can steer clear of such disasters.

As for environment vs. heredity, this is a problem I fear it'll take centuries (if not forever) to settle. I'd say it's pretty much a 50-50 proposition. Moreover, I'm inclined to believe that the emphasis on one or the other depends almost wholly on the individual. If it is the run-of-the-mill person you are contemplating, I agree: remarkably much can be done to salvage him from drossy living. But it seems to me environment has not too much to do with the really large person. All of us, of course, are somewhat vegetable & deeply influenced by the world we live in; some of us, however, are infinitely more than this world. We come into it with needs. But if we are vital, even out of apparent adversity we wring the food for those needs; if we are flickering & small we simply submit. One of the earmarks of superiority (a requisite to genius) is the ability to derive spiritual nourishment from its environment, ugly, cruel, inhuman, poverty-stricken though it may be. Often, by very hatred of such environment the artist wins through to the opposite: Blake, Burns, Van Gogh, Daumier, Joyce, etc. You do agree that character, reacting in one way or another, is purely personal, born & hereditary? Or do you?

I say again that man, to assuage his ignorance, has constantly invented myths. At one time it was God & predestination; now it's genes. One is no truer or more accurate than the other (& no falser either: words like truth or falsehood do not apply in this matter), simply clad in the terminology of the time: ours (genes), by the claims of science or technical language, gives the appearance of preciseness & reality; actually it's a story like the rest except that it no longer wears wings & commands us to love. So ours are exiguous myths.

You in your dear desire for order & improvement (your lovely rationality) overemphasize environment: you forget that a certain environment, except in cases of complete oppression, etc. (& so death), has always been accessible, fortunately, to man—that is, the environment of earth, sky, trees, animals, & other people. At best all environment can do is add faggots to the fire, bank it, shield it from too much wind, & clear away some of the ashes.

What does your Papa say about us? (Speaking of environment!)

~

T & R
HANGINGS

Over dishes clattering
and the chatter in the museum
cafeteria, a sudden hiss
breaks out.
        A crumpled
young woman, strained forward
at a table alone, hangs
listening.
        Then, face
contorted, chair screechingly
scraped back, she leaps
to her feet.
        Scuttling,
she shouts over her shoulder,
"I can't take any more
of this!"
        Wherever she
looks, some Goya, some Bosch,
in terrible mastery sets
off an agony:
        dangling
on hooks as from their bones,
flocks of Christs hacked
slabs of beef.

            Groans
transfixing her, how tolerate
this nightmare, the body,
half human
            and half beast,
incessantly gnawing at itself?

~

November 18, 1940

    Your wanting to marry as soon as possible is what I want & want you to want; the only thing that causes me pause is the "soon as possible": how tedious–long will that be? As for Minneapolis, righto! If I can hold off my desire for you till Sunday, surely I can put aside my Minneapolis-queries. The same applies to your Dad. Wait till we see each other. It would be dreadful if speaking to him resulted in a tiff. From now on, however, I suggest that, whenever occasion presents itself, you feel your Dad out about us. Whether he wishes it or no, he DOES occupy a responsible position. And even though, contrary to his will, we'd marry (wouldn't we?), I would like to know where I stand in his mind.

November 19, 1940

    Hit you & burn myself? I think not. Hitting's not in my tradition. Even my Pop, who is an incendiary if there ever was one, in his most violent, self-consuming moments has never descended to blows. Rather he's threatened to do injury to himself. This, I suppose, is the supreme egotist's way; he assumes that offering to harm his own person will enlist sympathy & consternation from the other more efficiently than any other form of torture. It is quite likely that in extreme rage I too might resort to such theatrical gestures.

I hope not. After all, I DO pride myself on my rationality (!). Despite his ragings my Dad never whipped me. I have thought that at such moments he was too immersed in his emotional mess to turn to anything as specific as a blow.

No, My Dearest, you needn't fear blows from me—not physical ones; but other kinds, those of the verbal variety, may occasion us a good deal more concern. THESE are the ones I'll have to learn to curb.

My Sweetest, forgive this treatise: I'm just back from a two-hour seminar; this probably accounts for my above pontificating. You see, I DO indulge in verbal batterings of you.

November 22, 1940

Day-all I've been carrying you in my body. So I've taken you to Newark with me where we Turkeyed this day away with my grandparents, my uncle, his wife, her mother, and my uncle's six-year-old son, Jerry.

I spent the hours telling my grandparents & family what (!) a person you are, how (!) much I love you, & how (!) badly I need a job. The remaining time I played with Jerry—sweet little fellow whose bright-eyes, always busy, seem to hail the rest of his face along, the way stars buoy the night. He's so full to over-flowing with allergies (he daren't eat any sweets, daren't be near dust, feathers, perfume, etc., etc.), one could almost say he's allergic to living itself. With such an abnormal childhood he should blossom into a first-rate decadent poet. Yet he's sturdy, spontaneous. Convinced that I, because of my bulk, must be a football star for Columbia, he informed the neighbor kids that today his football cousin was coming to visit him.

For a considerable space after dinner he & I wrestled on his bed; tiring, I pretended sleep in one eye & shushed him, telling him he'd waken my other eye. He took the fancy with great glee & gustily tiptoed through the house whispering this choice bit of news, hushing everyone into silence.

But I forgot to mention that, not only did my Folks listen sympathetically to what I had to say about you & me, but they heartily applauded the idea of a soon job & marriage. And, thanks be, my uncle pressed a $5.00 bill on me, just what we need for your visit.

On the long tube-ride home from Newark, I found it diverting watching one person watching another person watching another person, on & on in an endless chain till I realized with a start that right along someone'd been watching me watching. It's fascinating to see what one woman's hair does to another's eyes (then the latter turned her eyes, now symbols of contempt, to the crossword puzzle the former was doing), how young men's eyes gloss the legs of across-the-aisle women. These eyes & faces are subjective mirrors, reflecting what the person is seeing, but also what the person is—mirrors with a past & a personality.

November 25, 1940

Well, I've been around to see the Employment Lady. She was very considerate & encouraging. I told her I'd be willing to take even a Prep School job, in fact anything that might turn up. I assured her I can teach debating, oratory, dramatics, history of art, tennis!

Moreover, I've arranged for an interview this week in regard to any other job beside teaching. One o'clock I'll see Van Doren. Three-thirty I'm to meet David to inquire about civil service exams. So you see I'm beginning to do my bit; you'll have to do yours—that is, keep smiling; remember it may just be a dream we cooked up between us, & things can always be much worse!

It's grotesquely amusing: raw & overwrought as my feelings are, sitting in class, I can still write poemicules. You yourself, Dearest, prescribed poetry. As you said, "When you feel very glum, sit down & write yourself out of it." I hope you've been able to counsel yourself? So befogged am I, I don't even have to write, just sit & listen to the sun & my door rattling & my clock cricketing the time away, I a fly in the amber-clear of this autumn sunlight. Always, you know, when the situation gets too much out of hand, good old nature seems to inject me with some dope, just the way doctors do when their patitent's pain is too excruciating. Then I go through the movements of a day, attend classes, smile at people, talk, eat, etc.; but all the time my head's deposited asleep on some farthest shelf.

P.S. I've put away all of $7.00 for your next visit: marriage license & what not.

November 26, 1940

Save for the interview I'm to have this Thursday, Sweetest, I've just about completed everything I can do in regard to a job. Yesterday I visited several professors; one suggested I write off to a whole flock of better colleges requesting application blanks for fellowships & assistantships. I intend to do so at once. This morning I saw Professor Campbell, perhaps the most influential man in my department. Most interested, he said he'd certainly let me know posthaste as soon as anything turns up. If anyone can help, he can.

So you've come through as I thought you would. You're totally right about my talking too much. And I judge myself something of a poet! What kind of poet is this who is inconsiderate of, cannot recognize immediately, the feelings of his Dearest One? Your letter, I'm happy to say, makes all the things I've written to you sound like something out of a finicky old maiden aunt. Since I've come to know you, that is, since I began to love you, I've sensed in you, & overwhelmingly, an inner poise, a cool strength that you yourself probably don't yet realize. Instinctively, requiring such firmness, I turned to you at once. Now you completely confirm my feeling.

November 29, 1940

Every once in a while I catch myself smiling, smiling straight at you. I'm happy, quietly happy: the reasons: today the world's agreeing with me.

Then in the morning mail I received a note from one of my teacher-friends, Wells by name. Last week, carrying several poems with me & running into him, on the spur of the moment, pocket-hot as they were, I read them to him. And he wrote: "I enjoyed your poems greatly. In fact I hope very much some day to possess a copy of your latest joyful offspring. More to the point just now is my inquiry as to whether you would care to dine with Mrs. Wells & myself this Christmas. With a beard you would greatly resemble Santa Claus (?!). You have the festival spirit. And your company would be greatly appreciated."

Only when I reached my room, did the old glaciers begin to creep in again. But I locked them out by shutting the heavy door of sleep in their faces.

And morning's on the job once more, streetcleaner, dressed in gray and white, doing my street & sky. The sky-stage is perfectly set, with the curtain up, for another performance of snow. I suppose it's time: the last drama is now little more than grey-dirty blotches on roofs & ground— ragged memories.

Though we slipt through yesterday smoothly enough, my visit with your parents was a crowded day indeed. Just think of the things discussed: your-my situation, the world situation & that of the world to be, book-talk, talk about the academic atmosphere, & merely general Turkey talk.

After the first bit of awkwardness, the necessary adjustment moments, matters went smoothly. All the jerry-built resentments & complaints I had collected against your parents collapsed, like snow in the sun of their being, melted away. To my surprise, I was happy to be with them. Probably in part because I sensed (or am I egoising?) that they enjoyed being with me. My old liking for your Pop quickly reasserted itself. So I warmed to the pride-for-me expressed by your Pop & replied to the affection I met in your Mother. Or are these also figments of my hopeful, imagining ego?

Though it's been purely verbal, I cannot help believing that so far we've been pretty lucky. Suppose your Pop entertained a point of view similar to my Pop's?! Not only would he think me impossible, but he would undoubtedly forbid our meetings. Fortunately I'm doing roughly what your Dad has always yearned to do. And it's difficult for a man to sell out his deepest dreams.

December 1, 1940

This Saturday night I spent with the Schuberts. David & I sat up with the night till it was nearly over, almost five o'clock. What exciting talk he & I luxuriate in—to the head what being with you is to the whole of me. Mentally we kindle each other till I begin to see images approaching the glimmer of you. You see, you are the goal all my delights strive toward—my mica mecca!

The conclusions, provisional of course, David & I came to—in themselves commonplace enough, but mighty important for the thinker to reach via his own head (& heart ultimately)—are that the individual is at bottom totally unimportant, simply an accident, a throw-off of the general energy—meaningful only insofar as he serves as voice for this energy, which never changes but delights in showing itself in a variety of forms. The more the individual acts as a vehicle for this energy (forgive this looseness of language; but what can we poor mortals do?) the larger he himself becomes. So though this energy, like its attributes, love, etc. is anonymous & almost abstract in that it expresses itself in accidental faces & actions, these latter participate in its importance. So even the adventitious becomes significant; & the more so the more it reveals or the more we discover in it. This is where the hierarchy of values sets in: the artist must have his critical canon well-sharpened so as to be able to select the choicest details.

Actually, I'm not the egotist (or at least the kind) you & I believe I am. To begin with, recognizing the unimportance & accidentality of the individual, when I think so highly of myself, I'm merely paying homage to the essential energy, expressing my gratitude for whatever grace this energy has given me. What I know, what I am, is, of course, no doing of mine. Consequently, admiring my efforts, I'm admiring the whole. Love, Dearest, love for all, is the result of such thinking.

What has this to do with writing? Well, stylistic tricks, personal twisting of language, are worthless & meretricious. Self-parading, ego-hugging, can never achieve excellence. Already, as a consequence, many of the pieces I've written, for their fancy-fingering, do nothing but repel me. And yet, in a sense, since such a viewpoint really frees its exponent, he or she may indulge in almost any expression that pleases him or her at the time. See the difficulty?

~

T & R
FOR GIL AND OTHER INCURABLES

Matter? More than anything else,
getting yourself down on the page
as on a blank check that yields
whatever riches you declare.
                              No need
to consider the wild fluctuations
in the currency, the willfulness
of the traders, imponderables
like the weather, the size of the crops.
                                        You
assumed everything depended on you:
your words would easily catch all
the world's hungry fishermen.
                              Now,
though you finally had to let go,
your pride, ever defiant of reality,
still blazons forth,
                      a reality
all your own that only the impossible
can make possible.

~

December 2, 1940 (a note delivered by John)

Dearest, though I have neither you nor the achievement of fine poetry before me this morning, I feel well & whole, my body-brain-spirit all closely knitted together & my native idiom as articulated as it's ever been. The reasons are plain: you (letters, thoughts, etc.) & the commonplace ones—my thesis is wellnigh completed. All that remains is the compiling of bibliography, a boring business, I assure you, but the last & therefore almost a breeze. And this morning starts off propitiously: up before seven, shower, breakfast, reading, & writing to you—the whole wrapt up in a gentle rainy day. My Lovely, I have not felt so at one with myself, so balanced, in a long time: it is the calm that means intensity.

December 2, 1940

Yes, again, Liebchen, I repeated some of Thursday to the Weisses. They're very anxious to learn where they stand; more, impatient with N.Y., they're chafing at the reins of time. Renee's father made a tidy sum on a property he sold; he's written to tell them that he'll advance them whatever amount they need. Accordingly, they're all set. They press me constantly for a definitive statement. Meantime, I've been pushing on with my own little venture as best I can. I've sent off a raff of cards to a large variety of universities requesting application blanks for assistantships, instructorships, or whatever they may have.

Sunday, just before the Philharmonic program, I bumped into quite an argument with a fellow I've just met. He maintained that it is wrong (in that it obstructs the music) to create pictorial images while listening to music. The "higher" appreciation, as he put it—snobbishly, it seems to me—concerns itself with the abstract beauty of that which it is hearing.

Though I seldom see pictures while listening to music (unless I'm deliberately using it as a fillip to poetic images), I think it preposterous to limit music or any other art to one certain effect. The more one derives from it, the richer the experience, the happier he. If someone secures an additional pleasure by fashioning pictures, I can see no reason for criticizing him. If, however, this activity does screen off the music, then it ought to be stopped. What do you think? Your family's Sunday Philharmonic rides in the beautiful Pa. country-side, are they also pictures or a happy blend of music and abundant scenery?

Dec. 4, 1940

My You, I had no intention of launching the Minneapolis business all over again. Your conclusions are correct: I do not care to enmesh myself in anything as complicated & exacting as business, if I can help it. But the Weisses are not aware that I intend to exhaust the job potentialities here in N.Y. before turning finally to the bookstore. So, fixed as they themselves are, they constantly put pressure on me. I cannot tell them how little the bookstore plan attracts me. Nonetheless, it might be relevant to have your Dad over at the Weisses for dinner during the exposition. You remember, he said he intends to spend a day with me at Columbia.

You're very sane about music appreciation. I'm delighted that you have no art-snobbery about you. What you say anent music is equally pertinent to the other arts; & you are delivering yourself of a judicious diatribe against most art criticism. Generalizations about the arts are as odious (probably more so, since they deal with a specialization) as generalizations about life. Arnold has defined art as a criticism of life; then what is criticism, but a criticism of a criticism? (And what I'm doing now is a criticism of a criticism of a criticism!)

I've just received a note from John, whom I've not heard from in weeks. He's home again, "employed by the Whelan U.S. Cigar Corp. as a fountaineer at $18 per week." He ends, "We (Antoinette & he) hope to ask you to our furnished room soon." We'll go, won't we?

December 5, 1940

Almost four o'clock, My Love, & no letter from you, so I talk to you first. On the whole, I've myself pretty much in hand. But sometimes unaccountably I slip right through my fingers. Much as you are of me, you go too. Then I'm left alone with loneliness. This is one of those naked moments. When you dwell within my arms, Dearest, I'm a man who's finally found his country. If I sound like a bloated sentimentalist or popular magazine romantic, forgive me. It's not my fault, my loving you so extravagantly.

During the night, with a thousand, quiet, white, little steps—the air the road it took—Switzerland moved in. A thin, stingy Switzerland, it's true. Happily, while the flakes enlivened the air, I skied through the hours. It's great fun climbing the Alps of bushes, trees, & buildings with one's eyes, especially if one can watch the mountains grow into a million instant EdelWEISSES! But people seem very hostile to Switzerland. Immediately they fight it off with brooms & shrieking shovels. Poor Switzerland hasn't a chance. With a few last fluttery flakes it surrenders, soon transformed into a gray-dirty Venice; it requires rowboats to cross the streets.

O, Sweetest, do you truly miss me, or have you settled down to a comfortable, occasional memory? Have I faded for you like an old photograph, still dear, but daily growing more distant? Though this may anger you, I must write it, must read strong denial (I hope!) from your replying pen. I know, I know: this is the kind of letter I had made up my mind, had promised, not to write. What do the feelings

110

know of, or care about, promises?

Yippee!! Your letter's come. I've just gone down to my box (4:30) to look once more, steeled for no letter, & there she blows! Excuse me while I read you. So, Dearest, you jump straight through my loneliness & your letter, & I'm well & peopled again with you.

I'll have to have you around just to prod me out of the ruts I often slip into. Like everyone else, I have a tendency to paint the world around me in the drab hue of myself—that is, when I'm in the dumps. This is living by habit: seeing, touching, hearing, feeling things as one's always done; or not seeing or feeling them at all. Somehow we have to welcome NOW with innocent, firstime seeing eyes. So with your mother & father; how little we recognize the things (their immeasurable charm) we live with. But to live this truth requires tremendous vitality. Still the more beauty you discern in the world, the more beauty—& vitality—you yourself are. So we'll even revel in our differences, our logomachies: anything that can be done in this life (especially between thee & me), keep we but the proper perspective. So, Beloved, if it were just for a quarrel, would you were here now!

I look out my moving picture window & the world's all swaddled in blue now, even the snow—a blueish white covering the roofs like icing I can taste with my eyes.

THE BEST TIME
O now were slinky
Cleopatra, silky Helen,
willful Dido, shy Isolte
and those we've still to see,
all lovely, loving women,
ripe as love can be,
be it 4000 AD
or 4000 BC,

all rolled into one,
the best time been
or ever yet to be,
were you in my arms
underscoring me. . .

December 9, 1940

I know too well the root of the friction you mention; yes, it was the work of my dad, poor, misguided creature, & sinful too, taking other people's feelings into his clumsy hands. Grievous though the deed was, I don't consider it irremediable: I've written to your dad & I hope by now the matter is explained away. I'll explain it to you Sunday. Till then contain your curiosity as best you can.

You know the poem I mentioned? Well, I've finally typed it out with another. But instead of sending them, I'll show them to you on Sunday. I showed them to Van Doren today, & he laughed heartily over them. He descried in them (to my pleasure; for such was my intention) a unity of theme & proposed that I expand them (as I have also projected in my own mind) into a book. He suggested I submit them for publication & inquired as to the health of the Hopkins' paper (!). Then somehow we got into talk of laws. I mentioned the difficulty of marrying. We compared notes. He said that fortunately for him it was much simpler: he met his wife-to-be at her mother's; they decided to marry on a Friday night, & without further todo did so the next morning. Enviable people!

I hope someday you will know him too; without doubt he's been my most exciting academic (inadequate word to use with him!) experience. How can I help but be happy with your love & a company of such hearties as Myself, You, & Van Doren?

December 10, 1940

I've just come into the Schubert's home, greeted by some never-before-heard symphonic music on full trumpets & by David sporting a dish towel round his head turban-wise. (Judy's not yet home from work.) I'm sitting now in David's private dovecote of a study, a tiny pocket of a room you nearly have to put on like a tight-fitting uniform. A fat central pole, running throughout the floor and ceiling, leans up against me; David's typewriter crowds me.

Rolling up my sleeves (figuratively, for there's not room enough in here for such gigantic action! David probably uses this room to concentrate his writing), I release your dear serious letter about not being too serious. You're right about depression: we mustn't permit each other the self-coddling luxury of it. Of course, it's not so easy as simply saying so. But freshness will be ours, My Love, if we remember always the infinite facets each one of us is & has. Then we'll be superbly ready for whatever may transpire. (Zounds, Liebling, this room seems to be trying to shove me out; it hardly has room for itself!)

David just now dashes in & insists on reading two poems he's written, very proudly, in his staccato style, one called *Lullaby*. I renamed it Lulu-by; David admitted its validity.

LULLABY FROM THE JAPANESE
Koro, koro, nenkoroyo,
Where did your nurse go, my dear boy?
She went home to see her parents.
Did she bring you back a pretty toy?

What did you get from your nurse, my dear boy?
What did she give you, sir?
A flute to play on all day long
And sleep when day is over.
Lulla, lulla, lullabye,
And sleep when day is over.

This morning I subwayed down to City Hall to accumulate marriage information; the details are disheartening indeed. Save by some deus ex machina, I don't see how (for some time at least) we'll be able to engineer our being together. First, expensive tests must be taken, which require a lapse of three days after they've been OKed. Then the two parties must present them to the marriage license bureau. If either is less than 21 he or she must provide a birth certificate proving he or she is over 18. Otherwise one must have one's parents' consent. So what do we do? We must concoct some scheme; no stupid government is going to keep us apart.

December 11, 1940

So tired, Liebkin, even yesterday in me is tired. And no doubt tomorrow too. Days I've been writing & writing & writing, tens (or is it tons?) of poems clamoring to be papered; I chase frantically after them like a multitude of sparks from a single match: see the constellation of falling stars! I try catching all of them at once. Most of them are will o' the wisps (wisps o' the will?), but they seduce me. I sit here now with a few dead shattered words. Brimful Mine, when we're one, you'll have to say firmly, "Now, Ted, you'd better stop. Type & revise the best few, & let the others go." I'll have to give up being hospitable to every hobo poem whining for a handout.

This afternoon David came to my room. He plucked me out of it & we walked thru the twilighting streets. I took this sheet with me ("I've gotta write a letter to my Liebkin!" "What! again?!" David asks in simulated disgust), folded, but naked of words.

I'm now hunched up against a wall in a narrow trench of a restaurant, surrounded by men on stools & the behind-the-counter waiter's voice. (If you hear noises, don't

114

mind: it's the shoving around of chairs & people's appetites.) While David eats a hamburger, I write this on a table just the least bit larger than this letter. If there are any grease stains on this page, David did it.

Looking up, talking to David, I stop a moment to listen to the voluble waiter, very happy, it seems, at his work, with slick patentleather hair & a large, drooping nose in which his voice seems to live. He's a real salesman, persuading his customers: "How about some juicy pineapple pie? Or this fresh green apple pie? The apples are fresh & ripe, even though green." "How about coffee?" he continues. "How's the pie? Good isn't it?" He's puffed up with the importance of his work. Just now a bulgy girl complains "Your stools are too near the counter; I can't get my legs in." "Is it my fault if your legs are too fat?" What a mustard-drop of a restaurant! The girl behind the counter sighs, "Life's so BORING!"

Whoops! this cheesebox of a lunchroom is becoming chaos itself, like a nest of bustling mice. Fellows sliding by with their dishes, one bumps against David, & David spills half his coffee over the table. By a hair I save this letter from a darkbrown death by drowning. Talk about your ivory-tower writing? You can't say my letters to you don't come straight from the horse's mouth!

~

T & R
REAL ESTATE

She assumed she'd always be
where the wings are, but superior
to flight, a tree nestling birds
in song.
              There even mosquitoes hum
the dream of Mozart. And each night,
like a miser, counts over day's
sumptuosities.
                    But now she sees
that she at best is fugitive notes,
not out of Dostoievsky or Tolstoy,
but out of some second-stringer
much ignored.
                    And all those balls,
buxom ladies and mustachioed dandies,
turning chandeliers into a waltz
of happy tears?
                    Never to be invited
to The Summer Palace! How can she
master such a boundless affluence
of disappointment, poverty, neglect?

She would have been better
off itemizing every drop of rain
as it pirouetted in a puddle
loftiest stars, admiring, studied.

With such patience all kinds

of surprises might have arrived
to treat her—like Doctor Chekhov,
who could have saved her life
and maybe in one of his stories did—
as if she were a royal heir.

Every daughter has a place
prize as a first son's or a last.
Where would these be without her?
How, lacking her experience, expect
to calculate their real estate?

~

December 13, 1940

    I've just come from Van Doren's class all pepped up. With no letter from you I rush through my sandwich thinking: "I've gotta write my Liebkin about Van Doren again; she's probably tired of my incessant praise of him, but I can't help it." When I've finished lunching, however, there you are waiting in your envelope. I bustle up to my room & hurry on to this.

    How I wish you were here with me to enjoy him. I'm certain he's the finest, most cultivated man I've ever met. And I'm fond of him all the more because he reminds me of you. Of course, everything does—a hint (whether flower, smile, or word) to a renewal of you in my head. But he resembles you at a point which I love most. He has won his way through intellectually to what you realize instinctively— that commonly known as the Comic Spirit.

    The last few years I've developed a respect for this point of view (really all points of view in one: what I'd call a floating perspective, one that changes with each thing viewed—whether child, leaf, or mouse), till now I believe this is the best attitude a person, certainly the artist, can set up as goal, the final emancipation. You have it, My Dearest, in your thoroughgoing tolerance of people, your refusal to indulge in the "vice" of judging others, your capacity for acceptance & active participation in the pleasure of this acceptance. Van Doren in his classes espouses & enunciates this attitude better than anyone I've ever encountered either in the classroom or in explanatory books. And you, My Love, are my best living illustration of this attitude in practice. May you never lose this genius.

Yes, I too would gladly trade in all mind feelings for feeling thoughts, even better feeling feelings! But why not have—& enjoy —all?

~

T & R
Economies

I
Hiking along the foothills
of a mountain, you run into
an old farmer shovelling away,
the wheelbarrow beside him
heaped with rocks and gravel.

You ask, "What are you up to?
Digging for gold?"
　　　　　　　The shovel
flickering as it deflects
the sinking sun, the old man says:
"I'm taking down this mountain."

"This mountain! All of it?
By yourself?"
                    "Hardly a problem.
I've five sons. Each has his share
of sons. Soon they'll have sons.
In no time the job'll be done."

"But why are you bothering?"

"The mountain blocks the view
and crowds my property. And over
there a shining city waits
jammed with treasures."

                    "The dirt
piled up, dirt still to dig,
what's to become of it?"
                    "O we'll
make a wall, one high enough
to keep all strangers out."

                    II
A little girl in second grade
just learned this earth of ours
consists of everything that's ever
been, that's ever yet to be.

Broken bits, fitted carefully,
recover ancient toys and vases,
houses, parks, entire towns.

Why not put together pieces
of the animals that live
inside her dreams, the children,
strewn about like floppy dolls?

Promptly she gets to work
gathering up her booty.
                    "Rub
this stone. Can you feel the fire
inside? That's the dragon's breath."

Tuning in on her, he reconsiders:
And the shining from this rock's
no doubt a morning long ago
still dreaming in the cracks.

"Watch out!" She warns. "That chunk
of glass has got its eye on you."
But, alas, the smell is filling
up the rooms.
                    And fat worms,
wriggling in and out the dirt,
bugs, spiders, skittering around
as if the house belongs to them.

Mother, frowning, shakes a broom:
"You think you can stash away
the whole wide world in here!"

                    III
Whatever can we do with them,
panhandlers, drug dealers, bag
people, dumped like garbage,
in a traffic clogged enough
to seem one sluggish beast?

And consider the rubbish, noise,
and stink! Sewage that the city
is, there's nothing for it

but to flush it down the drain.

"I have a better solution.
Look at the Met. It goes on
serenely growing: thriving in it,
countless lost civilizations.

Why not enlarge it to accommodate
the city one and all?"
                              Con-artists,
salesmen, politicians, stock-brokers,
pick-pockets, pimps, and whores
performing their roles?
                              "Yes,
in a setting right for them,
a Mall, a Wal-Mart, a Macdonald's."

The headlines read the daily
happenings: Manhattan, Chinatown,
the Bowery become sell-out side-shows

"running," for the time being,
"permanently."

~

December 16, 1940
    So, Dearest, today's my birthday, & I celebrate it, give
myself a party by thinking of you. But if that's the case than
everyday's a birthday for me!
    Yet what a hellish morning I've spent. I brought to
bear against myself all the good things to small avail. Yesterday

I was flame; today, ashes that must somehow be carted away. But I refused to let it go at that; I battered away at my despondency with all the reason I possess. If I love you enough to suffer over us, surely I love you enough to do something about it so that I can enjoy us.

Anyway, I tired of being vinegary to myself as the day wore away—guess I'm just not made to be depressed very long. As my poem put it, The lilacs got a letter through. More, late this morning I connected the radio you brought me; there waiting to wish me a happy birthday was a Mozart symphony. As though the you-in-me feelings weren't symphony enough!

I've just returned from Van Doren; I showed him the poems you read yesterday. His first words were: "Say, these are swell! You're just about ripe for a book!" I'm thinking of sending four or five of the long ones off to some magazine to see what sort of rise I get from the editors.

Your letter, plus your direct words, makes me realize what anticipation your heart must have been—no wonder your eyes star-glittered so!—when you first saw me. But why do you use the cruel term "outsider" against me? Certainly it's hard to be understood or to justify ourselves to others; but remember how difficult it is for us to understand & justify ourselves to ourselves. You're going along pretty comfortably; you turn a corner & there, waiting for you, a feeling, a thought, you had least expected—one you can scarcely name or recognize. So how can one, not in your skin, do any BETTER? When you're angry or irritated, even your writing tightens up into itself. Right?

December 17, 1940

Several times I've attempted the Hansel & Gretel theme in poetry, but not too well. I'm girding myself to it once more: this time it MUST come through, underscored, as it is, by your remark & by the fact that the world is very much in a Hansel & Gretel way: the breadcrumb theories & faiths it lived by no longer suffice: it can't find its way back. So it will have to go through the witch, dressed in sugary attractions, of tyranny, saved only by love. I pause, Dear, to read Hansel & Gretel: I'll be right back.

I've read it: it's excellent material. In fact, all the fairytales are available for poetry: someday I hope to translate a number into verse. I hope, My Dear Gretchen, the next time I see you, through the glasses of my letter, I shall have written most of the poem. I've another in mind based on your father & my parents. The setting & the action are simple— his entering their home on a mission of goodwill. What I intend to do is wreathe the string of this setting with the pearls of their respective thoughts & feelings: the face each one shows & the face each one's feeling actually has.

My poem-writing now requires much more effort than before. Then I dashed off pleasant little poem after poem (at least that's what I called them); now I've the arduous job of condensing, stitching together, polishing. Easy going as I am, this is not too attractive a regimen. Yet if I am to write anything worthwhile, this is the only path I can take.

I've this minute returned from class & jogged through your letter. Your marriage news perturbs me no end. What are we going to do? More, your health worries me. Hereafter when you come in I'll have to see to it that we take the day a little less hectically. I'm usually so lost in my desire for you I've hardly time to think that maybe you're not in exactly the same position. From now on, however, I promise not to be so selfish—truly selfless in that at junctures such as passion (as we agreed Sunday) passion takes over & the individual is obliterated.

December 18, 1940

Seems we go so far as to share the feeling described in your letter. I've the ingredients, the flour too; but I lack the mixingbowl of you. And, Sweet, the feeling of instability, of incompletion, is further stressed for me by my writing. As I reported yesterday, it's become several times more difficult than before. Here I am trying to patch the rips in my emotions & also stitch together the odds & ends I've been collecting for the two poems I mentioned yesterday. I look & look down the endless landscape of my head, but can't seem to find the setting for the poems. Form is of course extremely important to me: & this Hansel & Grethel idea is the most ambitious I've ever attempted. Once I get down to the actual writing it's a joy; but till that moment I'm picking my way over a sword-paved road. But instead of stewing around so, I suppose I ought to sit down & write. For the more I think about it the more insuperably difficult it seems. Tomorrow (& all day), without further todo, I'm going to devote to writing.

Yes, you'll have to act your 17 & I my 24. But golly! 24 is so much, so long to act! It's not fair! You, with 6 years less, have it much easier than I. Think, Dearest, how hard it must be to act 40, say, 60, or 80!

~

T & R
THE STORY

Though they may have lent a phrase
or two, a lordly image wave-like
riding itself, this plot did not
derive from Melmouth the Wanderer,
or out of the cracked saddlebag
of Don Quixote.

124

Regardless of
eruptions breaking out—violent,
so distracting, say, as the volcano
on this island we are visiting—
the plot serenely reels.

Is that
it lurking between the slopped roof
of that abandoned Chinese temple,
piss-incensed, and the rainbow
mist diffuses?

Or among the buds
sticky on yesterday's bare branch?
Perhaps that butterfly, perched
on a brisk trade wind, describes
its course?

Why, given such elusive
clues, do I persist? This flimsy
leaf, twist it much as I like
around a stone, will not produce
the golden ring. My penny-whistle
plays no magic toot.

Yet squiggles
I obey, seemingly far-fetched,
for feelings first engendered there,
marked clearly as an X upon a map,
compose an apt accompaniment.

Morning's traffic rushing by,
snarled inside a loose-meshed rain,
we move from bed to chair to shoe.
We know without knowing that so
the tale gets told—
                    especially then
when the curtain drops at intermission.

~

December 19, 1940

To your questions, My Own Little Doctor, I can give
only vague answers. I can't recall the precise moments at
which my desire to put an end to it all appeared. As I told
you, the impulse has displayed itself only when I'm with
family, those women I love & only when I'm alone with
them, usually in a night-setting. I don't doubt in the least that
reading has helped to nurture this impulse, already rooted in
my melodramatic mind. The atmosphere of night very pal-
pably underlines the idea, affords it a dramatic (sensational)
background. It's quite possible a kiss would dispel the
impulse. This, coupled with my helplessness & cowardice in
the face of an infinitely uncertain future, evoked the feeling
with you. You're right: I am quite normal except that I pos-
sess or am possessed by an unusually overheated imagination.

I broached the whole business yesterday to Yun, My
Chinese psychology friend. He also said that the impulse is
common; few people other than the entirely unthinking
escape it. Most, however, suppress it immediately. But I,
eagerly as I welcome all ideas, have almost fallen victim to
this one. (This is an instance in which the idea cultivates the
man, not viceversa! It's like the animal tamer who has dealt
with lions all his life; suddenly one day a lion turns on him
& rips him to shreds. Well, I've been taming lion-ideas most

of my life; now an idea's out to claw me. We won't let it, will we?) Yun further emphasized the escape-motive. In a desire to run away from all responsibility, especially to those closest to me & so most exacting, I've an impulse to destroy everything.

Your prescription, Doctor Mine, is excellent. It's precisely what Yun suggested. Instead of running from the impulse & thereby encouraging it, face it, so dispel it. Together, My Love, I'm sure we can scotch this impulse.

I've vetoed coming home for the holiday, even for a weekend. I couldn't stand being there for just a half day & not seeing you, knowing you're just a wall away. No, I haven't imagination good enough to pretend a thin wall is a hundred miles or two hours between us. I might as easily (!) tell myself a hundred miles, etc. is only a thin wall! So for general peace I remain in N.Y. But you'll have to visit me.

Well, it is three o'clock; & I've finally reined in the flirty poem on paper: but like most seductresses, I doubt whether she was worth the effort. She's all talk & no taking hold, no action. But perhaps I can clean her up & straighten her out. Make an honest woman of her or, better, a genuine seductress!

~

T & R
CARGO

I

Like the sack a beach-comber
keeps for pick-ups, you bulge
with cracklings of a two-crowed
caw, now sprouted into a flock
making raucous music of the leaf-
thick sycamore,
                                as thoughts,
self-willed, sidle in and out
of you defter than glissandos
of a wind.
                        The frowzled plants
hugging the sill and the Hawaiian
Ti in the corner claim the room,
until a cat yowl,
                                breaking in,
reiteratively accuses the world.
A door slams like a shot, a life
in rumpled shorts rushes out:
a car rumbles off.

II

                        The vines
by the window? They are climbing
themselves as though the reining
moon were driving deep inside.

Meantime, this army of ants,
abiding by an identical impulse,
skit back and forth, flagging
butterfly wings many times
their size.

III
Consider the revolution
gathering forces in this body
of yours, wholly politic: patriot
on one occasion, terrorist the next.

At best its congress squabbling,
every cell, devoted to its ideology,
soon strikes to sack the world
surrounding it.

~

December 25, 1940

Well, My Beloved, here it is nearly 9 P.M.; & after this runaway note to you, I'm off to bed. Am I ripe for sleep! The explanation's obvious: working religiously, relentlessly, on Hansel & Gretel. Finally, last evening—to my surprise & relief—around 8:30 it finished itself (that is, a first draught—& draughty it is). Some 600 lines, it's exceedingly uneven. But at least I've the whole on paper. I plan to take a vacation from it the next few days, then return to the major job of polishing, etc.

In the afternoon Judy phoned to invite me to a little Christmas evening party. I declined on the score of work, taking it for granted the poem would carry me deep into the weehours. Done unexpectedly soon, I wrestled with the temptation of the invitation. I now found being alone oppressive. Conceiving a huge appetite for people, I called Judy back & departed partyward. This, mind you, against my "better" judgment. You know how little generally I relish parties with their forced smiles & artificial excitement. I figured, however, that anything would be superior to my own face & the profile of my poetising.

I was wrong. Last year (was it?) I had attended a similar affair at the Schuberts with most depressing results. The depression repeated itself. The people (mostly married couples, you needn't fear!) were as dull as people can be en masse & still remain people. I don't know how or why David abides them. I'm not sure he does. Last year he walked out on them; this year he was better behaved; but several times he escaped into the silence of himself. I believe he accepts them on two counts: 1) for Judy's sake: she has a very inclusive & enthusiastic receptivity; 2) because of a desire to reach people other than himself. No, despite my tone I'm not being snobbish: just admitting there are people not worth the effort of striving to contact. O, I realize that one by one they could show me many things; but together no!

Anyway, the damn thing dragged itself out till about four o'clock. Then as unobtrusively as possible I (first) sneaked off: they had attained the hail (hell) fellow, dirtysong stage. It was much after five before I got to bed.

Today I had to rise before eleven: Wells came for me after twelve & took me to his home way up town. The locality's as spacious as I had never suspected N.Y. of possibly being. The house must originally have been a barn; then it was transformed into a small theatre; & finally into the present home. The first floor's one immense room with a lot of intense windows thrown in everywhere: thoughts here can be of epic proportions. The peaked roof is braced by beams; upstairs, cuddled in a corner, their bedroom looks up at you obliquely.

Wells himself is a thoughtful & extraordinarily gentle person. Though physically angular (the kind of body you expect to kick over the teatray), he moves like a pleasant whisper. On campus, even as you are talking with him, like Don Quixote he swoops away & disappears as you, astonished, look for him. His wife whom he calls, & as often as he can, Katherine (names, you know, are mainly epithets of affection: Sweet, Brimful, Ember Bright, Liebkin) is also sharp-featured, but crisper &, I should imagine, more precisely tempered than he. A wellmatched pair, they birth an atmosphere of affection between them it's most agreeable to move about in.

After all kinds of fruits, candies, & cookies, out came the turkey—an unusually photogenic bird, stuffing, etc., etc., such as I've seldom tasted. After that, we rode over to the Cloisters not far from their home & heard medieval Christmas carol, MY Favorite Karol, recordings. Back again: animated talk, carolling, eating. Finally Mrs. Wells brought me back to Columbia. And here I am writing to you.

January 2, 1941

Stretched out here solo, no. 21 of this caterpillar bus, my emotions giving off their customary goaway shimmer, I hunger for the you-beside-me I wished for several days ago.

The bus, first sparsely peopled, slowly fills. An eight-year-old, red hair, shiny, inquisitive eyes & a lumberjacket, sits beside me now (what shapes you take!) eating a tootsie roll. As it stickies up his hands, he holds them away from him, as if in disgust. Meantime, every onceinawhile rubbing his nose, he glances up, wrapping his blinkless curiosity around me.

Through the bus window I see the cat-night silently slinking through the trees, pressing its belly against buildings & windows, casting off the sparks we call stars, to be chased away only by the scat! of day. Across the aisle two rubbery babes are busily rolling out a sticky-thick accent, like molasses from a bigbellied keg, but hardly sweet to hear. Directly across from us a young man & woman take turns at their tiny, bare baby, who frequently protests the indignity of the bus's jogging.

My seat-partner, his legs crisscrossed over my box of

books, clothes, etc., has slumped over, his lips puffed by sleep. His redknot falls to the side, looking for a shoulder to lean on else his head, too heavily burdened with dreams, may snap off. Finally his head finds my shoulder. As I look at him, the young man, the mother directly behind us, & his sister across the aisle all do the same: for a moment we're caught in one smile. The passengers continue to pile in, more than the seats can hold. (If they knew you were here and without a ticket, My Sweet Stowaway!) Meanwhile, the bus drives through the cold air night to its target.

Subway: a tall, narrow, craggy-nosed man raises his glasses to talk to, to look at, his friend: seems he can't open his mouth till he does so. Now, after hundreds of stops, hundreds of thoughts & yearnings, & eighty some miles, I'm writing to you at the same old desk, nearly 12:30 o'clock.

A few last thoughts: the only reason I become angry with your dad is because he doesn't permit me to love him as I would. If he were to act naturally toward my parents, I assure you (as you well know) I'd have nothing but affection for him.

Forgive me for my haziness when you spoke of wishing to provide yourself with philosophical & historical background before you take to fiction. Vague as I must have been (due to fatigue & the opium of your lips), I continue to agree with what I suggested: Durant's *Story of Philosophy*. Wasn't your father reading it? But read it with great boulders of salt. Any questions ship to me. Perhaps I can help answer them. After that, I think you ought to tackle some of the philosophers themselves. Write to me when you're ready, & I'll name some likely ones.

~ 3 ~

January 4, 1941

At last, My Liebchen, as though convalescing from a long sickness, the sky is clearing; morning has discovered a rift in the forest of rain & is crowding through. Not yet nine o'clock & I've already had Borodin & Bruchner as visitors. Daylong our radio comforts me. Last evening I heard, & in this order, Mozart, Beethoven's First Symphony, & Brahms' First. Some consorting with the Great, no?

Meanwhile, I've elbowed my way through two books; two more today, two more tomorrow. Then two days for the writing of the report. How noisomely dull all this is. I believe Professor Neff assigned this topic, biography, because he knows how vexing such factual writing is to me. He's giving me a lesson in discipline! Yet he favored me too by choosing me to do the report!

I've little good personal news to retail. The two poems were returned yesterday without comment. I warned you how unpenetrating editors are! However, rereading the poems, I must admit that I find them rather clumsy & wordy. After this report perhaps I'll rework them & send them off again. Who am I to expect a gentler time of it than a Frost, say, Hopkins, Dickinson?! Each of us, I suppose, must pay the price of years. People, being too lazy, refuse to make the effort requisite to the understanding of something they've not met before. Or am I absurdly consoling myself by laying claims to too much originality?

The other bad news? Two days ago I took my pin around to the jewelers'. I figured on at least eight dollars' worth of gold. The Muhlenberg catalog describes the award as the interest for a year on a thousand dollars. So I assumed its original value at roughly twenty five dollars. The jeweler offered me $1.80! The reward for four years' arduous work! So much for striving after medals!!

January 6, 1941

Time for just a little rickety note, Liebkin. I'm tired & clogged up as though corks had been pushed into me everywhere. Three books I've read & written up two, which means two more to read & three to review. It's not quite morning, eight o'clock: already sun's begun to touch up my eye-world here & there; in a remote corner of my ear-sky an anonymous bird is chirping like a vague reminiscence. Throughout the day I'll try to steal away you-seconds from my workaday. I've become a reading & writing machine, something that scribbles odd-looking characters on innocent white paper. So I've accumulated thirty pages of report.

When I was home why did you suppress your desire to whistle: at least I would have known where you were. Everytime your door opened or slammed I became pure expectancy: Did You go out? Where is She now? Till I heard your voice again, I was lost. Didn't you hear me hum, sing, whistle our favorite passages of Brahms, Sibelius, etc. just to let you know I was thinking of you? You're pretty lucky, Music Mine, everytime I hear, hum, think Brahms or any other of our favorites, you spring up in me. But what are the times you don't?!

Long ago I was struck by the truth that the world is crammed with, is made of, music, & I'm not able to release it! You, My Dearest, bring that music to a voice for me. The violinist is helpless without his violin. Playing it, he in turn becomes a violin vigorously bowed. Together, Liebchen, what a violin we are! You the instrument, I the bow (beau!), with love the genius-hand that plays us.

Mother sends me a postcard: "We sure miss you. Even

if you are a badboy and won't listen." Their love will eventually bring them around. I only wish I could be as sure of a job.

I've not yet reconciled myself to my Grandfather's death. Good, gentle, thoughtful man that he was, I feel some essential part of my vitality has been torn away from me, & from nature too.

January 7, 1941

Yippee! I've just finished the report (10:30 in the morning). Congratulate me, My Love. It's sixty pages LONG. I open the window wide, let the day in, & stretch luxuriously. But this afternoon I'll have to read the damned thing to the class; that's what worries me. Keep your fingers crossed. I forget: you'll receive this tomorrow.

But at least the sun's piling in here heaping golden dust—on my desk, my books, my hands, this letter. May the gold illuminate the letter when you read it.

Tomorrow I'm going to read around voluptuously & as I like. Possibly I'll look at Hansel & Gretel. I intend to finish my by now ancient thesis; I WILL have it complete before the end of the semester.

Tonight I've something like a date with my (our?) cousin Mollie Picon, the actress. I met her mother at my grandfather's funeral. She suggested I come around tonight to Mollie's radio broadcast. Who knows, perhaps something will come of it. (As her mother said, when I hesitated, "Blood is thicker than water.")

January 8, 1941

The day is cold, sharp, & shining like glitter from a giant icicle. This is how my letter to you began this noon before I picked Paul up & went downtown with him, I to convert mother's cigarette coupons into cash, he to hunt a job. He & Renée are desperate: they've all of five dollars for all expenses, including food, for the rest of the month. More, they're buried under bills. So Paul studied the job-ads, posted around cheap agencies' entrances: Dishwasher: $12, Busboy: $10, Doorman: $15. Terribly depressed, Paul decided he'd rather starve. This summer, however, if nothing better turns up, I intend to try MY hand at such work. A despondency like Paul's is exceedingly contagious; I sit here now with you in a milesdeep funk.

I read my report yesterday; considering what helterskelter way it had been prepared, I'd say it went off rather well. Customarily after a paper-reading, there are questions or criticisms; but there were none. Perhaps I used all the words up! In fact, Professor Neff congratulated me on my poem in the *Columbia Quarterly* & hoped to see more soon. Well! But despite my professor's expression of interest in my poetry, it's scholarly work the academy wants, NOT poems.

Save for a single conclusion I agree with you, My Dearest. When the wound (death) happens to us, too sharp as it is, at the time we must turn away & pretend to forget. But afterwards we must adjust ourselves to it. And that is my difficulty, My Little Philosopher, accommodating the fixtures of my mind to this new idea that has come to live with me. It requires a lot of furniture moving before my head-house is put in order again. We can never forget or forsake anything as deep as a death (it won't permit it, even if we would); we must learn to live with it, & positively—as I sometimes can when spirit-strength (you) is with me.

January 9, 1941

Ten thirty & I must begin my Tomorrow-Letter to you. Sitting on my bed in the magic circle of you, music, & Rilke, I (despite myself) cannot help being happy. Days now

I've chased around looking for me; this moment—for the moment at least—by way of the three of you I've caught up with me.

How much larger-hearted you are then I! Yet minutes after I mailed my last letter to you I regretted it. Had I occupied me totally, I'm sure I would not have written it. As matters stand now it has taken me over two hours to reach what should be instant. What am I roundaboutly driving at? That I don't care whether I'm published or not. But, Dearest, the burden (yes, burden) of beauty is so big; & in a time like ours, when many have tried to turn cruelty into beauty, one feels alone & helpless—particularly if the heart is hungry & a little closed. Thinking, however, reading & rereading your letter, & Rilke brought me around. What I think of you I needn't tell you; but may I continue my praises of Rilke?

It delights me just to write about him. He himself is his happiest word. A mighty, magnificent artist he was (is, & will be). Sometimes I feel he had been made to reply to my questions with you. As I read him I repeat to myself endlessly (what finer applause?): "I must read this to Renée! Wish she were here now so we could read this together." Few writers am I so anxious to do with you. To get closer to him it would be well worth rubbing the rust off my German. German in his hands is a uniquely subtle & supple instrument: Frenchmen & angels might crave the use of it!

But let me quote what just now urged me to write this letter. I've been reading his *Letters to a Young Poet.* You are bound to recognize the sentiments: "In one creative thought a thousand forgotten nights of love revive and fill it with sublimity and exaltation. (The very thing I try to say in Hansel & Gretel, how from behind a happiness all the faces past, present, & to be, pleased like cherubim, peep out.) And those who come together in the night and are entwined in rocking delight do an earnest work & gather sweetnesses, gather depth and strength for the song of some coming poet, who will arise to speak of ecstasies beyond telling. ...without knowing it...the great renewal of the world will perhaps consist in this, that man & maid, freed of all false feeling & aversion, will seek each other not as opposites, but as brother & sister, as neighbors, & will come together AS HUMAN BEINGS, in order simply, seriously & patiently to bear in common the difficult generation that is their burden."

Reading a little more Rilke, I come to this: I just have to copy it. Do you mind? even if it does keep you up a bit longer? "...those who are near you (You My Sweet), are far, you say,...that shows it is beginning to grow wide about you. And when what is near you is far (my work! school! most people here), then your distance is already among the stars & very large; rejoice in your growth, in which you naturally can take no one with you, & be kind to those who remain behind, & be sure & calm before them & do not worry about your doubts & do not frighten them with your confidence or joy, which they cannot grasp... love in them life in an unfamiliar form & be considerate of aging people, who fear that being alone in which you trust. Avoid contributing material (this, this! if only I could learn it; always, when the test arrives, I forget it or refuse to believe it.) to the drama that is ever prolonged between parents & children; it uses up much of the children's energy (Right!) & consumes the love of the elders that is effective & warming even if it does not comprehend. (This too!) Ask no advice from them & count upon no understanding; but believe in a love that is being preserved for you like an inheritance & trust that in this love there is a strength & a blessing, beyond which you do not have to move in order to go very far indeed!"

I was accurate, wasn't I, when I said that often he seems to be writing directly to me (us), with me (us) in mind. But that, I suppose (to reiterate one of criticism's stockintrade notions), is one of the essential hallmarks of great art.

Good (& it is!) night again.

Good Afternoon! (12:30). I still feel well—quieter, but steady. I've finished the Rilke. Curbing temptation, I content me with only one more quotation: "We have no reason to mistrust our world, for it is not against us. Has it terrors, they are OUR terrors (So, Dearest, one becomes fond of one's own sorrows, & sicknesses; often is loathe to part from them); has it abysses, those abysses belong to us; are dangers at hand, we must try to love them. (This I've tried to express many times: this is OUR world; consequently, everywhere is home, if we are but alive enough to know it. Nothing is alien to us which lives; & what does not live cannot harm us because it belongs to some other order or world. What we must do then—as I wrote you long ago—is prepare for the hardest, the "worst"—both in ourselves & the world; whatever happens less than our expectations will then be delight. But I'm supposed to be quoting Rilke! Poor Ted! he can never keep quiet—not even if God be talking!) And if we only arrange our life according to that principle which counsels us that we must always hold to what is difficult, then that which now still seems to us the most hostile, will become what we most trust & find most faithful. How should we be able to forget about those ancient myths that are at the beginning of all peoples, the myths about dragons that at the last moment turn into princesses; perhaps all the dragons of our lives are princesses who are only waiting to see us once beautiful & brave. Perhaps everything terrible is in its deepest being something helpless that wants help from us."

Of course, I do not accept all his words unqualifiedly. Not that he is wrong (In such matters one is not wrong, just different); simply that, at certain points, because of where I am in my age & experience, I cannot use what he says & must find my own explanation. But what one person (or even all) was ever God enough to provide all the answers?!

January 10, 1941

I march resolutely to the attack on "that" thesis. I MUST elbow it out of the way, as you say. But Dearest, your words on orchestra work (with the evident relish it gives you) & on the possibility of a scholarship through it at Miami University have afforded me long pause & deep concern. You SHOULD have the orchestra work & Miami too. I cannot help feeling that in this connection at least I'm in your way. Let's, for a moment, anticipate. Suppose I have no job next year? What then? Not only can we not live together, but you cannot go to school. But say I do get a job paying about $25 a week. On this we can marry & live together. If it's N.Y., you can attend Hunter.

Paul has just come in, asking me to go for a walk with him. Very restless, he paces back & forth, back & forth in my little sunbeam of a room, throwing the light of it into my eyes: his problems—money—are hounding him.

January 12, 1941

Ted's Sunday-morning Devotional Exercises, My Dearest, writing to you. You are right about David & me; in fact, receiving your letters Friday afternoon, that evening I visited the Schuberts to make the acid test. After a long talk with David & Judy, we decided that the true artist—particularly the poet—has no stake in this society: it recognizes him instinctively as a potential enemy. I stress the poet because in the past he, generally revered, occupied a position of importance. The attitude today is diametrically opposite. And the poet must choose either to compromise—finding some small, anonymous, distracting job, or to be defiant—refusing to come to terms, writing out of Promethean conviction.

David & I took a long moonlit walk in which, for the moon's loveliness, even the cold wind was breathless (& warm). The night was you, walking beside me, holding my hand; the stars, moon, & a gentle breeze were the lovewords you had to say.

Around two-thirty I left David; & after three-thirty I reached my room (at which time I wrote most of this). Yes, David's & my friendship, should I say love?, resembles your description. As we disclose to each other the traits in ourselves we most dislike, in the light of the other's considerateness & love even these traits become lovable if not lovely.

But, Dearest, let me report to you what I saw coming home. On the subway, bent over in the corner opposite me, like somebody's lost little sigh, huddled a shrivel of a woman, her wispy hair, save for outspinnings, wound up, & topheavy, in what once must have been blue flannel underclothes. She is halfresting (collapsing), halfcrouching (hiding as though her face imaged her shame) behind a large package whose cord is coming off. Two young girls come in. Gaily dressed, their features polished in laughter's oil, they exchange brightplumed words, rainbow-louder even than their clothes. Attracted by the brightness & the gaiety, for the first time the sigh looks up, sees them with unbelieving, content-less eyes, then hides again as though recalling that she might be seen. She ups & downs in this fashion many times like a fish drawn by bait. She opens her blacktoothed mouth as though to address them, thinks better of it &, knowing that a sigh cannot possibly join such gaiety, sinks behind her package.

Forgive the digression, My Patient One, I had to get it off my head. I am sorry about your School's leechiness (glad too, if it makes my letters dearer to you); this condition, unless you are extraordinarily fortunate & strike that rarebird, a genuine teacher, is what you are bound to encounter in college. I'm not trying to discourage you. On the contrary, you'd better write letters off immediately. College can be possible, even enjoyable, if you undertake work that engrosses you. And college can provide you with time (but this requires deliberate indifference to many compulsory studies) to read around & discover yourself, supplies you with books & facilities you might not have access to otherwise & with human material—faculty & students—for observation & study. However, most of it is likely to be uninspired, not to say dull. Yet despite my words, I DO want you to go to college. You understand, don't you, Dearest, why I'm excoriating college the way I do? I can't endure the thought of your going off to Miami. I'd infinitely prefer your going to a local college even. Is orchestra so important to you? I can hear your dad urging, "Look, Renee, go to Miami. You have a scholarship in the orchestra & you can live with grandpa as you did your sophomore year. Shelve Ted for the time being. If your love is strong it will last, & four years from now it will be better. Young as you are, you should meet other young men. Ted has nothing to offer you as yet. Furthermore, I can't afford to send you anywhere else." Words like these, sharp-toothed as they are, have been biting away at me. I hope, hope, hope I'm totally wrong.

January 13, 1941

Gosh, Dearest (setting aside our seven [!] minute phonetalk, the best—most human—we've ever had: we've reached the point where we're one even over the phone; congratulate us!), how you scared me. I come to your letter, thinking to find a reply to my Miami-qualms & I read "having people wait on me." Instantly my thoughts, far fleeter than my eyes, exclaim, "What's happened? Some accident?" With your parents in Florida & you left in charge at home, you write "Having a wonderful time" (!) Whether you intended it or not, your casualness & its blithe tone upset me only the more.

"The doctor ordered a nurse to take care of your brother & sister & to keep you in bed?" Please softpedal the "having a wonderful time": you're likely to encourage the grippe to stay. And tell Miss Hope I'm glad to meet her, like her if you do; but she better take especially good care of you, do better than be just hope, if she knows what's good for her. Here's my kiss & take from me whatever strength you require.

January 15, 1941

I'm glad there is a nurse to take care. Please do stay in bed. Now you'll be sure to take your cough medicine.

Perhaps it's because I'm tired of waiting so long to see you, perhaps it's the thinness my nerves sometimes become, trampling them as I do, perhaps it's the stupid parental bent I have; but be it what it may, on reading your letter & learning that you had begun *Days of Our Years*, I was immediately provoked. The reason? You were reading a book I had neither read nor suggested. And probably the realization that you have a life—the ability to do as you like & without my knowing it—of your own.

Instantly a throng of ugly thoughts sprang to the fore: "What is she reading THAT temporal stuff for? Why doesn't she give herself to serious work? Doesn't she agree with me that fiction is superior to any reporting, no matter how well it may be done? (This mind you, Liebling, though I've not read a page of the book!)

But my reaction, I believe, sprouts from a much larger background than that. I know how important the political scene has been to your father & what it must have been like at the same time to manage a thriving business & to run for Socialist mayor in a town as conservative as Allentown, & I respected him for it. But that is HIS past; not ours. I too have wrestled long with social & political problems. Last evening, visiting the Schuberts, I was submerged in talk concerned with such matters with downstairs neighbors, perfervid Democrats (with a capital D); the husband is unusually well informed & capably spoken. We harangued the night away with our "time-talk."

After they left, I suggested that I was finding such discussion more & more barren. David agreed & we concluded that tyrants & war had always been &—terrible to say—quite possibly would always be. But, despite the destruction, death, & suffering they spread, only in a most hideously negative way are they relevant. The significance of Hitler? I hardly minimize the vast havoc, the vast, monstrous suffering, he has caused, & the endless repercussions that must follow. But years from now a great writer may come along, pick up the Hitler story, & erect an epic from it—one in which values & feelings will flourish that we, too near, cannot suspect. Do I sound outrageously callous, My Love? I'm interested (or would like at my best to be) in the quality, not the quantity, of suffering, feeling, thinking—what it has to tell us about our world. Meantime I suffer, as do all, the irremediable horrors of daily life.

You understand me now, don't you, My Love? Actually, I gather that the book you are reading is firstrate, literature rather than reportage. In short, my response was a compound of jealousy & pique that you should "disregard" the books I gave you. Why do I expatiate on all this? To let you see what pettiness you will have to contend with. (But why DON'T you start those novels?!)

Take it easy, Dear, with the out-of-bed business: the weather's still very tricky; grippe's too dangerous to play around with.

By the way, did you know that James Joyce died? Do you know his work? I just learned of his death last night. A hard blow it is. What a lot of best-people have been dying! And with Europe in utter upheaval, what a lot of death there is around to take care of in thinking & feeling. Last night, subwaying & fiercely wanting you, pondering the clumsy unbelievable dilemma of death—the mind cannot really cope with it—I was as cold, lonely, & forlorn as I've ever been. Tears are the only ritual, the only tribute, meet to such men as Yeats, Bergson, Joyce &, yes, my gentle grandfather. Shield me from such thoughts & warm me with a cloak of kisses.

January 17, 1941

Yes, My Dearest, it's quite O.K. with me for you to love rather than become angry with me! For both of us it would be ridiculous for you to become angry with me for loving you—even though my love express itself in such roundabout ways.

On to your 2nd letter. Yes, I know that you are reading some of the poets I recommended. How do you like them & whom? You are, I fear, right about Van Doren, the parsimony of his poetry. Though he possesses facility & considerable gift for the pastoral, as well as a metaphysical turn with abstractions, fortunately the man & teacher only now & then resembles his poems. In person & in class he displays an altogether rare, dry, crackling intensity of intellect. Listening to him, one enjoys the privilege of witnessing a passionate thinking, the mind at full tilt, about literature, the great books that absorb him, especially the human situation they celebrate. He said he was eager to see my Hansel & Gretel, which I've not yet finished or typed off.

Doing what he does in his poems, plainly the academic atmosphere is not as pernicious as it might be. Still it is remarkable that he manages to keep his wit, his feeling, his thoughts alive & human. As far as I can see, he has all the equipment, all the ingredients essential to major poetry, save possibly (most important of all) a rich emotional fund. I've never been able to decide whether his reserve, his dry humor, bespeaks control or the lack of something immense to control. Fond as I am of him, I incline toward the former. His poetry does, on the whole, seem to imply the latter.

Right, My Urgency, I'll dash a letter off today, also one to Penn State. This morning I went to see Professor Campbell, a well-known Shakespeare scholar, for a letter of recommendation. He was extremely affable & encouraging. Old as he is, he's buoyant & warm. Usually when I ask a question in his Shakespeare class, he responds cheerfully, "That's too much for me. You'll have to talk to Van Doren."

He wanted to know why I'm not taking my orals this year. (Apparently he thinks I've been studying diligently all the while!) Then he asked if I had a dissertation subject. When I related my difficulty with Professor Neff, the man whom I'm supposed to be working with, anent Hopkins— When I proposed Hopkins for my subject, Neff said Hopkins in all likelihood was a flash-in-the-pan, & when I then proposed examining Hopkins' work with him to prove otherwise, Neff declared he'd rather not deal with Catholic topics—Campbell offered to take the matter up with the head of the Department. He said I should take my oral to get a fellowship for working on my dissertation next year. As I left, he said confidently, "You'll get a job all right."

A word, Lovum, about war & the future; I see you still entertain the idea of progress, the very notion I was questioning in my letter. Abhorrent as it may sound, I'm wondering whether man—made as he is—can "do" without war. Certain fierce, animal impulses in him (he IS a creature of nature), it seems, must find expression. Only if society can find other channels for them will war be exiled. What do you think of a world-wide baseball match ? Or a poetry contest?

146

~

T & R
ON THE SCENT

"At last, after sixteen years,"
the television announcer exclaims,
"the New York Yankees once more win
the World Series!"
                        It's enough
to unite the whole embattled city.
Politicians, stock-brokers, grocers,
cops, pickpockets hail each other.
The closest we can hope to come
to the paupers and princes rubbing
shoulders, stink and perfumes blending
in hosannahs, as they bore Chartres,
hallowed stone by stone, uphill?

"In today's parade you're a key player,"
says the announcer, poking her mike
at the man beside the truck grinding
out confetti. He stammers, "I'm proud
to be the one chosen for this job."

"And you," she says to a fat boy
squeezing castoffs into balls,
"aren't you lucky to be standing
next to the shredder? You've computer
discards, all the way from Wall Street
to Harlem, in your hands." A grin
brims his triple chin.

"This victory,"
she assures the audience, "will go
down in history. No Babe Ruth,
no Lou Gehrig, just great team work."
The TV cameras pan in on
"over three million onlookers.
Many of them, to snag front seats,
bedded down the whole night through,
beside the pros, along Fifth Avenue.

But here's the parade. What a spectacle!
One could get lost in this avalanche
of man-made snow."
                    Over-exposed,
we flick channels to find ourselves,
in a tropical setting, cheek by jowl
with a beetle scuttling after a family.

Determined little cuss, does he play
favorites: mighty at the plate,
batting out homers, Big Dick, say,
or Buxom Mamie with choice snacks,
or Mortimer Junior for his half-
baked, little breakfast cakes?

The beetle takes for granted
that these elephants are here,
digesting acre upon acre, mainly
for his welfare.
                    Hot on the scent,
he trundles after. And artfully
shaping one dropping and the next
into a ball bigger than himself,
he rolls it—as he rides it—
uphill, down, until he finds
a nook to hide these groceries in.

The herd lumbered on, hard put
he is to harvest such a bumper crop.
The best consumed, the rest will see
him through late hungry times.

Like many a devoted Yankee fan,
who, months gone by, will ruminate
on remnants of his memories.
                                        And we?
Also hard at work rounding out,
based on the ball we all live on,
our savory artifacts.

~

January 30, 1941

    Woven through my night, Morning Mine, last night
like a frozen thread, my thoughts—ghosts directly from the
world of death— with icy fingers gripped my heart. In one
horrible moment that lasted forever I saw our life in all its
pitiable flimsiness. Everything—my books, my poems, my
body, even my you—was frightfully far away. Why, My Love,
must we always try to give death which, happily, has no head,
our consciousness, try to make it feel?

    Don't worry, Liebchen, I'm better now. It seems I'm
making that painful transition between adolescence & matu-
rity: in extreme youth we (people as absurdly ambitious &
egotistical as I) strive to compel life to accommodate itself to
us; in later years, if we wish to stay alive, we seek to adjust
ourselves to life. Then, however, the flame is usually bent &
resigned, no longer boldly brave. Those who cannot yield
must die—the flame snuffed out.

    I've discovered that, days after I've written a long
poem, I slink about, a garden whose plants have all been

uprooted. To put it another way, I'm an empty flask, & not till I've filled up with new images & new ideas can I rest (in the action of renewed writing: this, I suppose, is the difference between busy rest & restless lethargy) & be happy again. Such uneasiness probably accounts for my here-beginning sentiments. Another fact I've observed is that writing at my best resembles making love to you: here too my name melts & the I is swallowed up by unmitigated joy. You don't object too much to the comparison, do you?

What's the idea attributing your violin dilatoriness to me? Don't you know you're supposed to gain only good things from me—if you can find any! I fear you're going to be (& are!) a musician in spite of yourself. One can't know as much as you do & then expect to let it go: the music itself wouldn't permit it.

Febuary 2, 1941

No, you needn't concern yourself about the future so long as we never forget certain fundamentals: patience & tolerance (how much you will need!); flexibility. A love that hardens in its expectations & exactions on the part of either partner is preparing its own demise. The only source of discontent I fear is the financial one. Want need not deflate a love, but it can make it exceedingly difficult. In this respect (& in most others, I suppose) I'm entirely, disgustingly bourgeois: not being able to give you the things I want you to have pains me even in prospect.

Sometimes now, when I am sure of your love, I find myself giving way to the exhilaration of mass-people. Yesterday, for example, I happened to be in a bank a few minutes before closing time. The press & pour of people made me feel as though I were partaking of all of them, participating in some vigorous sport, writing, or even loving you, until at its climax, for the intensity of my immersion, I felt I had had a hand in the making (!) of these human beings, as though I had been present at the planning & shaping & the breathing of life into them. Then such a love, like a giant bellringing, is wrung from me it embraces them all—MY people. But such ecstasy is woefully difficult to accomplish & even more difficult, of course, to sustain. We must be grateful for such moments. We WILL have them, My Love.

February 4, 1941

Your essay is excellent, Sweets. Of course, you realize that if you make such statements you may be dubbed "anarchist," "nihilist," etc? You'd better make it clear (hadn't you?) that all ideas are man—& woman!—made, mainly to adapt himself to nature. You err, it seems to me, in believing that as soon as customs outlive their usefulness, they are discarded. This is one of the tragedies: that men are compelled to abide by customs, worn out & burdensome. Most ideas are static; living, of course, is not; thus their conflict. Fortunately, in the end life usually wins out.

As for science, you might demonstrate via examples that science socalled has been a fairytale: man's attempted explanation of the universe. But a good, truly imaginative fairytale or myth is useable & therefore can be deemed "true." (True & false are words, no?, that must be confined to human experience, though man in his arrogance & need is tempted to apply them to the cosmos.) Philosophies, as you say, are mostly rationalizations of what men desire or apologies for the lives they have led.

Yes, I may come in (have to) for the draft examination. I'll let you know, of course.

February 6, 1941

After you & writing poems I like reading best. (I should do a little more of it!) Last evening I spent in my room with Blackmur's *The Expense of Greatness*. It's amazing how one man can be so sensitive, subtle, & perspicacious &, at the same time, such a log-jammed writer. Despite his style (learned mostly from Henry James?), his rare acumen comes through. Not in a very long time have I met criticism as stirring as his. In fact, excellent as he is, he's nearly rekindled my old desire to be a critic as well as a poet. But there are the even more rousing examples of Pound & Eliot. Well, the Hopkins is waiting!

What do I think of Milton? He made do without pictures except for those of the mind's eye (& ear)! I suppose my opinion is fairly orthodox. He's an often grand & great poet, but at this time of me there are smaller others I prefer—that is, he's not the kind of writer I care to have by my side to read regularly. But perhaps that's because I'm still too young (or he's too demanding: too undeviatingly, highmindedly moral). As far as I'm concerned, too often he walks on stilts. I'd rather share the earthy company of Chaucer, say. Milton's work smiles almost nowhere. In Chaucer, on the other hand, a smile—now & then a chortle, a guffaw—aerates & perfumes much of his verses.

Yes, the austerity of Milton's life & the hectic nature of his times did deeply influence his poetry. But don't misunderstand; boring though I sometimes find him—the great are (in part because of their great expectations), now & again great bores—I appreciate & AM grateful for the splendors he introduced into or, better, wrung out of English poetry, astonished it with new moments of its genius.

~

T & R
GROUND BASS

Libretti? They have their place:
prompting one chord and another,
a lordly phrase wave-like riding
itself, at best they underscore
the music.
          Even all-out eruptions,
spouting lava,
            "like that volcano
on the island we are visiting?"

cannot deflect the basic themes.
Enamoured of its trill, the tune
plays on.
        "Is that its shadow
sidling between the scalloped roof
of this forsaken Chinese temple,
piss-incensed, and a rainbow
mist diffuses?"
          Or among buds
sticky on yesterday's bare branch.

"Maybe the silk-furled butterfly,
a brisk trade wind conducting,
plots the music's score."
          Why,
given such elusive cues, persist?
This leaf, tracked to its root,
unearths no god-forged ring.

                              "Yet
the cramped squiggles scribbled here,
prompted by feelings they struggle
to obey, far-fetched though they
appear, surely compose a fit
accompaniment?"
                    Dawn traffic
snarling in a loose-meshed rain,
we move from bed to shoes to words.

"We know without knowing that so,
by what we do and do not do,
the song gets sung—"
                         especially once
the curtain falls at intermission.

~

February 7, 1941

        It pleases me that you should have started to appre-
ciate Shakespeare as early as you have. Retarded in this
respect, I tended to agree with Tolstoy that Shakespeare is
frightfully overrated. (Tolstoy at least had the excuse of a for-
eign language & his own blinding genius!) Not till my early
college years did I begin to waken to his magnificence. I was
too cocky, too green, too sceptical of established taste, too
self-insulated.
        And my first course on him at Muhlenberg did little
more than ruffle the plays' surface. Professor (Reverend)
Brown hardly disturbed their sleep! It's as though the plays
were being introduced & interpreted (?) by Holefernes.
Brown did share the damned reiteration of that pedant non-
pareil. Fortunately, in his love of theater, performances,
actors, Brown did have a tiny bit of Bottom about him. And

154

he fit in seamlessly with half-&-quarter-witlings like Simple (the lucidity of), & Silent, one or two brief bursts of his eloquence.

Van Doren, as you must have gathered by now, has liberated all that Brown failed to see, welcomed his lucky students to the endless feast. I went at once from fast to festivities! Shakespeare, I'm sure, more than anyone else emboldened Van Doren to the vision I described earlier & ascribed to you as well—namely, allowing every character, from noblest king to dusty clown, his own precious, unique voice. He showed us that the world can balance, if teeteringly—dance a little too—on such pinheads as Simple & Aguecheek.

Once Shakespeare caught on with me, I realized that if there was anything he couldn't do verbally (dramatically too) the race had not yet discovered it. I spoke of Milton's putting the language through unexpected paces. More than anyone else Shakespeare was THE triumphant Laocoön: gripping the slippery, lively, serpentine language, he twisted it into the miraculous shapes of his bidding, & we've relied on them ever since.

My chief complaint against him now is not that he occasionally falters or fails (or maybe better, overdoes: sometimes he resorts to ten words, ten images, when one would more than do), but that often he's TOO great, too much (blinding as lightning) to handle. And you've not yet done (or have you?) the largest plays—*Hamlet, Othello, King Lear*, etc. You & I, My Love, will luxuriate in them together.

I've not heard from Florida yet. Penn State writes that they'll keep me in mind. They are hardly encouraging, however. That's all so far. But I've gone around to two teacher employment agencies. Possibly when you visit again you will do some of your dances for me? Are you choreographing? Shall we see Martha Graham when you come in? Let that be an additional inducement. Do you need more?

As for your playing your violin on the radio, I'll keep my fingers crossed (though you hardly need it), if you promise to keep yours open, at their quickest & most graceful. February 8, 1941

Yes, Milton's mythological allusions do—especially for us with our little knowledge of the classics, a knowledge he could take for granted in most of his readers—riddle his work. Unlike most poets, however, who rely heavily on allusions, he does achieve remarkable effects with them. Seldom, also, has such polyphony been attained by the mere repetition of names. I urge you to read passages of it aloud to savor its sonorousness. Moreover—though one might accuse him of exhibitionism—he employs allusions so adroitly, their use seems casual if not inevitable, almost unconscious—as unconscious as my saying "apple." Conscious craftsman that he was, this is hardly ever so. The greater he for it.

This morning (it's nearly one o'clock now) I attended Van Doren's class. The topic of discussion was *Hamlet*. Oh the arrogance of man! Most critics have tried to "explain" Hamlet. They do not seem to realize that Hamlet (he's the one character a writer has created that approaches most closely to the multifariousness of life itself) is not to be explained, rather to be seen & wondered at. We human beings with our reductive passion for explanations! Shakespeare himself was great enough to admit—the whole play says it—that Hamlet, or any human being for that matter, is not to be understood or explained. Why can't our critics comprehend that art itself, in making the multiple mystery radiantly plain, is as close as we can come to explaining?

O, I'm not denying that for the sheer fun of it all kinds of speculation can be indulged in about the play: Hamlet is this, Hamlet is that, & a thousand other things. Such mental activity may strengthen the mind of the speculator; but he should have grace enough to recognize it as speculation, not conclusive truth. Van Doren usually takes this position. But Hamlet, wily as he is, tempted even him. Maybe that too is the play's point: life's baiting us through our infinite lust for explanations.

~

T & R
A CONFERENCE

"Everyone in this room
knows at least two languages."

The same languages
being known become different?

Twenty-two everyones
knowing forty-four languages?

Forty-four ways of
arguing about the same thing?

Forty-four ways of
making the same thing strange?

A new language flowers:
the forty-fifth? the sixtieth?

But a new language
as every poem is meant to be?

Everyone in the room
knows at least two languages.

Everyone in the room
longs to be free of language.

Everyone in the room
longs to be free of the room.

~

February 9, 1941

Dearest, it's not fair (you do get Saturday letters from me, don't you?): here I have to float my way, best I can, through a vast weekend without even a spar of a phrase from you to ride on. Now that I'm soon to be released (released's the word) out of here, now that I'm just about through with my grippe (& it with me), I suppose I can relate it to you—though you may have surmised it from the fuzziness of my last letter. This past night, turning from side to side, wearing them out, wondering why we haven't more sides, & finally resorting to the inside, I suffered the most fitful evening of bed I can remember & you present at every turn. (Is there a moment I don't think of you? If there is I can't think of it.)

On the wheel of fire I've become, I suddenly remember Milton & what I had said to you, marveling at my capacity for confusion: "polyphony..." polyphony? polyphony? polyphony! Giminy Crickets! I had meant "euphony." Yet "polyphony" does have some bearing on his work. But that's a subject for another letter (?). Obviously, My Love, even my thoughts & my vocabulary had the grippe.

Where am I speaking to you from? From the Infirmary, on my floor. You see, wittingly or not, I couldn't endure your having experienced something I had not. Obligingly, therefore, the grippe visited me too.

But let's compare notes; when it struck you, did it nearly knock you off your feet? I wandered about, reeling, as though my head were about to explode; I was convinced the staples had been pulled out of me & the only thing that held me together was my not having strength enough to engineer a collapse. (I'm exaggerating? Maybe. What am I a writer for, anyway?)

I staggered into the infirmary; the nurse takes one look at me: "You better move in here." I politely but firmly refuse: it costs $1.50 a day. "Well," she retorts, "go to bed, drink lots of juice & come in here four o'clock." I do so; this time she insists I stay.

My room? It's a little like a hotel room, but without you. As soon as I move in I write, "In this room, as personal as a railroad station or a corner drugstore, pains & coughs the climate, the pokerfaced walls throw off my every attempt at writing my private meaning on them. Even the mirror is a confusion, a negative of a hundred faces, confluent as a river. The bureau like the basin has given up its person, anonymous as no number on the door." However, by the very writing I began to feel a feeling for the room. And now that I feel well & WISH YOU WERE HERE, this room, I guess, is as good as any.

February 10, 1941

Well, I'm out, though I daren't go outdoors (the headnurse—a little whitehaired lady, spruce & quick-moving, warns me: "I'd stay in bed for a while, if I were you.") But I have to be up, dressed & shaved. I've a four-day beard, the longest my face has ever known. I look like a cross bearing a Messiah or a wildman; take your pick: one's as bad, I guess, as the other.

Considerately enough, here's your letter, bright & early (12 o'clock)—just the tonic I need. I'm feeling quite fragile. Do you mind if I lean on your letter, allow its sunny tune to play through me? I've been having a hard time with my moral self this morning, trying to prove to it that I'm not a wastrel, that my poetic efforts do mean something, etc. If only I could learn to let myself alone!

Do you mind if I drive with you, letterweiss? You must keep my window closed, however, & your right arm tight around me (to ward off the cold: I AM an invalid, you know!); & sometimes—the prescription says "often"—you must stop to give me a tablespoonful of kisses. Yes, I'll have some of the water & the sun & the humming mild air.

O, so it takes a pregnancy to make talk! I refuse to give you a baby just to provide us with conversation. Don't you think it's carrying (!) things a little too far? Seriously, if married folks have to resort to such measures for interest's sake, seems to me there's something drastically wrong. Yet grudgingly I'm compelled to admit that this more than not does happen. All I need do is recollect how abhorrently stale I often have become to myself the last few weeks (or is it the last few only because they are the most recent?)—I with my glorious ego! Sweetest, it seems there's nothing more arduous in this life than keeping "awake." If you do this, you ARE an artist, whether you paint, write, compose or just experience.

No, I've not finished the thesis. How could I with the grippe? (At least I do have something of an alibi, no? All right, so it's NO!) As for the colleges, returns from the applications do not appear till around April.

February 11, 1941

With the nurse's approval I've been outside several times. Last evening the Weisses bundled me up, took me home & doctored me. Today I cut my classes, but I felt I couldn't miss my appointment with the head of the department. He was surprisingly sympathetic & willing to help. He offered to write no-end of letters. Seems he doesn't know

I'm Jewish or else that Muhlenberg is a "Christian" college (those were the Dean's words to me): he asked if there wasn't place there for me & suggested that he & the other members of the department would be more than happy to write letters to induce the Muhlenberg English Dept. to hire me. I tried to tell him that it was fundamentally a matter of race, but I don't think he got it. After lunch I felt woozy, so I went back to bed, setting my alarm for 3:30 o'clock. I rose, dressed, plucked your letter—my codloveroil—out of my mailbox, & here we are. Yes, you must tell me; I love hearing it from you, love your concern & everything that goes with you. Now the eerie first strains of Stravinsky's "The Rites of Spring"—remember, we heard it at the Dell with your family last summer after your lesson—are beginning to engulf me. If he uses cacophony successfully it's certainly here. Great art is obviously being produced in our times, despite the times (but wrested out of them).

I've just come upon two postcard reproductions I had bought for you. May I tell you what, as I see it, the Cézanne does in action? As I mentioned, I had been feeling pretty slumpish again. Then I happened on that picture. In a sense it is what feeling you makes me. My Gaiety, had you it in hand this would be my injunction to you: wrap its sky-blue & tree-green around you, then run into yourself, what you best are: greenest gaiety. Don't, ever, cross the boundaries of your own blithesomeness. Let the mountains scamper down, bud-burst into shaggy whirlwind trees, dryads that, though entirely tree, can't stand still for joy. Zooks, My Love, how this man has absorbed himself into this world, digested & soaked it into his heart, then brought it out again completely transfused. Everything is sun-sodden, with the sun radiating from within.

This, My Patient One, by the way (anyway!), is NOT art criticism: dithyrambic word-hurling trying vainly to convey the amazement with which I always see Cézanne. It's the kind of marvel that everytime you look at it you're sure you've never noticed it before; but why didn't someone tell you about it, why did you (& how could you) miss it so long? Van Gogh saw the world on fire: he was the fire. But his fire sears as it fascinates. Cézanne's flame, however burly it may be, however massive and sculptured, is calm & self-possessed for the boundless degree to which it has been engrossed by the world it lights on.

February 13, 1941

It's almost worth it to receive no letter from you yesterday (since yesterday is yesterday) so as to receive TWO today. Had I my way, I'd insist on a letter from you at least every hour. But perhaps that's asking too much. Masterly as you are at spreading yourself through your pages, I manage to budget you so that I have just enough for the entire day.

Yes, I feel much better; the old energy, the old GRR, is beginning to race through my body again. Just wait till I hold you in my arms Sunday. Grr! You'll not get the grippe from me, just the tightest grip you ever did feel.

I spent this morning chasing around looking for a job. Doing so, I watched myself watching the world. It's fascinating, coming back to the world from an illness. I tried to write it out—that sickness is a journey far away from feeling & the strong earth. I'm returning; but the earth & I are like dear friends that have been separated for a long time, gone different ways, done different things. Meeting once more, we're a little shy & don't know what to say, what the right, uniting word might be.

And YOU sent it to me! The river rushing thru your letter, cascading redcheeked joy-words at me, this brought me back to earth faster & better than anything I've seen or felt since I've been ill. I lean on joy once more, a windowledge looking out on a mountain-morning made for you to walk toward me. Though I hate the days that part us, I love them too: they are the bridge over which we walk toward each other; & each moment is a step nearer. Run, Dearest, run!

February 17, 1941

Yesterday, after completing my letter to you, at eleven o'clock I popped into bed, as fine, as perfect, a fatigue as I've ever been. At that moment, as though I'd been watched, just as I was turning my face to sleep's, my telephone buzzer rang. Out I jumped & raced down the hall to the phone. It was Renee Weiss. She implored me to come to their place. Of course, I adamantly refused, stressing my weariness & my eagerness to rise early to work. Then Paul got on the phone, underscoring Renee's supplications. Tiring, he relayed the phone to Renee again, & she baited me by telling me that I better come NOW, I might not be seeing them soon. How could I ignore that warning? I went.

Out of desperation they've been considering return- ing to Renee's home. Their debts have been piling up, as I told you, till they see no way of extricating themselves except by pulling out. There's no reason why they should stay. They've developed almost no ties beyond me. And as lit- tle as Paul attends classes, he could dispense with all of them. In May, when he intends to take his M.A. exam, he could bus here for it.

But all kinds of conditions complicate the idea. Paul doesn't relish the idea of living with Renee's folks; they've an apartment lease to break, & so on. I'd miss them very much. Just by enabling me to talk out my woe, they've helped me a great deal, made it a bit more endurable.

But talking about woe, sometimes I seem deliberate- ly to plot out my own. This morning I couldn't find my poetry notebook anywhere. You can imagine my anxiety. In this notebook, off & on for the last few months, I've jotted down observations, etc. on a multiplicity of subjects; & it contains several longer poems I'm hopeful for, one particularly on my grandfather's death.

At once I started galloping all over creation looking for it. The last I remembered of it was Saturday afternoon. I'd gone to some wrestling & fencing matches with Paul. I dashed over to the Gym. Not there. And I was late for Van Doren's class. I sat through it on tenterhooks. After class I dashed off to another building. Not there. I pellmelled over to John Jay to telephone Paul. Maybe I had left it at his apartment. No, he remembered distinctly my carrying it away. And as a matter of fact so did I.

Walking toward John Jay, carrying the notebook in one hand, Paul's borrowed briefcase in the other, I kept saying to my egotistical self, "I bet people are wondering (as though they even noticed it!) why I don't put the notebook in the briefcase." That left only the art shop & the Columbia bookstore. I hotfooted it there. Not there! I rushed to the bookstore. Not there! Then to the library, though I was positive I hadn't gone there. No. There was nothing left to do but settle down to the loss as best I could.

I tried to console myself by recalling that Carlyle's whole big French Revolution was burned; & he had to rewrite it. But mine was poetry, much of it, spontaneous stuff not recoverable. I sat there forlorn over the months of living, an essential part of me, irrevocably gone.

I drooped up to my room. Aimlessly, not even reassured by your letter, I waded through the papers on my desk. There, Dearest, snuggling under a pile, was the notebook! My heart danced round like shouting kids whirling round a Maypole. The maid must have rearranged my papers, & the notebook wriggled down under them. I, accustomed to seeing it on top, took it for granted, with my nose for trouble & my overly anxious nature, that it was lost.

February 27, 1941

Dearest, I've suddenly understood why your letter stung me as much as it did. On several occasions the Weisses, seeing us together, after you had left, insisted that I baby you too much. Renee, whether she realized it or not, resented my attentiveness in the face of Paul's fairly indifferent treatment of her. Rather than admit this, she accused me of not acting enough the man with you. Vehemently she maintained that women prefer more domination & less catering to. Paul, not caring to increase his consideration of her, of course agreed. He would not want her to make odious comparisons. I knew that what they were saying is balderdash. But evidently it stayed, hiding in my subconscious.

Thus when you suggested I sometimes might be a bit more exacting, this sleeping thought the Weisses had planted in me sprang forth. Instantly, though I knew it to be false, eager as I am not to be dogmatic, I heard myself mutter: "Maybe the Weisses are right after all?" I'm not such an ego-fool as to think everything I believe must be true. And loving you as I do, I want to do exactly what you want me to. Surely that's not wrong?

February 28, 1941

Yippee! My Love, now, exactly 10:30 in the morning, I've completed the second section of that paper & have only a short piece, no more than a note, to do. By tomorrow, when I'll be reading this letterette with you, I hope to have finished the whole thing & then once more I'm free! With you no more than 24 hours away, this day's little more than a thin grey veil between us.

March 2, 1941

A little after one (Sunday afternoon) & a few jotter-ies now for my nextdoor, practicing Renee. At moments ten-derness & yearning, some giant unseen hand, wring me. All I can do is mumble: "My Renée! My Dear Renée!"

I've stayed in bed through the morning to eschew parent-talk about you, my lack of a job, etc. Pop came for me last evening. Immediately after my getting into the car & the greetings, he showered me with I-told-you-so talk. I breezed it through with cheery words, but felt very much the rotter. Yet reaching home, sitting in the glow of my Mom's & Grandmom's love, even my shame melted away. After all, what I (we) had done was thoroughly right. My present duplicity? Well, it's bad only in so far as it makes me feel that I've committed a misdemeanor (naughty?).

(But I have to be careful: Pop's walking in & out of the parlor. So I conceal these pages within my poetry note-book: here he comes! Hide, Dearest, hide!)

Pop & Bubi are arguing in the kitchen (in Yiddish) as to who of them is a better prophet. (He's in again!) Bubi: "Wait! Wait! You'll see. He'll fool you all. You'll be proud of him (naches). You must just have patience (geduld). I knew Herschel (my Zadi: this offered as proof of her powers) would die first." My Pop meantime scoffs, "Yeh! Yeh!" but hopefully.

It's after three. Your radio has just gone on. I hasten to switch ours on too, to catch up with you. (I have to be extremely cautious; Pop's reclining on the sofa, liable to look up any moment.)

It's dreadful, Dear, (my Pop's just gotten up & gone out for cigarettes: a few minutes of peaceful writing) the bur-den of my folks' expectations, of their belief that someday (soon!) I'll do something "great" &, even worse, "great" in their sense of the word. At least you have the wisdom to accept & love me for what I now am (no?).

166

This noon John telephoned me from Bethlehem, much to my Pop's smoldering rage, even though he was my best friend throughout high school. He has nothing but wholecloth hatred for John: "A boy like you should look for better company! With his opportunities see what he's not made of himself! When you come home for a day that day should be for your parents!" So you can understand why I must restrain with all my might this impulse to cast all restraint away & dash over to see you (& your Pop).

Mom, Bubi secretly informs me, wanted to have you over for dinner; but Pop wouldn't have it. Does your Pop know I'm here? Has he said anything about my not coming over?

Mom just came in, sat down beside me & with tearful eyes began to speak to me of us: "You think your Pop doesn't like Renee? There are lots of things about her he likes—if only her Pop would act like a Mensch. Everytime Pop tries to make the best of it, Abe laughs and teases him."

This is hours later. At the end of Mom's words Pop returned. Friends arrived. Then as though to corroborate Mom's insistencies, Pop suddenly decided to invite you to dinner. You know the rest. I hesitate, however, to retail what transpired after you left. But since I long ago resolved on complete honesty with you, I do so, begging you only to be patient.

My parents have no charges to bring against you (how could they?). Once again it's your Dad's conduct, his refusal to act as a potential in-law. The conversation galloped through hours, Pop reviewing with infinite patience & pains all my flagrancies: "Taking English, getting mixed up with a girl so soon, & just a little one at that," on & on. Finally, at about 11:30 he stumbled on a proposition, one he wished to execute no later than tomorrow. Being as objective as I can, I must admit the proposition has much to recommend it.

As you know, Pop is worried about my slim prospects; nor can he endure the thought of my working, say, at some shoestore (let alone a furniture store!). Teaching, he now begrudgingly admits, is my profession. Since I made the mistake of selecting such a miserable occupation, I must make the best of it. It seems clear I'll not be able to get a job without my Ph.D. Unfortunately he can no longer support me. Therefore, he wants me to go with him to your Pop with this proposition:

I require at least a year of just basic support (no tuition, etc.) so that I can study toward my oral & my Ph.D. Abe should provide the minimum amount of money necessary to see me through. In the meantime (immediately after high school, say) I marry you. Either we live together or apart (!) as financial conditions permit. So Abe will be helping not only me, but you.

The plan does attract me: were your Dad really interested in our happiness, I can see no reason for his refusing it. My Pop, I know, expects him to refuse, so hopes to make me realize how stingy, etc. your Dad is.

Well, I've persuaded my Pop to postpone broaching the plan for at least two months till I know definitely whether I'll be able to find a job or not. At that juncture, if I've not located something, I don't see how I'll be able to rein my Pop in.

What do you think of the idea? Do you consider us too hard on your Dad?

~

T & R
FOOTWORK

I

Pots and pans. Pins and needles.
But mostly women's bargain shoes
jammed his father's barn of a store,
East Greenville's Grand Emporium.

O yes, he was into dresses too.
In the big window programs changed
with the seasons:
                       mustache upturned,
felt slippers donned, father
waltzed his three svelte mannekins
to their stations. There he arranged
them in their most seductive pose.

(Like those figures lounged about,
winking out of his past, showing
off second-hand goods in well-lit,
roomy windows on certain streets
in cities masterly at merchandising.)

But however fetching dresses were,
for a man new to this new world,
ever on the move, shoes seemed
the thing to put one's money on.
Boxed two by two, each shoe bore,
ornately stamped upon its sole,
Doctor Weiss.

II
                In the hamlet
where he grew up, folks squished
their toes in mud.
                Shoes? Trotted
out for special occasions only,
while boots were meant for parades,
drums rolling as the recruits drilled.
The wooded birds nearby, a winged
tweeting to father's fiddler tunes,
muffled that constant, rumbling beat.

Until, one cold October dawn,
feet tramping a thunderous march,
his shoes jiggling round his neck,
he fled into the thickening mists
swirled out of the Black Forest.
Twitters lighting up his steps,
he made his way to the sea.
                Sea-sick-
weeks later, his past washed clean,
he landed footloose in a clog of streets,
among towers clambering the sky.

Its traffic tangled, crowds headlong,
how survive? A little village,
open spaces serving men and animals,
must be the answer.
                And there,
streets and pavements spreading,
shoes would lead him to his fortune.

III

Fortune nothing. Chores and bills,
collecting, and a rooted restlessness
drove him from one two-bit town
to another; each, a bedazzled beckoning,
quickly dimmed.
                              Still, hunched
over the backyard stoop, he spent
countless, engrossed hours looking
after his penned prize birds.

A brooding hen flying the coop,
ladling whiskey down an old hen's beak,
he set her on the orphaned nest. Come
to, soberly she took it for her own.

And when a new-born, runty pheasant
wobbled on a twisted leg, father carved
it a twig-crutch; soon it fluttered
with the rest.
                              Even in his last
shoe store, midtown bustle screeching,
the whole back wall sported cages.
There, as he warbled gypsy tunes,
kicking up his heels, the canaries
two by two trilled a shady forest
round him, drowning out the din.

FOOTNOTE

A college boy, he strutted on down
in skyblue boots, their hollow heels
atingle. Following his father's steps,
Saturdays and Summers he sold shoes.

And like his father bent on pleasing,
there was little he wouldn't stoop to.
Pumps too tight? He'd stretch them
till their stitches broke. Or stuffed
floppy sandals with inner soles.

His customers, mostly working girls,
tittered as, fallen to his knees,
he regaled them with sweet talk.
And as he tried shoe after shoe,
recommending this one, too snug,
for its now perfect fit, that one,
too loose, for its easygoing comfort,
his sweat splattering their legs.

They, for a moment in the spotlight,
saw themselves—O dem golden slippers—
twirling, starry eyed.
                    Afterwards,
nestling in his book-lined room,
a dream harem or a one-man rocket,
bits of tunes garlanding his head,
he, via words like meteors, swooped
down upon his first, half-made-up
gosling poems.

~

March 3, 1941
        Speeding toward N.Y. loneliness again, in this stream-
lined, chromium-plated train, I wonder how it is that I can
ever be casual: that times sneak through in which I'm amused
& carefree? Don't think, however, that I'm not grateful for
these occasional releases. Madness otherwise would be the

172

only consequence. Now I race toward misery again, trying desperately hard to patch up my want of you with memories. I needn't tell you I'm sure how rapidly they fade &—especially with the hard use I put them to—wear out.

My yesterday letter didn't frighten you, did it? Don't take it too seriously: it was written on its (my) back. And horizontal, long-after-midnight letters must be swallowed with a mine of salt. Even as I wrote it, groggy as I was from my Pop's everlasting iteration of my errancies, I realized how distorted my words must be. But I lacked the will or the coherence to control them. Also, I felt that qualifications were unnecessary; I could rely on your acuity to make the relevant modifications. But wouldn't it be wonderful if your Dad surprised us all & came through? I'm afraid I'd accept the proposition. And you?

But to return to the beginning of this letter: what amazes me most is that I, who tighten up so, & ignite too, at the thought of you, when I'm with you, can lapse into ease, like a steady breeze, a smoothly flowing river. Yet surely this is all I could desire. Happiness, you know, a large part of it, is to be comfortable (I don't mean smug), at home. We can't expect to travel at breakneck pace (something I've exacted from myself in the past) all the time without a breakdown. Real love oils functioning so that it rolls hummingly along. O, don't worry, I'll supply us with plenty of snags to make us appreciate all the more the smoothness.

~ 4 ~

March 4, 1941

It's after five o'clock, Tuesday, & I've not yet heard from you. Nor am I likely to anymore today. Did my Pop's proposition frighten or anger you? Or my near acquiescence to it? Or is it that at last you think you realize how devoid I am of consistency?

I know, My Love, how interminably I've inveighed against the academic world in general & Columbia in particular. By now I must have conveyed to you how much of graduate work I loathe & how much I'd dislike continuing toward a Ph.D. Why then, you may justly be asking, do you display this sudden access of interest. It isn't that I've changed. Simply I've been thinking that, little as I like the grubbiness of graduate study, I've even less yen for other work—the kind I'm likely to get.

As you, Abe, (I mean your Dad!) & I agreed, when we were together in N.Y., the business world is scarcely for me. But with the situation what it is, an M.A. is hardly enough. I do believe, however, that armed with a Ph.D. I'd be fairly certain of finding a position. And with assiduous application I think I could get the degree within a year & two summers. My Pop, if he could afford it, would see me through. Poor as his business is, his further support is impossible. If your Dad is financially able to do so, do you deem it wrong for him to help me (us)? After all, as I understand it, HE was given an initial push by your grandfather. I'm confident that with you behind me I could gird myself to the monotonies, & irrelevancies too, of graduate study.

March 5, 1941

And My Dear Sensible One proves herself as wise as ever. Yes, I know too well how potentially rife with hostility such a situation must be: put two such conflagrations as my Pop & yours opposite each other & what can we expect but explosion? That's mainly the reason I insisted on being present—to act as referee. But your proposal, Beloved, is better. One question, however: how do YOU take to my Pop's proposition? Yes, My Only One, you will get into my family all right—&, I hope, never get out!—even if you have to use the backdoor of me. Already they are adapting themselves, with difficulty it's true, to the idea. The actuality is only a step away. But nowhere in your letter do you permit yourself one word of approval or displeasure. Would you like me to continue Ph.D.ing (especially if we could be together)?

I suggested to my Pop that if his plan were to materialize it might put a hitch in your college hopes. But he poohpoohed the idea, "Nonsense! You'll teach her what she has to know." If only he realized how much My Liebling has to teach ME! Other ideas have been simmering in my mind: if Abe enabled us to live in N.Y., Renee could attend Hunter.   I've a class now; I'll be seeing you: an on-the-run kiss.

Yes, it's amazing how one beauty (as in your instance of music cum landscape: your Sunday afternoon drives with your family, listening to the Philharmonic, the rolling, rounded, immaculate Pennsylvania countryside & the music echoing each other) underscores & substantiates the other. But you appreciate, of course, that it's the beauty of you that first births their beauties two, & then compacts them into beauty one. You have, I'd say, hit on one of the characteristics of beauty—its adjustability & flowing-togetherness with whatever it meets. You know how gracefully/effortlessly rain & snow, sky & music accommodate themselves to everything & everywhere.

Such beauty is our obligation: achieving in the every daily the effortlessness, the grace, you do in your dancing.

March 6, 1941

Waiting for your letter, I'm all ready to spend my usual happy letter-time with you. But other things, other people insist on intruding. In the same mail with yours I receive a letter from my Mom. To show you why I do not at this moment entertain the kindest (!) feelings toward your Dad, I quote my Mom's choicest passage: "Well, Mr. Abe Karol has been talking again. He is telling people he doesn't want you at all for a son-in-law. He sent Renee to Florida so she'd forget you. And he also claims that she doesn't play her violin or study her lessons on account of you. It seems you are making a dope out of her according to his talk. So you see, Ted, what you can expect from a man like that." And so on.

I know, My Dearest, that I ought not repeat this to you. But it's filled me so I can't help spilling some of it on you. Exaggerated though the above may be, I cannot believe that the whole is fabricated even though I didn't really SEE you until AFTER you returned from Florida. I still remember your descending those stairs as though you were opening my eyes, descending into me. Before that it was your father who was my friend! Why, My Gentleness (& however much you may have curbed your anger in the past, please do it now!), can't your Dad keep his mouth shut? I know there's nothing you can do. But at least I can talk the present bitterness out of me by discussing the matter with you.

The irony of it, My Love, that, for a moment even, we expected your Dad to help us! His conduct is, I fear, too plain. He's preparing himself & his friends for the time when we are to marry; then he can tell me & THEM (he wants them to think him a good fellow) that, since he had nothing to do with promoting our affection—in fact, he frowned on it, he's no way responsible for us now. Some way we'll have to fend for ourselves.

Forgive me, My Patient One, but I can find no excuse for such actions. You do understand my animus? Though I've tried my hardest to stem its growth, the hope has flowered in me that perhaps, after all, Abe WOULD extend a helping hand. Now with a few words he's trampled the whole underfoot. Not only do we have the difficulty of finding a job to contend with, but apparently we must cope with his disapprobation.

What reasons has he, My Wise One, other than financial ones? If you can remark any logical others, please send them to me; willingly I'd supplant what I believe with them. But, My Sturdy, instead of permitting such inconsiderate-nesses to come between us, we must forge greater love & strength out of them. Some day soon, I fear, your Dad & I will have it out. I pray your love for me will prove so substantial that such a fracas will shake neither you nor your love.

Don't worry, My Precious. This bitterness will shortly melt away; it's only because this letter is written on the heels of my Mom's. Yet I can't help resenting being duped so easily by MYself. How eager I was to believe the patently impossible! What an impractical fool I am! Do you remember in the hotelroom how your Dad bridled at the thought of my approaching him for a loan? Then too he had excuses galore. NO, he refused to buy (his word) a soninlaw. However, because he would gladly help any deserving young man, he would sign a note for $250 IF I could first get my Pop to do the same, & then six or seven others!

I realize, My Love, how all this must goad you, yet some sadistic devil insists on my writing it. But the whole effect of this is to make me more eager than ever to pluck you out of your home & leave it far behind. Paul, despite the goodness, the openhanded generosity, of Renee's parents, resents them. Then am I not entitled to ONE letterful of spleen?

And then you write: "Please don't ever worry that anger or anything else would keep me from writing to you"! This is certainly the acid test. Had Mother's letter not upset my applecart of plans, I would have asked, "You say you don't object to your Dad's helping, but do you APPROVE?" Such questions are now obviously irrelevant.

March 7, 1941

Of course, Dear Heart, I regret my yesterday's irascibility—first, that I should have experienced it at all &, second, most important of all, that I should have vented it on you. These last hours, thinking to myself, "Renee must have received it now; now she's reading it!" the best thing I've been able to do is to work away industriously biting my fingernails. My Poor Dearling, from your Pop (the fire) to me (the frying pan)! Then, as though things aren't bad enough, you have to come along with your sane, carefully pondered today-letter. (If you don't beware, I'LL get sore again!) You're so much more levelheaded than I'll ever be. Are you willing to think for both of us?

Yes, I recognized that your approval was tacitly expressed in your acceptance & suggestion. But I wanted to read your say-so. That's something you often do—or forget to! You can't realize how jagged my next hours will be till I receive your tomorrow letter. Seriously, My Sweetest, what I've been doing all along here is apologizing, apologizing, apologizing. I know I deliberately spill the milk; then I cry over it & expect you to wipe it up, pat me on the back & say, "What a good boy YOU've been!"

I know I've been wrong (see how my guilt insists on pushing itself through all my other thoughts) to give any credence to such gossip, repeated by a very jealous, hardly dispassionate mother; then, to become angry about it; &, finally, to reiterate it to you. Is there anything I can do for penance? Were you here such acts wouldn't happen: you'd fortify me against my gusts of anger & petulance with the colossal sanity of a kiss.

March 9, 1941

It's still snowing. I haven't sent you any weather—other than personal; stormy as it's been, it's blocked out all other—in some three days. But that falling now is only tiny specks like an afterthought, as though some flakelets, a remnant in the bottom of the bag, had been overlooked.

Now that I've settled the weather & you can sit back in it with me, I'd like to tell you of my room weather; My Love has brought me not only my private music but public as well: last evening I heard a magnificent rendition of Brahms' *First*; this morning I basked in Beethoven's *Egmont Overture*, three of Brahms' *Hungarian Dances*, etc.: rainbows all to festoon this gray trellis of a day, heavy with the threat of additional snow.

This leads me (us) a step deeper, so that I reach my most intimate climate—that of head-&-heart. You must learn to disregard my bluster. I needn't tell you how interfused you are with me. When I receive such choice snippet of gossip as Mother's, I—the merely me & not the you-in-me—am shaken. I know this shouldn't happen. But without you I'm a haunted house. (A ragged little dog is running snowwild on a large roof across the street; he tries to pee on all of it: is that HIS way of declaring his love?) When such ruthless words sound, the boards begin to creak, the mad ghosts begin to run. You must come then to drive them out with a smile & a kiss, sunshine flooding the dusty, gloom-ridden rooms.

Two days, My Ghost-Chaser, I'd been accumulating anxiety about my letter. No-letter Saturday morning determined me to telephone. And just as I call, you come home. (See how Love takes care of its own.) But, Dearest, let me describe the motions of my wayward brain during & after our talk. I want you to know the amplitude of my jealousy & suspicion. Your dashing to the phone, your breathlessness, the fact that it was Saturday night, noone in the house, instantly aroused my suspicions. O, I know I have no reason (or right) to think such things. But realize that the insult falls not to you but to me for thinking such thoughts. I trust you, Liebkin, yet I've seen, heard, read so much, know how easy it is to slip, that I wouldn't put any faith in God Himself. (Lord, look what he did to Mary—poor Joseph!) You MUST understand, My Tolerance, that I really don't think these thoughts as much as they think me.

Finally, I recall my letter to you. After sending it off, retesting its barbs of rancor, I'm appalled at myself. How can you help but be angry? So I called. Nonetheless, when you told me that for a moment you WERE angry with my anger & considered yours justifiable just for the moment of heat in which it happened, I was angry with your anger for a moment, angry that you didn't justify my lack of justification. Greedy as I am, I resent that you should harbor ANY affection for your Dad; I want it all. Such times as that letter, I, at my invidious worst, set out to make capital of the situation & to deracinate your love for your folks. I fail to see that such tactic can do nothing but drive you to their defense. And yet (!) if your Dad DID utter such sentiments, to people who have no right to hear them, don't you think it fair (beholden upon me even) to feel some resentment? I know such anger's not justifiable under any circumstances, but...! Unfortunately I'm what we call too-too-human.

March 10, 1941

Good morning, My Morning. (Though it's a little after twelve, morning is still bustling about, humming away in tiniest corners, as if it's just arrived.) Again—& I've become so accustomed to it, I soon probably won't remark it, but take it for granted as I do the morning—you display your unusual common good sense & wisdom too. What's the idea of blossoming under my very fingers (would it were so!) into such a profound soothsayer? (My little roof-dog is frisking about once more as though anxious to rid himself of the roominess he's collected. He races round & round as though every flake were a fluffy white rabbit &, catching one, he drops it to dash off for another.)

You say that you are not so hurt by my remarks as by the fact that I become so involved in them. Dearest, such remarks can't be uttered (at least by me) unless I AM involved in them. Heat, as you said, partially forgives them. As for involvement, have you forgotten how indulgent I am of all my feelings? But isn't this the only way to "enjoy" them? I agree, however, that restraint & control, even in the case of our love, should result (if possible!) in deeper, fuller joy.

For instance, the day I waited & waited & waited for you at Penn Station, finding you in every face, chasing from face to face, like the pup his bits of snow, till I seemed a revolving-door. My energies that should have been husband-ed (I use the word advisedly) for you were practically dissipated. All my surface fluster means that, not only is the feeling often exhausted rapidly like top waves, but the depths get lost in froth. Don't misunderstand. If there is anything deep about me, it is my love for you. Still I DO object to my adolescent giddiness when feeling saddles me rather than I the feeling. And loving you as I do, there is an element of dissatisfaction in my love (at least no complacency yet): it insists on going on, beyond itself, deeper & deeper & deeper.

You are wholecircle right about your Pop. He does allow you to see me, & I AM thankful. Believe me. It's amusing how we expect & would exact nobility from OTHERS. Thus I am irked when your Dad doesn' t act as magnanimously as he might. And yet why should he? Were I in his position I'd probably experience the same uncertainties. But that's precisely what provokes me. I would have HIM dismiss what I so constantly & unhappily recognize! I would extract from your Pop the full measure of HIS idealism! But always remember, My Sweetest, that I DO harbor deep affection for your Pop; that's why he can wound me so.

March 11, 1941

Now that the letter-flurry (all mine) is over, I can say, My Loveliest One, that in the face of our letters alone (mine, nasty, snarling; yours considerate as ever), you have shown yourself the infinitely larger person. Perhaps that was the "justification" for the entire (my) todo: it enabled me to see once more (as though I need it any longer!) how inexplicably lucky I am to have had YOU fall in love with me. How can I tell you the pride your sweet reasonableness engendered in me? Sweetest, had I dwelt, after my dolt-letter, on what reply I would most wish from you, I'm sure I am not fine enough to have hit on the ideal answer you DID send. Have you ever thought of studying law—that is, if law were lawful & just? Or politics?!

The days after my letter I had time enough to ponder my conduct & yours. It's always I who foment these affairs. In the past I've found what I deemed ample vindication for my actions. (One always can.) "My Parents are doing the senseless things they do because they love me. Out of ignorance rises all their folly. But your Pop is a person of pretensions & ideals. Didn't you tell me that in the old days he even helped striking workers at your grandfather's silk mill?

Now look at him. His concern, as far as I can see, has not been your welfare & happiness but his own financial fears."

But, My Love, examining the above, I'm forced to recognize how riddled with errors my thinking (rationalizing) is. I'd been giving myself—very graciously—a green light to anger. MY Parents DID start the whole rumpus. However much they adjudge their actions ones of love, they stem from reasons as petty as (if not more so than) Abe's. What are they emphasizing but matters I claim to contemn—money, position, the opinions of other people. But past times I had excused them on the score of ignorance— they don't know any better & don't pretend to. This is my mistake: I still ascribe too much importance to intellect. I forget that your Dad is as spiced in passion & pride as my Pop. Because he has read more, thought more, is hardly reason to expect nobler conduct from him. (Look at me! probably more read & more thinking than either!) Clearly I'm still too much the moralist; for all my claims to the contrary, I'm still trammelled to "good" & "bad," "right" & "wrong."

You are moved by love rather than by "morals," too often a way of living for those who lack love. It is plain to me that people passionately in love have not become, as the poets maintain, momentarily at least, divine. More important & nobler than divinity, they've ripened to the ultimate of human becoming. I cannot say this of me; I CAN of you. By the example you've set me, by the shame you've shown me, you've helped to make me more human.

Don't misunderstand me, My Heart; I'm not making you out a gilded goodie, "too good for life"; on the contrary, one good enough for the all of it; one so large because she knows how small she (we) is (are).

But I forgot to finish my odious comparison. Your Dad's fears, if chiefly financial, are certainly as legitimate as my Parents': WILL Ted be able to take care of Renee? A very good & huge question it is! So he's caught between his respect (what's left of it) for me & his concern for you. But once more I'm doing the very thing I set out to eliminate: finding "justifications"!

It's four o'clock, & reading over this letter, I have to laugh at its pomposity. It occurs to me that only those may judge who love & those who love will not care to. I've come up to my room clutching your letter. Recently, every time I rush (my first reading IS a rush) through a new you-letter, I heave a heavy sigh of relief—first, for receiving it; second, for learning that all is well, that our love is still intact; &, third, for having you in paper-&-ink to dwell on a long thinking evening. The second though has come to be the cardinal fright. There is that unpredictable time between your letters when anything can happen. I feel like one receiving a report from a battlefront (how much the world at large & I agree!) & learning that his loved one is still untouched.

March 12, 1941

What's this My Bubi (she's in N.Y. visiting her sister) tells me about your having ANOTHER cold? What's the big idea? What's the idea also of driving alone in this big snow to hear Traubel? Jees, Liebkin, you're making a regular old grandmom out of me!

A few minutes ago as I'm returning, about 11:15 p.m., from Aunt Jenny's—Bubi's sister, the intellectual among the four sisters, now virtually immobilized, who is so huge she, afloat in her self, seems to flood the room—striding up the long walk that leads from Broadway to my dormitory, a swiftly running fellow dashes by me. He reaches a break in the wall, abutting on the Columbia race track, leaps wildly through the tremendous snowdrifts &, still in his heavy over-coat, races madly around the track.

Did I ever describe a similar moment involving my main seminar professor, Neff? One early morning, as I returned to campus from the Schuberts, I saw Neff, a sober, skinny, Andy Gumpish sort, looking about furtively. Failing to see me, he gathered himself up, then took a run & a great leap up all the steps. (Maybe I should forgive him after all for his failure with Hopkins?) Smiling triumphantly for a second, he drew his coat around him & soberly strode off. Good night, My Love. It's time for bed.

Now on to your letter. Your "I have a confession to make" frightened me! Never, never do that again. Of course, please commit such "crimes" as writing a poem a thousand times. But why call it a "crime"? Because you evaluate your attempt as inferior? "Apologies"? Folderol! What you ask of me, however, is just about impossible. Long I've wondered why, nearly resented that, you hadn't written some such expression of your love. I receive it finally, & you ask me to criticize it!

Can I criticize your love, tell you what to do with the line breaks, where to punctuate, etc? I'm not being critical or objective? Of course not. All I can suggest (& importune) is that you send me more. Perhaps, once I accustom myself to such expression, I can make suggestions—but even then, I assure you, most hesitantly. (It's snowing again! I bet it's My Parents' doing!)

One large hard suggestion I would make however: instead of describing your feeling & yourself in a straightforward, leisurely gait, try to DO the feeling & yourself: give the poem action & pace. Make the reader feel that the mood (or feeling) is happening under his eyes. This is the difficulty I have to struggle with, ALWAYS. Once one masters this, the rest becomes unimportant & readily learned. Yours is a fine, lovely (for me sweetest) statement; for other readers it must be more: infectious, it must make them participate in the passion or delight (whatever the poet presents).

But, My Dearest Dearest, do not take my words too harshly. I've been writing almost three years now continuously, fervidly; & save for a few fleeting touches, I've hardly been able to do what I'm proposing here. PLEASE write & send me more.

Hurrah! though the flakes are fluffy-fat, it's no more than a rain-snow. It can't last!

March 13, 1941

Sun's returned & gay again. The birds are gushing over with song, as though anxious to make up for lost time; & the light dashes about everywhere as if eager to investigate what might have happened while it was gone—like our snowdog it frisks about, beside itself (& around itself!). It's ten o'clock & there is work to be done. Yesterday I typed out a long poem, pretty stiff going, about you-me. Today I've another, about the Weisses' mother. And tomorrow *Hansel & Gretel* will be waiting. So I'll see you later, My Love. (The maid's making my bed: "You're the worst one here! Some of the boys have their girls' pictures on their bureaus, but you right on your desk! Doesn't she interfere with your work?" And I: "Sure, when I haven't her with me. With her here close to me, she oversees everything I do. I weave her into my work, she the best part of it." Leaving, she throws back over her shoulder: "Well, I'll lock you in so noone will steal you; so you can be alone with HER!" She doesn't know how right she is!

It's a little after twelve, My Darling. (The word "Darling" is no easier to say or to write than "My Wife"; is it because they're feelingful, so reverential, nearly ineffable?) I'm sitting back in a cellar barbershop, waiting for Paul who is getting a 35 cent haircut. A little box radio is singing in a scratchy voice, "I'm lonely & you're lonely too." I'm entirely sympathetic. Paul's getting a semi-crew haircut. As he emerges from his forest, he looks like a Goering, but a good-natured, grinning one—if such is conceivable. Finished, he

186

smiles sheepishly (a shorn one!).

You do me an injustice to assume that I am "not sufficiently aware" of what you really are. My Darling, I DO appreciate what passions you are capable of. And so I would have you be. A person devoid of the potentiality of passion scarcely deserves respect or praise for his-her restraint. The fact that you contain your passions, yet have them too, wins my always burgeoning admiration. Instead of using your feelings as knives against others, you employ them as lenses to understand them better.

The scissors are cricketing away: with my eyes busy studying my thoughts & your letter nestling in my lap, I can pretend this is that spring Allentown day, with you-&-me sitting in our little wellbehaved, if pampered, cricket-orchestrated park.

Of course, you know I'd be the last to deny your remark that I expect too much of people. I even do of myself; unhappily my expectations are seldom fulfilled. This is something I've never—though I HAVE tried—been able to overcome. I consider it a strain of the Puritan. It began at my first thinking childhood & it's been extorting tribute ever since. In part, poetry has emancipated me. You'll have to do the rest.

What do you mean by "keeping images straight"? Are you thinking of mixed metaphors? Such can be employed very successfully. But their use must be deliberate & skillful. Modern poets exploit this device often to excess. More of this, however, when (& if!) I see you Sunday.

Congratulations on the 95. That's as high a mark as Gerhard ever gave me. Your indifference to marks I applaud, of course. Can you sneak any time away these days for reading? You'll send me (or bring) your spring poem, please, won't you? You'll learn soon, if you keep at it, to wing your thoughts rather than mutilate them. That's the magic & the delight of mastering the medium. But such ease requires work, more, I admit, than I've been as yet willing or energetic enough to give.

All the way home, Paul's been darting glances at himself, his latest acquired disability. He's crammed up with apprehensions about Renee's reactions. I propose that as soon as he enters he hurl up a wall of words too thick for her to look through. But R. gets through the barrage at once & freezes us into silence with a glacial glance. Paul finally kisses her into acceptance.

No jobs yet; it's still too early. But we must be prepared for the worst. I think I see my way clear to a dissertation-subject, something I hadn't been able to ferret out all year.

March 14, 1941

It's almost nine o'clock, with crams & crams of work to be done. But I must rush this letter off to make sure you receive it tomorrow. Forgive it, therefore, if it appears distraught. Toiling away at these poems is not exactly the easiest work in the world. I've just about decided that such writing is as fine a training as one could desire for marriage (we'll see!); after dealing with & controlling (to a degree!) my poems, I'm fairly certain I could handle almost any Xanthippe of a wife. (I DON'T mean YOU!) Seriously, I don't think artists in general & poets in particular are as impossible husbands as they are assumed to be. It's simply that they've a larger job, a more elusive, complicated one, to contend with than most men. (I'm NOT making a plea for myself!) Poetry at best is a pretty shrewish mistress. O the capricious, exacting Muse! Then if the poet happens to wed a vixen, well!

But, Dearest, are you or are you not coming in Sunday? (Menuhin is playing Lalo's *Symphony Espaniole*, & I can hear again your cousin Abram's performance, your father accompanying him. When did he study with Flesch in Germany?) If you don't soon assure me of your visit, you'll have—if you should come—a nervous wreck on your hands. It's bad enough the moments (I say hours, years) before your train arrives, yanking me up & down like a yoyo. But to do it days!

March 17, 1941

Depression, depression everywhere; & nowhere concentration enough to allow for thinking or work.

Paul's just come in. Seeing me so wildeyed, he suggests I accompany him downtown. Morose as I am, I shan't be able to do anything except minister to my mood; so I decide to starve the damn thing to death by leaving it to itself. Paul picks me up with a blotter, somehow pours me into my coat, & we're off.

Well, here I am, My Sweet, slightly less tangled, more tied together: the outside demands at least a modicum of attention. But everything is wind. We run into the Irish parade. Poor kids! Many little girls clad in thin silk frocks, socks & bareness! No doubt, though, the Irish have enough such wild wind running round loose in them to resist. I watch people reacting to the wind. One man, crossing the street, twists his face into a sneer—his defiance. So cold it is, I wonder how the trees, the statues even, manage to avoid pneumonia. Thus, though I've carried you every bit of the way, I've nestled you in the warmest part of me. I know too well how susceptible you are to colds.

March 18, 1941

What insidious weather, My Permanent May! Here I've been looking forward to spring & winter stabs me in the back with an icicle. I've been chasing after my nose all last evening & this morning; it's running faster & faster. And I'M the one who showers you with counsel on colds! But the career of this cold is easy to outline. Your leaving me pulled the plug out of my spring-strength. Then this cold-spell hit & I, poor fish that I am, swallowed its rimy bait without a second's demur. Perhaps when we're together the two of us can keep colds at bay. I hope THIS TIME you've escaped?

Sunday when we separated I found a note at Columbia from David apologizing for his not coming to see me Saturday as he had planned. He insisted I visit them. Thus last night, against my better judgment, I ventured out into the dark wilderness of wind. It struck the face like a forest of attacking trees. I wouldn't have minded even this, but when it begins to use my face as an ice-rink, zooms over it with razor-sharp skates...!

Pushing my way through the mob of winds, I arrived at the Schuberts, to find that Judy had gone out to a "must" teachers meeting. The apartment, perched on top of its building, asks to be attacked. Repeatedly the winds hurled themselves against the thin walls. And while they nearly blew the place down, David & I sat huddled in the kitchen before the all-burning fires of the gas-stove & the fireplace of our words. We did our best to keep a blaze going. But the winds shouted us down. And I had little more than David's ego to keep me warm. You think mine bad? Well! nightlong he plied me for specific praise of the novel he's written (I had read about half of it), fed me such leading remarks as "Don't you really think it one of the great masterpieces of prose?" As I suggested to him, but obliquely (he too engrossed in his ego to appreciate the innuendo), he had so monopolized the territory of self-love no room remained for me. This went on till two o'clock, & still no Judy. I hinted he might begin to worry about her. Recalling his obligations, he pulled himself out of the quicksands of self.

190

As you know, I'm hardly one to deplore ego. In some respects (probably when I find it respectable!), I applaud it; for the artist, nearly inevitable, an essential evil, it affords him a vantage point from which to view the rest of the world. The danger, of course, is succumbing to Narcissus: falling in love with the focus, so seeing nothing else. Only when the artist, recognizing the uniqueness of his work (rather than of himself), steps over himself to other things does he put himself to happiest use.

I suspect a large portion of my objection to David's attitude derived from his ego's trampling mine. In the past, however, when David's self-wonder has been equally unbridled, & when I've not been cold inside & out, I've found much to amuse, even delight, me in his peacockeries. Often he's boyish & ingenuous about it, & therefore quite infectious. "In the next twenty years," David continues, "if I write the other two novels I'm planning, I'll be the most influential man in America—except for Roosevelt."!

Liebling, please excuse me if, before the cafeteria-rush begins, I hurry off to lunch.

I'm back. I just now telephoned my Bubi. She told me that last night Aunt Jennie died. Poor woman! Did I mention how long & intensely she had suffered? She had almost everything you can think of, & many things you can't. For the last twelve years she had been occupied with heart-trouble, asthma, arthritis, dropsy, rheumatism, obesity, & other ailments, large & small. Have I described her physical appearance? Short (no taller than my Bubi), she weighted over three hundred pounds. Walking, just moving from one room to another, was a prodigious expedition for her. She was moored to herself like a wrecked ship to its rotted dock. I've never seen anyone quite like her. Folds upon folds of flaccid flesh enveloped her like ten loosely fitting cloaks. Sometimes I had the impression of a slender person imprisoned in this fat, for from her neck to her bosom she was thin; but at that point she waxed horizontal. Remember Rodin's statue of Balzac? Out of a huge mass of marble Rodin fashioned the head & shoulders of Balzac straining to pull himself out of the rock—his spirit striving to escape its fleshy trammels. In HER case the spirit, except for her mind, capitulated a long time ago.

And my poor Bubi! Here she's still fresh from one—the closest possible—death & she's thrown into another. It's pretty horrible & clear, isn't it, the way Death early on begins to dog our footsteps, shadow-boxes with us in our loved ones, our friends, & the people about us till, tired of taunting, it takes us too.

But I left David holding his ego, didn't I? About two o'clock Judy telephoned, saying she'd be home soon. Several times David inquired about her whereabouts. She refused to answer. So he hung up in anger. More than an hour later she arrived. As she came in she giggled girlishly; David welcomed her with "Next time you better be a little more careful with your lipstick!" Though I usually spend the night with them, I decided that THIS was my cue to leave.

Cold with dread & pain for them, unable to avoid their preliminary reciprocal scathing remarks, I could scarcely help thinking of us in a similar situation. Just imagine the suspicion & jealousy that crackled in that room, & the mutual (if only momentary) rancor & hate that echoed round.

The last time I saw Aunt Jennie—Friday, four days ago—she had just come out of a heart attack ("They're frequent," she told me) the night before. Sitting on her bed, a disconsolate hillock, hardly able to move, she moaned: "If I weren't such a coward, I'd have killed myself long ago. What's the use? What kind of a life is this when you can't do anything? I wish God would come & take me away." But then she spoke enthusiastically of spending the summer near the ocean, "That will help me." Later, when we were alone, Bubi strongly doubted her sister's surviving another summer.

March 19, 1941

So we trade winds, My Liveliest—yours, despite its power, pleasant, democratic; mine, uncongenial & fascist. Maybe, all this wind will help to sweep our heart-heaviness away. So thank you for yours. Thank you too for remembering to send the music dictionary; I WILL use it. Paging through, I've already hit on a likely term for one of my still unworked poems: KINDERSTUCK or CHILD'S PIECE; & CAPRICE is even more adapted to my needs than I had imagined. Our little book defines it "a whim; freak; composition without form." The last especially appeals to me. I have a series of such poems—airy, whimsical, given to thumbing their nose at hidebound forms, yet (I hope!) finding form in their very tumultuousness. CAPRICE is just the name for these.

I'm still coldish; it dampens my imagination so that I can hardly rise to the dear occasion of writing this to you. But to return to your wind, I'd say what you are doing with it—defining its form, capturing its spirit—is what the poet attempts to do with all feelings, things, etc.: indicate wherein precisely the object of his attention differs from all other objects. So doing, he can next heighten the similarity & unity too. Your quoting Hopkins much pleases me. I can think of no finer immortality a poet can enjoy than to crop up so in the thoughts of a living young person. For a moment Hopkins breathes your breath, feeds on it by affording you the storedup fire of his.

For some reason a bit of the *Lord's Prayer* (through Hopkins?), "greenpastures," flits through my head. Instantly the phrase lets me look through my memory to our past. Do you recall the summer-time moment, like a gem in the gold-green setting of our little midtown park, when it began to rain & we sought refuge of a tree & one another's arms—a kiss our best sanctuary. As we stood there, the rain plopped itself with fat sounds on the shielding leaves. Several drops, leaning over too far, lost their hold & fell through to us. The rain, a fairythread, wreathed us round, till someone, seeing us, might have thought that we had just burgeoned from the tree & the rain.

March 20, 1941

Now that my cold's just about over, it can be told: since Tuesday, at the insistence of Paul & Renee, I've been staying with them. Renee has played the veritable Florence Nightingale, nursing me night & day, & Paul has been correspondingly attentive. I write this just after his bringing your letter to me from Columbia.

You can imagine what this has done to my writing— save for a few poemicules & several lines & ideas, nothing of note. You remember the Weiss apartment, how huddled in it is between high buildings like a poor relative. Occasionally a stray sunbeam, one that must have lost its way, slips off the beaten track & reaches us. But by the time it does, usually it's so pallid we scarcely recognize it. Slight as sunbeams are, they need their sire sun to keep them alive. And you know how much I need sun. The semidark we're forced to dwell in here won't do.

Paul, coming in, has brought some of the outside & the day clinging like a burr to his coat, his fingers, & his eyes. And your letter of course—a day all by itself.

Hours through I lie here looking at the blankfaced walls that stare back at me like some prisoner held in a cellar, & somehow I have to make a world out of this twobit area. With my imagination & my recollections of you I succeed, translate it into material for a letter to you. Paul & Renee have imbued this two-by-four province with motion & emotion; & beside my always active thoughts of you, I have the company of a graceful, green-leafed plant. (How it prospers in this dungeon is a miracle.) Between us we erect an entire spring. By tomorrow I expect to write off this cold & to get to spring firsthand.

March 23, 1941

My cold? It's still around, but casually; our intimacy has "cooled" to a coughing acquaintanceship. I'm doing my best to estrange it entirely. But without you why shouldn't I have a cold? At least it's something to keep me occupied (!).

I'm enclosing the rejection from the University of Miami. Should I say, I told you so? It sounded like too perfect a set-up, with your scholarship & a job for me! The fates won't have it. Nonetheless, though I anticipated the rejection, it's very disheartening.

Yes, David's finished his book & submitted it too. What do I think of it? Well, I read over half, but I can't speak of it as a unity. In many spots what I saw is brilliant: daringly, yet without seeming effort, David breaks through the trammels of literary traditions; almost as much as I can imagine, his characters think & speak as they think & speak. But his episodes (the material & treatment is episodic) seem arbitrarily selected, uneven, & therefore sometimes monotonous. Moreover, in his deliberate disregard of direction David may be neglecting what is, after all, the lifeblood of most novels— plot. But I reserve judgment till I read the whole. After all, David is first & last a poet, & as a poet he may bring off what most novelists cannot.

Of course I want to see your dances! Even if the only thing you could do for me NOW would be exercises in a chair, I'd assay them ballet sublime. You so satisfy me, I'm compelled to wonder oftimes whether you shaped my appetite or my appetite shaped you; appetite & gratification are identical here, you see.

Your dreams, My One Dream, think me long; their career & consequence please me short. An old play has it that "in dreams begin responsibilities." Someway you & I must ponder out a plan to develop your dreams. But how shall I? I dream so little (at least consciously), you must be making up for me.

~

T & R
THAT SONG

While the others' ears are stuffed
with wax, you dare that song.

And, wafted over the sea,
steepened by a summer meadow scent,
it sweetens with your story, noted
as it ought to be.
                    O that music
beating through your ears, pulsing
through your veins. You strain
to give yourself, to join it.

Writhe as you will, ropes,
hard-knotted, tearing your skin,
hold fast.
                Then, past that fatal
shoal, you are, you think, finally
free.
        But some passion gripping,
a gust from an inmost nook of sleep,
and instantly that music crests
your blood again.

Years collecting,
waters crossed, notes grow wilder,
bloody cries there's no escaping.
Ear wax, hardened, seals them in.

Your heart a channel to the pounding
sea, you struggle as those beats
strike the cordage of your body,
ever tightening.
                    Until that rocky
inlet looms once more.
                         And waiting
there, faithful beyond any woman,
any goddess,
                    those music makers
twine their arms around you
as they sing you, everlastingly,
(at last!) into a dreamless sleep.

~

March 25, 1941

Early this morning WQXR is serenading me with
Mendelssohn's Violin Concerto. Weren't you playing it when
I was home last summer? On every slide of the bow like joy
you are riding up & down my heart. How can a day help but
be happy, launched as gaily as this one is? But I'm off to
INVASION. I've neglected it too long already. I'll be seeing
you later.

Late afternoon & I've just torn myself away from
gorging on your letter. All morning I worked away at the
poem, turned out another (5th) typewritten section &
roughly composed a missing transitional 6th. I hope to com-
plete the poem by tomorrow morning to take it to Van

Doren. The going, as you can see, is damnably difficult, but soon it should be able to stand on its own feet(!).

You know, the more I love you, Sweetkin, the harder it sometimes is for me to write to you. A paradox? Not really. At least not in this respect: my love has achieved a degree of stability. Whereas in the past I could describe the doubts & vagaries of my baby love, I can no longer do so. And I'm too proud, arrogant, to go on repeating "I love you," "I love you." Do you appreciate the difficulty? But since I'm supposedly something of a poet, it's my "profession" to quarry out variations in the apparently unvarying.

Last night I saw my Bubi at my uncle's. I told her of your father's proposition that he support us and we move in with them. Bubi greeted the proposition with some hope—perhaps NOW it may work out!

I agree that my living at your house seems unlikely. But if my parents accept the rest, it is conceivable that they MIGHT not boggle even at this. What concerns me—paramountly, if I may say so—is all of us living together. Much as I love your father, he's a very volatile fellow. Pray tell, though, what other arrangement would make our living together possible?

My Judicious One, afraid to criticize my little poem! But when you invite me to criticize your criticism or at least to defend myself, you realize, I'm sure, what temptation you set before me. It's always dangerous for an artist to explain his work, especially after it's done. Involved as he or she is in it (response to adverse criticism often becoming self-defense & not poem-explanation), the writer is likely to gloss over its faults, even endeavor to convert them into virtues. Furthermore, he is likely to suggest all kinds of immensities of meaning & emotion that may or may not have made their way into the work. These are the Scylla & Charybdis I have to steer through. May the presence of your song drown out the sirens in my travail/travel.

Thus you did understand what I wished to do, but you didn't care for what I did. But tell me, My Understanding One, why do you dislike playfulness? Do you refuse to admit how important & necessary it is? I'm sometimes inclined to judge it (here I go wildly generalizing again!) more a male than a female attribute. Many women, I've often suspected, however much they may have of wit & intellect themselves, are suspicious of them, or denied since women, suspicious of them as frivolous & so refuse to indulge & delight in them. I recognize that the generalization may well be absurdly erroneous. Yet so thoroughly do I wish us to avoid its possibility, I am willing to make the mistake.

Don't you think poetry—even the best poetry—can countenance SOME playfulness, especially if it does not swamp the essential seriousness of the poem, but accentuates it? Must it be all Milton, never the consummately sportive Shakespeare? Remember too that such playfulness usually denotes spiritual wellbeing, an overflow of gusto, & happiness. What more do we want?

March 27, 1941

Would I live at your house if my parents objected? I believe that, once we were married, their objections would crumble. They'd be forced to realize the absurdity, futility too, of such objections. But what do you propose in its place?

Yes, My Critic, nearly half the critic's task is to determine what the writer originally intended. Then the critic decides how well the writer achieved those intentions &, finally, whether the intentions were sufficiently large. But I never mentioned, did I, how intelligent & judicious your criticism was?

It's plain, despite your bubbling self, that you are a meditative poet after major conclusions rather than the urgent, fly-into-your-face kind of poem I was attempting to ram down your mental throat on Sunday. By this I am not in the slightest implying an adverse criticism. Both kinds are equally desirable—though I, since I try to write so!, prefer the latter. A generalization like Life is not amiss in your poem: for profound statements you need the "grand style", least of all the one I tend to employ. But the poem does ask for more attention. Lines like "Taught each to its habits" particularly please me.

Yesterday David phoned. His book, he told me very tremulously, has been rejected, though with greatest praise. The trouble, the publisher assured him (he read me the letter), is not with the writer, but with the material! This is one of David's charming qualities: he seldom conceals his feelings. So his voice came over shaken, hurt, incredulous, like a reprimanded child. I was deeply moved. This side of him is much more attractive than the other ego-flaunting one. But they probably have the same source & are two sides of one coin.

~

T & R
BOXED IN

      "Already
the year is more than half way
here, to be followed by snow,
at first hesitant midair,

going up and then,
to go farther, down in a very
ecstasy of windy cold. Pleasure,
pleasure and the darkest light."
     —from "Pleasure, Pleasure"

I

This man: "Stevens? Never heard of him."

That woman: "Of course I know what
a Stevens is. A garden implement.
Maybe a spirit-level?"

This woman:
           "Oh, yes,
I've read some Stevens. And I find him
quite seductive. In fact, I'm eager
to read much more."

That man:
           "I've read a lot
of Stevens. But he does often go round
and round in one small plot till I've got
quite bored."

This man: "Wait a minute. Now that
you ask, I recall a portly old gent
by that name. Wasn't he an important
church official? A bank president?"

II

Reading poems to a Melbourne audience
and come to "Pleasure, Pleasure,"
I see, leant forward in the front
row, a young man, brow knit,
scribbling away.
         As I finish,
he scoots up: "May I, Liang Jingong,
Beijing citizen, but now a graduate
English student, talk with you?"

His papers heaped up between us,
he questions syntax, punctuation,
grammar, every casual idiom.

Indeed, shadowing his English
from down under, fan-whispers
rustle round, silken innuendoes,
all shot through by punctuating
shouts:
   "Pleasure? Pleasure!
Bourgeois swine, gorging delicacies
while the masses starve!"

III
      Lunching
with Stevens at his Canoe Club,
I watch as he reviews the menu
like some cherished poem and,
as ever, orders a martini,
vichyssoise, a quiche.
      Awed
by this big red diffident man,
at every word unsaid a deeper red,
I, a total teetotaller, repelled
by gelid soups, accepting doom,
nod "The same."
      Then, gulping
down the vichyssoise and choking
on the drink, as if inspired by
my misery, I desperately blurt
out "I also come from Reading."
Presto, the soup heats up,
the wall-hung, stuffed canoe
glides over glittering breakers,
and we, landsmenner at last,

like birds united in a skein
or pecking gravel side by side,
communicate and perfectly
beyond all words.

IV
The artist,
whose powerful portraits I admired,
greets me cheerfully.
Wizened, stooped,
half blind, still he paints away
in the old folks home, hand shaking
like the strokes in this new work,
landscapes precisely mapping his age.

"You see," he says, "It's all a matter
of schooling, what it does for you
and what you do with it.
That year
the Wiener Kunstschule offered three
scholarships. I, merely sixteen
and a Jew, took third place.
The sober
young man who came in fourth, speaking
only when spoken to, producing
sketches competent, but utterly
conventional,
what would have happened
had I not stood in his way? What kind
of art, what order of world, would this
world have become?
Why make so much
of him? That runty, swarthy, self-
effacing youth was Adolph Hitler."

V

"It's all a matter of where one
comes from and what one makes of it,"
the Chinese student says.

                    "This poem
of yours, 'Pleasure, Pleasure,'
I think I understand. But 'the darkest
light,' what does that mean?"
                          My face
clouding over, he beams: "I know!
I know! We have a phrase for that
in my country."
                And to my skeptical
"You do?"
              "O, yes. 'The pig can fly.'"

Now, dawn just breaking over Beijing,
a pig zips through that poem and,
treading down its trotters, rows
on rows of headlong cyclists
furiously pedaling.
                Some stop
at stalls to wrangle over writhing
eels and octopuses, ducklings, piglets,
dangled over mangoes, cumquats, nuts,
clattered up by shiny pots and pans.

VI

In the Melbourne supermarket
we see the Chinese student slumping
over his cart.
             He shakes his head:
"So many soaps and soups and cereals,
jammed shelf after shelf of cereal,
each the newest, each the best,
and all put out by one big company!"

VII

But now, the Chinese privatizing,
their world aglut with multiplying,
poems a surplus as their progeny,
how deal with it?
                Maybe they'll
be trading in their top rhymer Mao
for some big-time CEO, a poet
in spare time.
              As for the clamorous
rest?
      Stevens urged satisfying
two old masters as the surest test:
"Write for Mallarmé and Valéry."
But they, elitist through and through,
had always been committed to a hard-
won economy,
              whereas he, resenting
poems that niggle, fancied "what
flies in the window."
              For unless
such lucky moments come, he knew
that, habits boxing us in, we tend
to write the same poem over and over.

Whom then trust to choose the best?
Rival poets? Professional critics?
Or, as last resort, the public taste
which, one day acclaiming some poet
its supernova, over night rejects
him or her, a fizzled meteor?

VIII

                           Yet who
can long resist those rows on rows,
even if reiterative as Warhol serials?
Boxed grape-nuts, corn flakes, cheerios.
Or books wedged together, cricket cages
in which their makers imperiously
drone.
                Already Beijing's swarms
are peddling furiously in a chain
of outdoor shops.
                      Or else they join
the throngs lined up around the block
before MacDonald's in Tiananmen Square.
Hooked in to stereo, computer, walkman,
they front Mao, dumbstruck on his last-
week-featured billboard.

IX

                       One noon
a young man, head abuzz with chasing
overheated figures, breaks away.

And loitering by the lake on
the Institute's plush grounds, he dips
his hands in the sparkling water.

At once a look winks back at him.
Bedazzled by the hypnosis—call it
paradise—of that gaze, has he found
at last what he was looking for?

206

Paradise? Look to your eyes, man.
Paradise or teetering on the abyss?

What glance ignited Einstein's look,
unlocked the power in a pencil's tip?
Was he, like Stevens, bent on hatching
supreme fictions? Certainly a unified
field theory? Or the final solution?

X

Still, as long as the world wags on,
like that ragtag band of jagged beards,
chanting as they jigged into the furnace,
with our last breath let's celebrate
each plum, each rose, a moment's boundless
vista and a super-bistro, no more,
no less, than the fiesta Picasso,
the revelry Stravinsky. (Even, alas,
the long siesta Glass—tedium=
Te Deum?)
                    The planet humming on the table,
Stevens? Whiffs, a shapely phrase or two
of his recalled, breathe out some rare
aroma from the earth he walked.
                                        Ah well,
pleasure, pleasure. Balked though we
may be, this poem of ours, like Stevens,
one pig and another winging through,
goes on, at least for you and me,
revising endlessly.

~

March 28, 1941

This early afternoon I saw Van Doren. He "regaled" me with his customary cryptic remarks. Yet hard as it may be for him, he does try hard. I showed him three short poems. He summed these up as "very successful," at least not his usual pokerfaced "very interesting." Then he went on to another. This, he felt, benefited beyond the short ones through its direct dramatic speech. One section he particularly applauded, indicating certain subtleties of technique or, as he put it, "artifice." Then he commented on my "gift," "talent," etc. of "volatility"—the swiftness with which my words move—this, paradoxically, since I employ parentheses so teemingly.

This launched us into a discussion of the importance & place of adjectives, be they words, phrases, or lengthy clauses. A discussion amusing & no doubt apt with someone as reticent as he. Here too he ventured little. He's as sparing of criticism as he is of imagery generally. Probably his very spareness helps make his remarks seem so pithy & reverberatory. And why do I barrage you with this say-by-say description? Just to have you with me in my doings.

Living at your home, we could at least spend our evenings together studying, etc. But you know how I feel about your working. Not that I object to woman-work if it's a worthwhile sort; on the contrary. It's the waste of time I abhor. And more, I'm much too selfish to spare you so much of the day. But your learning typing & shorthand would be of value to us. I say us advisedly: you could use them in college for lectures & papers, & you could be a great help to me.

March 28, 1941 (Special Delivery)

Matters here have not been very encouraging. Paul tried to get a job today with the Columbia University Press. Through his Wolfe manuscript, his MA thesis, he came to know one of the Press's men pretty well. Not only did they have no job to offer him, but they doubted his finding work anywhere in publishing—a closed shop, they called it.

To cap it, the editor of the Press, also dean of Newark University, when approached by this man for advice for Paul, strongly counseled him to stay out of academics—particularly since he's Jewish! He retailed all sorts of depressing stories: because of the draft most colleges will be reducing their faculties ten to twenty percent, others will be folding up altogether; then he said he had a mountain pile of job applications (& for any kind of job) from Ph.Ds., many with a long list of published books & experience.

As in almost everything else today, the only remote likelihood of securing collegiate work is via pull—strong pull at that. I'm not trying to make you unhappy, My Dearest. But you see it would be wellnigh impossible for me to accept your Pop's proposition if I were to realize that a job is beyond my grasp. What then?

Last night I visited the Schuberts. I reported your Dad's offer to them. They took to it not too kindly. Judy maintains that if I were to stay home with my parents & accept your Dad's loan, my parents would be only further insulted & infuriated. And living with your parents? You've sufficiently pointed out the difficulty of that. Judy accused me of being too soft. "You should get a job in some bookstore here, making $18 a week, & then bring Renee to N.Y." I replied that, first of all, such jobs weren't as abundant as she seemed to think. (Why doesn't David get one? She HAD said he'd be infinitely happier if he didn't have to depend on her. Furthermore, she may lose her job any day: her school's on the verge of collapse.) She agreed. Then I said I could see little future in such work. This she also admitted. So where are we?

The whole morning & noon I remained with David, he lamenting the madness & barbarism of our society, indifferent—except for animosity—to culture & art, till I, nearly prostrate, had to leave him. What he says is terribly true. Here is David, in many respects as talented a person as I've met, yet he can't find a job, can't find a place in the world. But, it must be said, he has immense personal problems that make him unavailable for most work. His heinous past did much to make him what he is; & our wretched present intensifies his problems. (Heredity versus—rather, in his case, &—environment again!)

March 30, 1941

I've just finished Sunday lunch, talking with several about the war & its terrible future, the killings by the millions in store, the universal agony. Is it only in such mankind is kin?

Did I tell you that not only was David contrition itself for his egoing the other day, but he asked me to reread & criticize his novel? At this I felt emboldened to remark the weaknesses I had noticed before but hadn't the heart to mention. Admitting the validity of my criticism, assuring me that he values my comments more than anyone else's, he requested me to criticize the work detailedly & precisely.

Last night I visited the Schuberts. (They've been berating me for not coming to see them often enough.) I took along five poems, the typed crop of two days. Both Judy & David, to my pleased surprise, were taken with them. Judy, probably the most caustic critic I know (I'm usually hesitant about showing her poems), burst out after reading one, "How utterly charming!" And David beamed at me so that I felt I had indeed wrested a bit of revelation from the stingy gods! Never have I seen David or Judy so ebullient about any poetry. Of course, their affection & so their eagerness to applaud stimulated their response. In the past, however, their praises have always been alloyed by adverse criticism.

Few pleasures compare, My Dear, with beholding others kindling to something you've made. Today, however, I've worked & worked to discouragingly little avail, put down words that seemed at once to take conscious, stubborn root. To change them is like breaking bones.

But I almost forgot! Martha Graham is dancing this coming Saturday, & Humphries & Weidman on Monday. Could you maybe New York for them? Especially Graham. Nobody in dance, & few elsewhere, can equal her intensity, her capacity to blend all elements of the arts & staging into major drama. Or do you think it better that I Allentown this weekend & pop the proposition to my Parents? Aside from my hesitancy at posing it, I've been thinking that, after all, there are two months still before the problem becomes imminent. If I present it too soon my parents may in the interim cultivate all kinds of difficulties. What do you think?

April 1, 1941

Yes, My Love, it's April first. Till now the day has been playing April-fool, flirting & hiding behind a cloud, pretending a soon rain. But as though it's been reading your just arrived letter over my shoulder, it's this minute blossomed into gayest light. (The maid, who is carpet-sweeping my room, interrupts me again & again to beg my pardon for the noise & to hope she's not disturbing me! Suddenly she breaks in, "Does your girl know you're a good boy?" I smile, "Of course she does; else why do you think she's marrying me?" She shakes her head: "Sometimes they learn too late." Then I ask her, "How do you know, what do you mean, I'm a good boy?" But she hides behind the hedge of the carpet-sweeper's burr-burr. Do YOU know, My Best Girl, that I'm a good boy?)

It's almost five, & David's come, with his manuscript & his charming intense stillness. He wants me to read it at once. But I beg off: "I have to write to Renee first." I read him your dream fairytale. We agreed that much of it's delightful. Before he came I had thought to say, "So, My Love, you've stolen a march (marchen, German for fairytale) on me! Written your dream before I could." How far you've winged away from your beginning lockedupness!

As David said, "If Renee writes so well now there's no telling where she'll go." Not to say that the piece is perfect. Occasionally, it seems to me, it lapses into less than happy phrases & disproportions. Tomorrow, since David's waiting, I'll try to make some suggestions. All right?

I don't know that my eyes are bad (good?) enough to keep me out of the draft. Of course, if war is declared—as now seems certain, I fear nothing will.

April 2, 1941

What a tureenful of a day, My Heart's Heart. I drink at it & drink. (I know I talk to you about days more than anything else—except my Love for you—but they're the best, the most colorful & almost only things I see these days.) If you can't read this, blame it on the sun, it's blinding the paper so. Geewhillickers! Outside's more like inside than inside. At least I can hide in the shade here—if I'm mole enough to want to!

I've just sauntered back from Van Doren: I showed him several lyrics I've typed off the last few days. He was unusually enthusiastic: "You're coming ahead by leaps & bounds: this group's by far the best you've shown me. It's remarkable how you leap from one set to another." —which makes it only harder: Hansel & Gretel just gotta' be better than these. These, to be included among others, I intend to call CAPRICES. (Remember?) As he read off lines & phrases he especially liked, he'd applaud them with comments like "that phrase could be in any poem" or "these poems are

212

WITTY," high praise indeed from him; for wit, as he defines it, is a laudable achievement—his reading aloud, however, was applause enough.

Sitting back a moment, I find poem phrases I recently wrote creeping into my thinking, but awkwardly, like strangers or casual acquaintances; they taste strange. Nothing is our own: we simply borrow it or, perhaps more accurately, things borrow us. I sometimes think artists are little more than bits of glass of differing color & shape through which shines the light of life. The greater the artist the more varied, the more prismatic his piece of glass is, till we reach a Shakespeare who, more than any great cathedral's stained-glass windows, seems to reflect all the myriad hues.

But certain items in your letter are awaiting answers. I see eye to eye (lip to lip, body to body, & heart to heart!) with you anent woman's having some mental job. I've nothing but abhorrence (at least right now!) for housework: I've seen too many women waste their lives on housekeeping. I've no intention (nor do you, I know) of allowing you to squander your life so. If only society would respect our day-dreaming! Oh well! One can't ask for everything. (And why not?)

~

T & R
PERHAPS

Perhaps it was perversity.
But when Hop delicately stepped
among the papers piled-up on the desk,
we did not mind, nor mind his tail
brushing new designs from ink
still wet. Wasn't he, if not
our muse, our mascat?

But sniffing,
as if to catch, crouched in the black,
some little critter meant for him,
and finding not a one, he saw
he had to take a different tack.

So, settling in his makeshift nest,
he placed his paw upon my wrist
as if to steady, if not steer,
me on my way. Perhaps he'd heard,
and long before we could, the music
coming in.
            Meantime, he purred,
perhaps to let us know how much
he reveled in our partnership.
Or else to note some pun cat-nippy
through these verses he alone
had sense enough to fathom.
                        Pun
or not, his purring said he savored
every tidbit of these scratchings.
For who knew better the allure,
itself a joy, of such an itch?

Scratch, scratch, and lo, by cat
account some epochs later, Hoppy,
tail asail whipping up a storm—
and no perhaps—slips in again,
himself a little critter shining,
like an extinct, furry starlet,
through this night-lit ink.

~

April 3, 1941

You're right, as always; but what am I to do? Can I help it if this poem lies before me indifferent to my most vigorous appeals? I've done almost everything I COULD: sat over it like a friend with a sick patient; caressed it like a lover. But either the bastard's dumb, deaf, & dead or else I'm not employing the proper tactics. Save for a few word-shiftings, I've not been able the past two days to get the poem to budge. But it's hardly conquered yet. After I've mailed this, back I go to grapple with it.

You suggest that you didn't poem the dream "because of the clumsiness of some of the lines." Great Gulliver, you've gotta sandpaper the lines if you expect to cast them into decent verses. You can't (although it HAS been done) break up prose & call the fragments lines of a poem. (Or am I misunderstanding?) That's one of the reasons for writing poetry: if we're keyed up to it, we're forced to sharpen phrases, tighten the thought, & clean the emotion— somethings not so exigent in prose (though the best prose DOES require such application also). One often improves one's prose by writing poetry. So try, will you, My Dearest, to mold your already excellent writing into poetry?

I didn't write you, did I, that Paul unexpectedly received his draft-questionnaire the other day? He & Renee, miscalculating his number, had concluded he was up somewhere in the six-thousands. You can imagine the consternation that possessed them. Renee was nextdoor neighbor to hysteria. Gloom continues to be the atmosphere. Though married, Paul's not supporting his wife. More, there's nothing wrong with him to make him ineligible. Perhaps he & I will be bunkmates!

In some way I wish you could persuade your Pop to come out of his indecision (liberalism!) at least regarding your Eastering with me. Gee whiz! What more does he want? Doesn't he know YET that we love each other & are eager to marry, tomorrow if he approves? Your choreography delights me; that's another reason for my being in Allentown this summer (!)—to see you perform, of course.

The other day talking to David, I asked him as a professional husband what he would prescribe as the best measure for permanising a love. He replied grimly, "Frequent vacations from each other!" Sounds pretty absurd, doesn't it? Yet from what I've seen & heard, I'm afraid it's too often true. He modified his statement, however, by admitting that he believed you & I, our tempers being sweeter, (!) more equable, & more considerate than his & Judy's (I'm inclined, grandly enough, to agree! At least in your case), would enjoy much larger likelihood of preserving the fervor of our love.

April 8, 1941

I've been thinking of us as married people: all kinds of domestic saws have been buzzing away in my head—things we already know, but truisms hard to remember at the crucial moment, & harder even to practice. I repeat some of them therefore for your benefit (& mine!).

First, we must never blame circumstances, particularly those outside ourselves & our control, on each other. Full of resentment at something that may have happened, we're easily tempted to pin the responsibility on someone other than ourselves; & naturally we hit upon the one nearest to us (because loving him or her as much as we do, it gives us perverse pleasure to hurt that one; & because we know that this person is the only one likely to accept—& most suffer from—our abuse). The advantages & favors of LOVE!

Second, we must never ascribe our boredom to the other. If only we can remember how frequently we are bored with ourselves; yet we do not castigate ourselves! (Maybe we do?) In short, we mustn't expect too much of each other. Rather than be nettled with the other's malaise, we should patiently with love endeavor to draw the other out of it. Big things I'm asking of us, no, My Dearest? I'm certain our love is worth them; I'm equally certain it will be I rather than you will have to keep them constantly in mind.

This afternoon I spoke to Neff once more about the feasibility of my continuing Ph.D. work, whether it would be worth the effort. He was nothing but encouragement. In the past, he assured me, the department has always placed its Ph.D.'s in college positions. Of course, he qualified, he couldn't promise me the position I'm entitled to: our world's hardly as fair as all that; it's pretty much a matter of luck. But, he continued, a person of my talents, etc. should certainly complete his graduate work. Then again, the world being as shaky as it is, it's impossible to predict its status one, two years from now. So what do you say? I guess it's Ph.D.ing for us, no?

And you take up where I leave off, most pleasingly lecturous! What delights me in these generalizing letters of ours is that each of us is writing to his (my) & her (your) own ego: we're warning ourselves, rather than the other. You will agree though that in many instances the difficulties arising between two marrieds are external? Of course, as you say, most people don't know they're happy. It takes insistence & vigorous living to make happiness a glowing-every-where atmosphere; most of us are too passive & casual for such weather.

But what's the idea trying to fob off on me the balderdash that you're no better than others?! What the devil do you think I'm marrying you for?! I'm the latter kind: I want to know you—through & through. Not that I don't like glamour, if that's what you're implying by men's not really wanting to know their wives. Certainly a wife must remain a woman, attractive & alluring, (mysterious?) even—especially!—after she's married. That's the trouble with many married women: they let themselves go & with it goes the husbands! Such women, it would seem, regard marriage as a variety of hunting: having bagged their quarry, why bother to keep the bait around? And the same, alas, is true of most husbands.

I'm hardly offering this as a description of you. I'm merely suggesting that if we want our love to live, we must keep on our toes. Nothing's more exacting than love, nothing more easily insulted & frightened away by lack of attention. Love persists only if the conditions & attitudes that parented it continue. A big order, no? (And a hell of a lot of preaching too! Love, to preserve itself, better be wary of that also.) But never fear—I'll never let you forget what you've written here.

Miss Leeds is right; but, what little I've seen of these dancers, wrong too. Humphrey may be simpler; but as much simpler as she is, so much inferior she is to Graham. I don't know anything about dancing? To begin with, how much must be known? You are, after all, dancing; THAT teaches me most of what I need to know. And good dancing, like the rest of the arts, & maybe more so, appeals to all levels. So I may not have understood Graham too thoroughly; the spirit of her dancing, however, was so infectious that it immediately involved me. Humphrey, on the other hand, stirred me almost not at all; her interpretations seemed pleasant, lively, entertaining, but not much more than that.

~

T & R
THE BAG LADY OF SUTTON PLACE

In her crammed apartment on the 19th floor,
the sun, sparked off the river, squints
through grimy panes.

                    Calling "Play,"
back-hand, from her wheel-chair, she bunts
the ball Aztec-wise to any catcher
dares to visit.
              Wheeling and dealing,
   "Foul! Most foul!," she keeps the score:
   at what hour this one failed to honor her,
   on which corner that one snatched
   the precious thought she first conceived,
   who cashed in her dead husband's art,
   who stole the scene in which she saved the day.
Soon, soon, as time must tell,
she plans to bring these culprits to the bar.

Close by, books loading the couch,
on dance-legged tables, grandstand chairs,
the News—still waiting to be read—
lies moldering.
              On buckling shelves
the Olds collect their sacred dust:
   Chinese horsemen and Aztec masks,
   stuck snubbing
   upstart portraits
   darkening the walls.

Like the couch: time, sprung, sinks
into itself.
              But Time is being called.
Knowing her own true worth, like theirs,
these paintings, dishes, porcelains, silver,
vases that must be sold,
                    "Not now!"
    she cries. "But soon, soon.
    Exactly when the time is right."
For how can she abandon them, her courtiers,
her servitors? They keep her regal place intact.
They circulate her always-bluer blood.

                              ~

April 15, 1941

    It's nearly nine o'clock & I'm wondering what I do
with time from now on. I've stript off my sweat-&-despera-
tion-drenched clothes & changed into pajamas & a letter-
writing. I've opened the window as far as it can go to let
what's in here out & to let in the easy night wind to do what
it can to calm the place. Choral singing climbs up here, the
swish-swish of the ocean waves of city noises, & a gang of
young boy voices hurtle up, "2,4,6,8, who do we appreciate?
Girls! Girls! Girls!" The singular's enough (& more than
many now) for me. But then I've never been good with
numbers! There's a waftiness in the air, a kind of sigh, as
though finally the winds have pulled free of the heat-grip of
day: a sea smell it seems or the moment before a cool, grace-
ful spring rain. And for the very loveliness, My Loveliest,
more hideous without you, as though nature itself (egotist
me!) were outdoing itself to mock me.

April 16, 1941

Good morning, My Darlingest; for though it's after twelve my morning's just arrived. It's amazing, but I'm happy! Somehow through all the blur of me. Even misery must smile. So, considering how rotten I feel, I'm feeling very well.

I spoke to David on the telephone to tell someone how lovely you are & how much I love you & how I miss you, yet happily! My love's too much for one. I had to have a wall to bounce the ball of me against.

The amazing thing to me this moment is, not that we are ever dull for being one person, but that, as many as we each one are, & ever changing, we can recognize each other, say "this is he, she, you, I."

I'm off to see *Night Train* now. I'm back. What a ripsnorter of a picture! A most skillful, almost patentleathersmooth employment of excitement & melodrama, done with gloves & a tophat—a thrill a second in the most English unruffled manner.

But sitting in it, watching with horror the Nazi invasion of Prague, a Nazi-thought suddenly invaded me. What's to prevent Renee from experiencing a recurrence of the indifference she felt for me when we first met? Nature, & human nature, always has something potentially Nazi, as unpredictably invasive, in it. Alter as love must, what's to assure its not wandering off in a direction quite different from me? You see what a sad state I'm in that I have to resort to the Nazi horror to describe it!

Oddly enough, this morning Van Doren was discussing women who insist on being told they are loved, but hate, & avoid as much as possible, direct admission of THEIR love. Thus they can hold their men dangling. And men, I suspect, prefer this with its agony & all: it keeps them on their toes. Had I been "smart," I would never have declared my love so openly, so unqualifiedly, & kept YOU guessing! Such tactics, however, smack too much of a game; & my love for you is too sacred (yes, I use this godawful word) for me to play with it. Please understand, I am NOT accusing you in the slightest of such stratagems. After all, you HAVE told me you love me, haven't you?

April 23, 1941

So, My Love, I'm back in the saddle again—& riding hard, rounding up my scrawny herd of scriblets. Writing & reading, that's the way I shape my days these days, & muffling my ears not to hear the beat of time, racing heartbeat too, as it stabs away.

O.K., Mrs. Weiss, I shan't Mrs. Weiss you anymore in public: I like Mrs. Weissing you under cover(s) best of all anyway! It doesn't matter too much though whether my Mom was disturbed or not: now that we're "officially" engaged, it's a disturbance she'll have to get used to. So you're "more used to the idea" of our engagement than Shirley is?! Does that mean that I'll have to unearth something new that you're NOT used to?

You know, I do not miss you now—& naturally—the way I did before. At long last you are mine officially. So you live in my heart easily, indistinguishable from heart itself. If I ever seem to take you for granted, know it is not so, but simply that I accept you as the best of me because you fit so amazingly well.

But have I mentioned how proud I am of you & Abe? Abe, of course, because of the grace with which he conducted himself when I suggested marriage that enlightened (!) Sunday morning: heavenly sun, a choral of birds, all waiting to minister to our desires! And your father once more the man of considerateness & enthusiasm I used to think that he was.

And you? I suppose I scarcely need tell you why. Yet for retasting's sake I recall the latest delicious provocations of my pride: the skill with which you conducted the entire affair at my house—your tact & understanding. But, even more tangibly, the courage you displayed, DESPITE yourself, in venturing into that lions' den my house was that nightmare Saturday night. The shouting occupants were certainly surprised to see you; but I think you were even more surprised than they to be there. It was as though your love & concern for me (or am I exaggerating?) had catapulted you to my side even before your thought could apprise you fully of what you were doing. I shall always remember how you stood there, defiantly juggling your own surprise as much as theirs. Apparently you, like your Pop, can especially mobilize your forces at the moment of crises. (Forgive my landing you pacifists in the middle of this military metaphor. You were, after all, the peacemaker!) But I hope I shan't employ this talent of yours TOO often!

~

T&R
NINE PARTNERS ROAD

> He traveled through life as though it were
> a Sahara, and he changed abodes like an Arab.
> Baudelaire on Poe.

> all the perfumes of Arabia
> Lady Macbeth

PREAMBLE

Every person is a place,
every cat and dog and rat,

every elephant and every ant,
every plant, tree, slug, and bee.

Wait. Turn the switch off
and start over.

Every person is a place,
every family, tribe, nation,
every country, every world.

Take your foot off the pedal.

Every person is a place.
Is every place a person?
Every rain sauntering by?
Every drop given a name?
And each snowflake, its special
flight, its unique fingerprint
Keep your eye on the road!

You wouldn't want to miss
the landscapes of your mind,
its mountains "no-man-fathomed,"
its chasms crammed with void?

Then there are all the detours,
endless deadends, and the traffic
congestion of a passionate thought.

Look out. You'll be totaled.

Meantime, we've studied maps
of the fabulous past, charts
of a never-never-land,
and maps of the future,

of the heavens and the stars,
so far and yet so near, so near
and yet so far.
　　And what about
　　　　the maps themselves?

★★★★

Preoccupied with maps, he dreams
one big enough--its folded avenues
smoothed out, the ruffled rivers,
and the crumpled parks--to fit
what's out there.
　　　　　　At their boldest
in the dark, great windows flashing
shops, fountains quiver naked scenes;
sleek autos hum, and revelers hoot,
so many notes upon the lovers'
braided breath.
　　　　　　But now he wishes
this map, growing bigger than all roads,
would envelop it in sleep.

★★★★

　　　　　　Still some colors,
he admits, surprise. Like dawn
radiating from his loved one's eyes,
a dawn preserved, ink-smudged,
in a certain catalog.
　　　　　　Or was it
a moth that sped him, swifter
than any Rand-McNally could,
to a buried treasure
in some forgotten spot:
　　　　　　　　that field

sprung up, more taking than the sky,
as a rush of fragrances swirled them
into that passing moment.
                    But, exposed
too often, wintry decades settling in,
the field faded to a wispy ghost.

★★★★

                    The highways,
no matter how exultant on his setting
out, now founder in a tidal wave
of movement.
            Of allies now
become the foes.
                    So he sighs for atlases
of cities, of himself, set free:
the roads loitering, men, slouched
in doorways,
                    repeating ancient
stories, as clouds chase
 themselves like kids holding hands
in ring-around-the-rosie.
                    He'd play
the prodigy of being nothing more
than being, happy to go as the moment
does, wherever wind or, in its slant
on things, moonlight sends him.

★★★★

But what can justify the far-
fetched maps, unbidden, cropping
up still: the hidden, desperate
desires, bent on converting,

not only breath, but life itself,
its local plenitudes, its platitudes,
into enduring words?
                    That time
his Latin teacher confronting him
with the blackboard map, the sun
rose for him
                    (he always counts
on lucky hits) in Portugal!
She, her fiery eyes riveting him,
supplied what Scylla he required.

No wonder he took to scribblings
complicated enough to bemuse
such monsters, if only momentarily.
So he's spent his time composing
maps on maps minus a country.
Sentenced to be a mindful wanderer,
he's anxious to join up with those
contemplatives of such travel:

                    ★★★★

the modern Magi? Einstein,
Marx, and Freud, for their life-
long, hot pursuit of the radiant
dark,
        believing they had gripped
the slippery scruff of the real;
yet like fugitives never able to settle
down. He feels love- and duty-
bound to ponder,
                    not only
harried prophets, but father,
sped from one village to another,

seeking fruitful pastures.

Instead he found his days
gritty air, heaped up, and dusty
water, sand-storms burying
every prized landmark.

★★★★

Hell-bent
on change, men, catapulting towers,
competed successfully with Arabs
and their pitched tents.
"Let us
build a tower, whose top may reach
unto heaven; and let us make us
a name." But the towers,
projected
through the sky, burst into flames.
And the roof fell down on them.
The Wrath seized them
from all directions. The huntsmen
up all over America,
how will we outfox them?

★★★★

This map itself,
properly read, affords a place
where one can stand (almost)
anything that happens. Better,
it locates us in our selves.

But why blame me
for names absorbing things,

names, time passing, ever more
telling than their coiners
could have predicted.
                    Towns
we grew up in, sporting sacred
names--Bethlehem, Nazareth,
Bath, Emmaus--
              for cultivated
desert stretches far exceeded
their originals, mirages hidden
behind mirages.
                If it's the literal
you want, men in their day-
by-day antics, taking things
as they are,
            consider this:
"Nazareth, Moravian-founded
1740; then, with a population
of 24706,
          had cement mills,
factories for textiles,
musical instruments, four
churches,
          five banks, four
gas-stations, and three
liquor stores, Elks, Moose,
Rotarians, Legionnaires."

                ★★★★

Too humdrum? How's this?
Bethlehem, the little town
of, famous house of bread
and also God,
            its steel-

mill flames at first sight
mellow as that manger scene,
its wondrous star,
                    yet lurid
in the dark, ingots molten
plunging like a lava flow,
the way the world began.

Still the music sounds:
a giant archangelic host,
joyous against the blasting
flames.
          At least you admit
stirrings round me. Know
that, for now, I'm set
on scrutinizing nothing
past the path that's mine.
I lean on my naked wits,

on hunger lighting
me, as well as on that
beetle flitting across
the path, the moonlight,
and this moth, all borne
along by winds inside them.

★★★★

But of the many times you whizzed
by Nine Partners Road, did you
ever pause?
          Or stop to listen
to the fragrant airs warbling
from wild things? Never telling
who those Partners might be!

Nine Partners? Maybe
it's American vernacular
for the Muses. Or a gang
of crooks out to import
the Wild West, making it
into their local mythology.

O you'll not find,
it's true, a bountiful
Arabia, puffing out choice
perfumes these cunning words
store up.

And not even the voices,
identifiable, of those
who help us, not so much
to find our way, as to keep
going, making destinations
of where we chance to be.

★★★★

So we're in this world to make
what we can of it, like a bug
that blindly eats whatever leaf
it's sitting on?
                    Sucking
and culling being one's nature,
it's no great feat making honey
out of fields of thyme.

But to discover heavenly
nectar in jagged rocks, distill
out of iron woes lightsome songs,
deserves all praise.

At times
a traveler, beset by howling
squalls, by drifts chin-high,
the night grown perfect,
                    must,
to descend a mountain, find
a flat rock that, like a sled,
glissandos down the ice-caked scarp.

★★★★

Occasionally a leaf's
the only raft sufficient
  against that stumbling current.

Perhaps you can provide charts
of a wind's route, that moth,
say, fluttering like an eye-lid
inside the oasis of a rose?

Or another map that traces
love's mutable landscape,
tropical lolls side by side
with Alpine storms.

★★★★

Whatever my skills or lack
of them, I can draw diverse,
wayward greens, mountains
massed, hemlocks
intertwining: draw lucid
blues, lakes brimming.

And I can also mark
the sites where crucial
this or that took place:
East Greenville, Zephyr
Promenade, Lark Highway,
26 Saint Cloud Street.

Or Nine Partners Road,
unexplored, but packed
with promises, their days
and nights more savory the more
they're locked away.

~ 5 ~

April 24, 1941

As I told you, I wrote to my parents at the same time I did to you of the Weisses' offer to put me up this summer. With your letter comes one from my Mom. You're right; they approve. Mom says, "Dearest Ted, yes I think it is a good idea living with the Weisses. If you like it it is O.K. with us." But she still harps on the notion that "it would be a very good idea if you could get some work over the summer." Obviously, I was utterly unable to make them realize how Titan a pile of work I have before me.

I suppose that proposing our marriage to my parents at this juncture would be premature. Best to let them get used to the idea of our engagement first. It would be wonderful though, My Mrs. Weiss, our living & studying together here in N.Y., wouldn't it? As for your choice of your Mom's rings as an engagement gift, my opinion is not the point. Which you choose & which you leave for Rowie is your decision.

Your "Are you working?" squirms me somewhat. I'm writing & reading; but though this work will certainly have some bearing on my exams, it's not of the direct nature it could (& will) be this summer. As we figured it together, this may be my last chance in a long time to devote myself wholly to my work. I deem it not wrong, either to you or to me, especially in the long run, with the world bent on destruction, for me to invest the last month in this writing.

Here's an old poem reworked—improved?:

Imagine it: a timeless summer day,
Leda playing with the lapping surf,
her thoughts as easygoing as the waves.

Desire, spying her, fastens on a swan,
the nearest thing, and soft, to sidle
up to Leda with, vague, white, billowy
as her breath, that she accept it
casually as a dream or the welcoming,
deep bed she spends her long nights in.

At once it is upon her
like a tidal wave. She shrieks
with joy and terror, passion
wakened by the ecstatic strike.

Only then, the feathers nesting her,
she knows what savagery had taken her,
a wave that would, swept on through her,
rise up to drown a nation in its pride,
its stormy story riding on,
a crest the timeless,
an ardent summer day.

April 26, 1941

It's nearly noon, Sunday. The day's stretching to touch everywhere. Like someone between us, it holds your hand & mine: can you feel me through it? O, Sweets, I'm a rime that's lost its mate & its reason too.

Yesterday early morning, far, far up in the "bewilderness" of the Bronx, in a high school, I took that Civil Service exam I mentioned. I've given the government its opportunity to employ me; if it's too obtuse, well, too bad for it. There was a most disheartening mob waiting to take the exams (hundreds here & thousands throughout the U.S. for who knows how few jobs).

But now I'm afraid we have little to look forward to from the government—unless it be the draft. After the exam I learned that the government doesn't inform the examinees of the results for a year or two. So, battered, I came home to grumble & gnaw the rest of the day away—& no consoling letter awaiting me.

Slowly, however, more of me is emerging. Today I'm good as old, & writing away again. But this week, for reading & other writing, I'm giving Hansel & Gretel a vacation. Poems, you know, have a life—& a will—quite apart from their writer. Perhaps those two will have something new to say to me when I return to them this afternoon.

April 28, 1941

My Love—Whoops! I just now dropt my bottle of ink all over the floor & splattered my pants! Everlastingly clumsy me! Seems I've tried to make a grace—at least a habit—of gaucherie. Left-handed my whole body is. Will you have love enough to put up with my awkwardness, especially since grace is yours? Oh well, I intended to have this suit cleaned soon anyway. This afternoon David splashed melted butter on it. Plainly the gods have it in for this suit!

As I began to say, I've just subwayed home. Last evening the Schuberts visited me at John Jay. Later they took me home with them to spend the night. Walking, I told them what had happened. (I hadn't seen them since I was home with you.) Both agreed with me that you & I ought to marry immediately now that our parents are straightened out. Judy, however, voiced some of my unarticulated sentiments—David's too, I know; & yours: she cares little for my accepting assistance from our Pops: she dislikes immensely my being treated almost like a piece of property with an arguable price & my being at the mercy of their whims.

To a degree I was compelled to concur. When I went on, however, to remark my lack of an alternative, she & David begrudgingly admitted that acceptance on my part would probably be the wisest course. In our Pops' way at least we have an eventual chance of breaking free. Of course both Judy & David were thumbs-down utterly on my (perhaps our) living with the Weisses. They consider that quite impossible. Yet here also they were forced to admit that it seemed the best—nearly only—course that offered itself. So?...!

It's amazing (I never seem to get to the end of it!), the proportions of David's ego. Sitting alone with him, he busy carrying the burden of his "greatness," I realize how terribly much the notion of that greatness has taken hold of him. Walking me to the subway, he abruptly stops to ask me, "How is it, Ted, I feel I am such a genius?" Yet it's not too noxious: almost the way a child asks his father, "Why is green? is sky?" or "Why do I have five fingers?" So long as he can salvage his humility, say, before his "genius," he's not too bad. But what if that too is swallowed up by his ego—a danger I suspect were he "fully recognized"? Or even fully unrecognized? Sometimes he & I, given my own ample ego, are like two proud blades hacking away at each other; yet this way we hone each other too.

Suddenly I sat back a moment thinking—(do you mind the silence?), & the following thought somersaulted into my mind: You are still in some ways shy with me: you still retain the feeling of responsibility for yourself to me. I, on the other hand, have completely (I think!) thrown off the trammels of such feeling. Thus when we are together I do not hesitate to show you any part of me: thought, feeling, body, or what have I. I'm eager to satisfy your curiosity as well as your physicality. Knowing that my body, for instance, is not really me or at least that I had negligibly little to do with making it what it is, I've no compunction about disclosing it to you; nay, my overwhelming desire is to share in it with you—the way, & eagerly, a child might share a gift recently received. (That's exactly what you, when you're with me, make of my body & my me FOR me—a gift, all new, by the gift of your love.) My desire is only accentuated by your desire & openheartedness.

April 29, 1941

What fears! especially for the waywardness my mind has been tending toward these last uncertain days: here it is way after twelve & STILL no word from you. And John writes from the Veterans Administration (officially!): "You do your damnedest to get married well before July 1st. From all I've read & overheard, your temporary student's deferment will be up then." With war probably just around the nearest corner, I have to content myself with—your Pop's words— maybe marriage in a year or two! Am I really speaking only for myself? Do YOU participate in my desire? After all, you haven't written to me in all of more than two & a half days!

It's now four o'clock, & like a good, healing sun My Love's letter dispels all, or almost all!, my clouds. For a moment I feared you hadn't changed to daylight-saving time, were limping a whole hour behind me. How would you ever catch up?! But now you tell me we're in step, dancing together, exactly synchronous.

A card from Mom apprises me similarly of the amity between the Weisses & Karols. As she says, "I think our peace will continue, for Dad is acting very nicely. I only hope Abe will keep up & act the way he did when you were here. So don't worry about our peace. I'm sure all will be well. Just worry about you & your studies." But what did my Pop give you? Such giving has always been his way of expressing his affection. O, My Love, continue to do as you have done to preserve this so precious—precarious?—peace.

You're too right: I've job enough with those damned language exams to be hurdled. As for feelings themselves, My Dearest Feeling, I suspect they are "always new," as you say, because they're always now. Feeling (the word by its very "ing" ending implies progression) is something living, growing, changing: least of all things can it be pinned down. Feelings refuse to remember—can't—because they're too busy being, doing, to have time for the laggard pace of mind.

You ask how you can be passionate with words. Act as though those words are the listening, lovely face of My Love. Of course you are hindered in expressing yourself by your feelings. That's the paradox: the artist wishes to articulate precisely these feelings, often more him than himself. Yet the larger they are, the more pressing, the more difficult they are to tame & cage into words—especially if the artist wishes to retain their life & fire. The only thing, I guess, he can do is to learn to hold them at arm's length, to skillfully step away, yet like a master lion-tamer keep as close as he can. And to study, study, study their characteristics.

The antithesis, however, is perhaps possible: let the feelings flood through & say themselves. But this I doubt: the most one's likely to get is Babel. Hopkins is so passionate precisely because he is so controlled (& controlling): though one part of him is involved in fire, the other part is steady, cool, removed. I DIDN'T intend a high-falutin literary tour! I hope you haven't fallen asleep?

I intimated above that you had chased all clouds away but one: no you this Sunday? Damn violin! I never thought that music would come between us! Three weeks before I see you? & Hitler trampling the earth! What a world! Chaos everywhere! How will we, as you say, "hear the sweet, life-giving tunes of poetry & music through those deadly booming blasts?"

April 30, 1941

It's wonderful what a complete experience your every letter has become—just the act of receiving & reading them. Forgive me, if I describe it physically: you know how physical I am! First, there are the so familiar prim features of the address; second, there is the letter itself neatly tucked in. And I hurry off the envelope like some stiff frock (as though I, poverty-stricken for ages, a whole day!, am expecting some mammoth check for my feelings—emotion-money; but my image is sexier than that? Or is that what money is? It must be for many people, engrossed as they are by it!) to reach nearer to the you within. I smooth out the creases of the letter, cramped from travel; dwell on the lovely little words, the thoughts & feelings made & meant just for me—enjoy the body of you, breathing, living, feeling beneath the thin shift of writing. Then, swept away, I strain to push the words aside, to break through them to the perfect body of you waiting beneath. You see how egregiously physical—for want of the physical—even thought, yes, spirit can become! You don't mind, do you, my having such a thoroughgoing relationship with your letters?

I apologized for my lecture because I appreciate that no one could possibly love my voice as much as I do. But I have, as you well know, a perpetual tendency, at the slightest invitation (& often no invitation at all!) to go off on a verbal binge, the professor in me shouting to get out such bobble I abhor—especially when I force the one I love to endure its droning. I wouldn't want myself to listen were I someone else, so why you?

May 1, 1941

I'm afraid, My Sweet, something I had hitherto strenuously denied, I too am capable of: boredom! In truth, I've flirted with the idea of wallowing in it to discover what

240

scenery, what drama & sensualities, it possesses. Baudelaire—
to name just one of the many modern connoisseurs of bore-
dom—dwelt in ennui so religiously, he succeeded in elicit-
ing excitement out of it. Not, however, that I'm lapsing into
such malaise out of literary interest. If I can dig myself out—
as I know I will—of this present monotony, I've still a more
than sufficient lively vein of me to mine. Guess one has to
experience everything. Nonetheless, this moment I'm so fed
up on myself I'd like to spit me out!

As though I had been tript suddenly, my appetites
pilfered from me, or the world jolted under my feet, I feel an
alien—a stranger through too much intimacy: I see the same
trees, people, rooms, desks, so much, I no longer notice them;
or at least they stare back at me as though we had met for
the first time, & unfortunately.

Writing at such hyperbolic length about this apathy,
I've nearly extricated myself! By the very friction of pen &
paper, ideas, & images—thoughts rubbing against each other
in the effort of thinking—I've managed to shoot off some
sparks. Ennui, except the highest (lowest?) best, cannot per-
mit such energizing & survive. I hope though in ridding
myself I haven't dumped my load of lethargy on you.

May 4, 1941

I spent last evening, overnight, breakfast & a large
chunk of the morning with the Schuberts. I left because I
had to get back for further conversation with you. And here
we are. It's sad the way Judy & David bicker, sometimes over
a single word-selection or a tone of voice. "You're too
emphatic!" David shouts emphatically with brimming bitter-
ness. More times than not it's David's fault. He's the most
irascible person I know—more so even than myself. He may
be experiencing some unhappy thought or mood & he
immediately pins it on poor Judy by pouncing on some

minute fleck of speech or gesture as the cause. Frightened by their example, I wonder if you & I will quarrel so after we're married—

(Hearing a voice, I look out. There on the opposite roof, clad in a tight green bathing suit, a very shapely body, & tossing, shiny hair, is a young woman, shouting & gesticulating wildly—never fear, it's not to me—doing her best to get some sense of this fellow in my wall whom she plainly doesn't know. She yells, points, arabesques, writes on the air. And succeeds: in finding out his age, studies, how long he's been in N.Y. She's studying too—ballet. It all ends happily; they arrange a meeting.)—Judy assures me we won't: "You're much more reasonable & considerate than David." But I can remember only those times I've been illogically & cruelly angry with you, the many times I've unjustly hurt you. Instantly geysers of guilt, gentleness, & love well up in me.

But about my rejection. I wrote you how little it touched me. In fact, so potent rejection is, I wrote furiously after receiving it.

Several hours later the truth began to catch up with me like a fall that doesn't pain till some time after its happening: this much writing, after receiving the rejection, was chiefly a surge, a rage of defiance & attempt at convincing myself of my indifference, my superiority to the blow. I'm better now though. And the rejection DID prod me into poems.

There are only three things to do: love you more—if possible!; write more & more & better; & send many, many poems out to many, many places. I'm afraid, My Darlingest, I'll have to travel the road most poets—even the best—have been forced to take. I warn you, it's a long, dusty, upmountain, often washed-out trail. Will you come along?!

~

T & R
THIRST

I

Robert Lowell, the last time
we saw him, hunkered down,
his eyes hooded, fixed
on some rapt scene.
                    Throughout
the ceremony—Ted sharing the stage—
Lowell seemed so lost in himself
we insisted on driving him home.

As we sped along, the sky a screen
tear-streaked by lights, bits
of cinema Manhattan flitted past;
through the din we heard him mutter
about love's excesses, errancies,
neglect's corrosive torments.

"Why, Cal," Ted, humoring him,
demurred, "when it comes to neglect,
your fellow scribblers leave you
far behind."
                    And he, turned
to us as from a vast distance,
head cocked to the side, glance
owl-wise set on its prey, scowled
as though to say

                neglect should be
weighed against talent.
                        Then,
as if summoned, he plunged back.

                II
Thirst is all, an overwhelming
gift, deep as the world is wide,
and deeper.
                Even water thirsts.
A cataract, tumbling over itself,
yearns to drown deep in the sea.

So too fire, enjoining
everything to merge with it,
rests only when it's turned all
into ash.
                Unquenchable no less,
the earth, absorbing floods and sun,
out of the dust sprouts rampaging
woods, herds, tribes, then smites
them back into that dust.

                III
 So too,
wrung out of Lowell's fathomless
thirst, a clamorous music.
                        Wrung
as he foundered in the dream of what
had been, what might have been,
and—worst of all—what would have
to be.
        "I am companionless;
        occasionally, I see a late,
        suicidal headlight burn

244

on the highway
and vanish."
                    Companionless
except for the innumerable cells
informing him; and even they, always
thirstier for freedom, plotting
to depose him.
                    And still, intent
on directing the show, he strained
to aim the spotlight of his art
upon the cast—earth, air, water,
fire—seething deep inside.

~

May 5, 1941

Righto! Since you wish it I'll Allentown this week-end, but only if you N.Y. the following Sunday. I do have some demurs about Allentowning. My folks will catechize me as usual: "Are you studying hard?" Also, your Pop has now become a responsibility of mine. (And I of him?!) Understandably he'll likewise inquire.

You better not tire yourself, Country Club or no Country Club. I am eager though to see you in your evening gown & silver slippers. But tell me: whom are you playing for at the Club & why the evening gown?

Which reminds me of a horrible dream I—who very rarely dream!—struggled through last night. Here it is. I'm making a surprise visit to Allentown. I learn that an older relative of yours, a cousin, a violin-playing one (someone like Abram), very handsome, is staying at your home. Out walking with him & seeing me, but thinking I've not noticed you two, you hurry away. You can imagine what anguish this bit of "entertainment" caused me. If my dreams must be of such character, I gladly relinquish all rights to them. No wonder I dream so little!

May 6, 1941

High ye, My Sky-High. I've been out walking in the morning like some paradise-park even to the noise, the smells, the dirt. What a lot of sun & spring & love can do! All it needs, this Eden world, to be complete is my Eve walking beside me.

This afternoon I took my German language exam. It was encouragingly easy. In fact, I was tempted to take the French exam too. But then I thought it wiser to wait. Of course I may be unduly sanguine, but I'm fairly certain I sauntered through. Perhaps I've been overestimating the difficulty of the Ph.D. all along!

O.K.! O.K.! You win. I'll meet you in Philadelphia. My hesitancy about coming to Allentown grows out of my awareness that my folks do not share your parents' respect for Mothers' Days & would accuse me of wasting money & time just to be with you—which would be the truth. So I'll be seeing you Saturday early noon. This time though I'll sit in the car; your teacher may not approve my presence, may even consider it a disturbance to your playing—& maybe it is?

May 8, 1941

One of the principal things I dislike about writing is that when you inscribe a thought you exclude all the others. How to learn to make the one suggest all the rest? See how pregnant silence is! So when I kiss you, I usually cannot say a word because all the words are there fluttering like same-time birds inside my lips. And when you reduce (rather RAISE) me to silence, understand that I am paying you the finest, fullest love-expression a lover can to his loved one. (But DON'T take this as a hint & stop writing to me!)

Are you familiar with the measure afoot—senators,

etc., it seems, are attempting to put it into effect at once? to bar all married men from the draft, supporters of wives or not? Will you marry me in two weeks, say? I expect to appear before my board the first of June. This might—should—be argument enough for our parents. I'll give you till Saturday—one whole day!—to decide. Am I not being magnanimous & above the fray?

And speaking of being wrapt up, I'm daring Shakespeare again. The more I read him the more my wonder grows. I'm reading one of his "lesser" plays & suddenly some lines pop out at me totally incredible, impossibly magnificent, & most imaginatively accurate. I no longer chafe under his immensity as I once, preposterously, did. There are, I'd say, two levels of great writers: he's the first level & all alone, quite beyond the grasp of the others. How did God—or Whoever—let so much escape Him (or Her)?

May 13, 1941

Once more begins the lean & lonely vigil. The maid has finished cleaning my room. As she leaves she says with a flourish, "Now, Dearie, the joint is yours." I promise her promptly, "I'll get drunk in it at once!" And I really will through thoughts of you.

I still carry the fragrance of you within me; I proudly wear your kiss's inscription on my mouth.

Paleontologists have reconstructed creatures supposed to have lived in prehistoric days with as little as a shin bone. Why shouldn't I, just fresh from you, be able, with this kiss, to shape for myself your you? These markings in my mouth tell me of your lips, your cheeks, your face, your throat, your breasts, your waist, (I forgot your arms!), your belly, your thighs, your—& so on!

Some time this morning I read an excellent review of some young poets. The critic describes poetry as "the very act of loving, the profoundest sort of acceptance," exactly what I've always tried to write. As you may remember, I've spoken of poetry as making love—to you, the world, or whatever object I may be dealing with. You are my way of making love to the world. Now slowly through growth—both of my love for you & of my nature—the world must become my way of making love to you—the largest mature step you have been helping me take.

Just now Paul's dropt in when I'm near to erupting with poems, so many I have to sit still so that they don't knock up against each other & wreck ME....

It's hours later. Shortly after Paul arrived, Jack, the chap who owed me money, came in. And a fascinating session took place. The few times he's seen Jack, Paul has objected to him, principally because of Jack's pronounced homosexuality (particularly obtrusive in Paul's presence because Jack, as though sensing Paul's displeasure, deliberately flaunts it). I've often been forced on the defense for my friendship with Jack. But as I've tried to explain to Paul, I sympathize with Jack rather than contemn him.

Well, today Paul's aversion was especially patent, & Jack's mien accordingly flagrant. Except for the strain & unhappiness of it, they struck me as extremely funny—Jack a little lap dog, curled & ineffectual; Paul a big bulking bull-dog—Jack yipping, Paul growling. A falling out between them seemed inevitable & imminent. At this juncture, however, Jack withdrew to get change. When he returned, without any preliminary remarks, he threw himself into the breach: "Why do you dislike me so?" And out of that stemmed a very moving, unique conversation. Paul accused Jack of being vulgar about his homosexuality & Jack retaliated by arraigning Paul for being a smug thick business man mentally as well as physically.

I succeeded in straightening them out, however: Jack was "vulgar" or outspoken in the first place because he assumed that Paul, being my friend, must be as "tolerant" & "understanding" as I am. "I have to have some outlet for my secret occasionally," Jack protested. Furthermore, Jack acted this way in self-defence & defiance. Paul, I pointed out, on the other hand, did not object to homosexuality (as Jack thought); he was much more emancipated than that. But he did object to Jack's display of it as though it were a prize or a special achievement.

Anyway, this ironed out the crinks between them; & Jack lapsed into a most ingenuous & disarming exposition of his condition & its hardships. He spoke of his terrible unhappiness. "Most fellows my age (he's about 22) have a girl-friend they go around with steadily; they're looking forward to a happy normal homelife with a family. But what have I to look forward to but loneliness?" He doesn't want to be homosexual, wants a so-called "normal" life: "I'd give anything to get over this!" What he desires—like everyone else, but more so because of his diminutiveness & his infantile paralysis—is love & tenderness. At an early age girls, because of his size & misshapenness, seeming inaccessible, he turned his attention to handsome big boys. As soon as his fourteenth year he conceived a huge crush on an older blond boy. Slowly this desire grew.

Finally, last year, he fell in love with a virile tall handsome blond fellow. This chap was ripe for Jack because he had just come away from an unhappy love affair with a girl who jilted him. He & Jack became ardent lovers—this other chap's first case of homosexuality. For a time their relationship was as idyllic as young lovers can be. ("I lived for him; I would do anything for him; I loved to work for him; he possessed me utterly.") Jack assured us that this was the first time he had "given" himself entirely. After a period, however, the other fellow's interests began to wander: he had relationships with other homosexuals. And Jack was as frantic as a lover could be. "How would you feel," he asked, "if your wife were to go off to bed with someone else & you had to go home alone to bed & your thoughts?"

This is Jack's tragedy. As he says: he cannot love anyone but the most thoroughly virile of men (homosexuals like himself positively repel him); & such men, though they may occasionally, & usually in passing, be loving, after a time return to women. Already Jack's broken off with this fellow. Jack can have relationships with women—& has had, but he feels no slightest love for any of them. Thus he voiced surprise, & wellnigh disgust, at my recalling my excitement & delight when I was about to see you. "I've tried to understand it, but I can't." The episode was tremendously moving. And Paul most pleasingly apologized to Jack for his boorishness.

So we talked the afternoon away. It's nearly nine o'clock now, & all the poems that were waiting for "next" have just about fallen asleep inside me. They'll have to wait, I fear, till I'm more awake.

~

T & R
COMMAND PEFORMANCE

As capable a troupe of super
stars as we could hope for.
But which one, having dressed
in hand-me-downs out of a skimpy
wardrobe, is acting up?
            However
each exhorts us, we can hardly
tell them apart. Is this what
ensemble playing means?

But now
a grizzled king, tricked out
in assorted stinking body rags,
lurched roaring
across the boards,
wields a dagger athirst for blood,
the rest of the cast swept along,
subject to his madness.
And we,
less than captivated, yet a captive
audience, also play our bit part—
clobbered zany, butt, whatever—
in this command performance.

If only, our cast ever rehearsing
their roles on us, we could find
it in ourselves to appreciate
their art, their ardencies!

~

May 14, 1941

Of course, My Darling, your desire to help, to type-write my poems, pleases me. But aren't you too busy to learn now? My poems are supposed to bring joy, not fatigue! As for educating the editors, I agree. But deeply stained as they are with the present vogue of depression, misery, naysaying in writing, educating them is going to be a big job indeed! The charge of optimist, escapist, one refusing to face "reality" is bound to be brought against me.

Most people do not appreciate the truth that it's a good part of the poet's purpose to maintain joy, never more so than in a time like ours—that it's his difficult, yet certain duty to penetrate the dead (like mummy-folds) layers of greed & hate, wrapt around the human flame (WQXR is just beginning Sibelius' First Symphony. Its sounds shiver through me like cat's claws) to rescue joy & restore it, with gratitude, to the race.

Your plan excites me: an apartment of our own! But I don't care a jot for the idea of your working. Have you forgotten that we want you to go to school? I can't believe that marrying me is worth such a sacrifice on your part. Nor can I applaud the thought of your working for your Pop. As for wishful thinking, however, add my bottomless dish to yours. Maybe then the wish will become a will & from a will a what-is. Whatever you suggest I'll do.

May 15, 1941

For months I've kept several potential articles in my mental closet; every once in a while they insist on doing a Jack-in-the-box. There's my Wolfe paper. After that I've a paper to do on *Beowulf*, an idea that came from my Anglo-Saxon class. And Hopkins, of course, is still waiting for the attention he so richly deserves. Actually, I've done him a grave injustice by neglecting him as much as I have. Just by probing around in my thesis I'm positive I could mine one, maybe two articles out of it.

If these were favorably received, I'd be encouraged to revise the thesis itself into a book. Finally, I've a crop of ideas for a Shakespeare paper. So, instead of devoting the summer to grubby language study, I should return to Allentown to write these articles. Utopian, no? Quite impossible, I fear. O well, at least we can revel in our ideas.

Jack IS interesting, but from a human, rather than a psychological standpoint: he held us nearly spellbound like some profound drama. He did us the honor of letting us into his heart, a rare experience indeed, especially when the heart is of such a nature.

I quizzed him about the possibility of his falling in love with a "feminine" woman: he frowned the notion away. HE wants to be dependent, not depended on. He assured us he derives physical pleasure from sexual relations with women, but nothing more. He cannot achieve an emotional tie with them. So Oscar Wilde was a homosexual at the same time that he was a husband & the father of several children. Yes, Jack does lack self-confidence, but chiefly, I believe, because of his condition (not vice versa); he recognizes how insecure & lonely his position must make him in our present society.

May 18, 1941

Last night I tried to lose myself in an Elizabethan play, *The Duchess of Malfi*, by John Webster. It's amazing, the distance between this & one of Shakespeare's plays. Webster has great dramatic skills (a sense of theater) & at times superb, memorable, verbal verve—luxuriousness even. But he's lacking in a central energy or emotional might. Thus his characters, though they mouth & strut wonderful words, seldom get up & walk—or even move—across our hearts as Shakespeare's people do. Rarely do we imagine Webster's men & women real flesh & blood. Paper & inkbloods they are.

Why, if your Hopkins paper is due Monday, didn't you ask my assistance earlier? Receiving your request late noon Friday, I thought to airmail my thesis & my book to you. But I decided by the tone of your letter that it was not too important. If you had wished help you'd have solicited it sooner. Anyway, what can I, who required several hundred pages—& even then scarcely satisfied—to say my say about Hopkins, write you of him in this brief page! My feelings for him you certainly already know. I go on regarding him as in many respects the best of the Victorian poets after

Browning—a poet who never swerved from his, & poetry's, roots, never forgot his integrity. In his work, however restricted, he kept his balance at all costs in the very midst of ecstasy or misery. Hardheaded & seldom sentimental, he criticized, & strove in his poetry to correct, the essential shortcomings (& longcomings too!) of the romantics.

May 20, 1941

Goddam it! My Heart's Keeper, but I'm irritable, have to do everything I can to keep me in hand: a fellow whistles on the elevator & it claws at me. The reason? I'm rubbed sick waiting & waiting & waiting for you! Even Roosevelt has proclaimed a National Emergency.

And then you send me a chewed-off letter, no bigger than a cigarette butt! But me no buts! Keep it up & in a few days you'll need no more than a postage stamp to letter me. O, I know you're occupied: last days of school & what not, but couldn't you save just a bit of you for me? Here I wait impatiently for a word from you all day long. It's as if we'd been married twenty, thirty years! I'm exaggerating? All right, ten years. You're mumbling to yourself "For goodness' sake I'm going to see him in a few days! What the devil does he want?" You forget that those "few days" must be somehow lived through.

I'd be delighted to read my Hopkins paper with you. Perhaps that would get me into it enough once more to rewrite it. There are seeds of a good book in it, if only I could persuade myself to cultivate them. If any poet now deserves such attention, it's surely Hopkins. I've been keeping my fingers crossed & my eyes half closed for fear I'll wake one day & read that such a study is about to appear. As vastly influential as Hopkins has been the last 15-20 years, the time's ripe for such a work. O well!

May 21, 1941

What now, My Nearest? Isn't it enough I fed my more than lion-ravenous appetite on your birdseed of a note yesterday? Now no fare at all! Guess you want me to eat myself. Already I've done away with my fingernails & several times. Now on to the fingers!

But that's not all! About nine o'clock this morning Judy telephoned: she was deeply concerned about David, about leaving him alone. They had had some falling-out about his novel. Depressed by its rejection (& probably Judy's & my comments), he simply tore it to pieces. You can imagine my horror. Hyperhypersensitive as David is, it must have thoroughly depressed him; Judy was afraid of what his mood might do to him. So she called to beg me to phone him at once & persuade him to visit me for the day. I did so. David replied in a very scattered voice—a turmoil he tried to conceal. I feigned our sunny usualness & asked him over. He assented, "I'll come about four." "Couldn't you come sooner?" "All right, around two; but I have to hurry now." And before I could say another word, he hung up. Well, here it is after four & still no David! I've phoned his place three times with no response. I'm very worried about him. Then to top it off, YOU don't write.

Twelve o'clock I hugged my mailbox way beyond the time of the mail's distribution. Came two-thirty & I began to pace my cheesebox room, unable to go out because of waiting for David. From three o'clock I rivetted myself to my wristwatch, hung on the minute hand as though my life depended on it (like Harold Lloyd hanging from a clock hand high up in a skyscraper). At three-thirty I could curb myself no longer & burst from my room. Still no letter. But mail doesn't arrive till four o'clock! That left me with a half hour to dispatch. Talk about killing time: if only I could get my hands around that half hour's throat!

I called David again: no reply. That meant I must stay
in the hall, fidget there; if I left it, I might miss him. Thus I
pranced back & forth, back & forth. Four crawled around. I
dashed to the box. No letter. I pawed inside myself for fifteen
more minutes, then back to the box. No Renee! I rushed to
the information desk. The mail had been distributed a long
time ago! What a merry (merry?)-go-round! Dizzily I wait-
ed. Are you ill?

~

T & R
TO A SUCCESS AND OTHER FAILURES

Long you've worked and, planning,
prayed to whatever god looks after
dreams.
      This whole morning buried
In your complex schemings, at last,
Bleary-eyed, you wander round
The lake.
      A breeze is swirling
the waters into a spendthrift cast
of coins, as rustling leaves,
past reckoning, riffle by.
      Reeds,
edging the lake, over and over
whisper sibilant sounds.
      O to bank
this moment into a monument!
      An itch
flits up your arm. You flick it
off.

Plummeting into the grass,
it hardens into a scarab.
                    Dipping
a hand into the ripples, you brush
a darting rainbow trout.
                         The water,
stiffening, the fish becomes
an artifact stuck in a museum's
case.
          At last the world, turning
to you, is turning into what
you've longed for?
                         Now, dogging
your tracks, your greyhound races
round.
          Stroking, you bid "Stand!"
At once, fixed on some mammoth
chase, he heels.
                    You, astonished,
stare.
          There, far off, as if
morning-minted, a figure glitters.
Is it a statue?
                    No, she waves.
And as she speeds toward you, nears,
her every look strikes your heart.

Your daughter!
                    Should you flee?
It is too late. The reeds rasping
"Midas! Mid-ass!"

```
                    too late you see
and, blinded, see what bankruptcies
you've deftly wedged
                           between you
and the world.
```

~

May 22, 1941

Whoopie! My Sweets gifts me with a bumpercrop, a cornucopia of letters! Comes JUST at the right time too. In this sweaty desert of late May, there's no water to drink, & you send me a wellful. Somehow I'll have to contrive to spread these letters over the dullness of days till you arrive: not, as my voraciousness would have it, gobble them down at once; but store them away for the next lean days. Yet your letters are like Jupiter's present to the old people: the pot that never emptied. The more I eat the more I have!

It's a wry business how I plot to do away with these days, almost as much as we scheme in all directions to devise a way to marry. This is what I've arranged: this afternoon I'm going to a movie with the Weisses; this evening I'm visiting the Schuberts.

Oh, yes, David finally turned up. Around five o'clock, when for you & him I was beside myself, Judy called. She begged my forgiveness for David: he had simply walked off with himself—a little like KIDnapping—had roamed the streets all afternoon looking for peace & himself. When he at last remembered his visit to me he was too ashamed to telephone, so he had Judy do it. Well, the upshot of it was they asked me to spend the rest of the week with them. I'll probably stay there overnight, but no longer. David in continuous stretches is too exhausting—though you're right, we do stimulate ("inspire" as you say) each other; but you know how tiring inspiration can be!

I told Judy over the phone that the Weisses were leaving. She again suggested I stay with her & David. And if I can't come home, I may after all. I could spend most of my time in the Columbia Library; that way I'd avoid the storm & stress of David.

I looked through all my papers & found my draft-card: I needn't present myself before July first.

Yes, my not staying with the Weisses is not too bad. Their urgent presences would make study most unlikely. But being alone in the city, I'll have nothing but loneliness & scholarship. People ARE necessary.

You propose that I delay my summer-work a little to do an article. Unhappily I can't delay the language exams: they're offered only every three months. So I'll have just enough time (I hope!) to prepare—that is, if I apply myself most diligently.

As for your other idea—our marrying & living in Allentown, your teaching violin, my taking on some students, etc.—pleases me much more. But you ignore one uncomfortable little fact: our parents did NOT come to terms on my staying with the Weisses. Their treaty, you remember, was based chiefly on my Pop's insistence that I remain in N.Y. If I were in Allentown people could say, "Well, Mr. Weiss, what's happened to your wonderful son?" Remember how he paraded my report cards before one & all!

What I'd most wish to do this summer—aside from You & Poetry—is rework my Hopkins paper. If I could convince our Pops that with the investment of the summer I could finish it & then get it published, don't you think that maybe they'd listen to reason & allow us this summer?

May 27, 1941

I've been sitting out here in the neat little quadrangle before John Jay Hall—a thickly treed, heavily leafed garden-spot, watching the students, the winds, & my thoughts pass by, swaying like the leaves & the vines on the walls. A little fat brown bird, hopping sideways, almost blown over & away, hides a moment behind a tree till the danger's past. Motion is so important, especially motion contained within a well defined form, like that within the tiny compass of a kiss!

This damn uncertainty is further kindled (if you can imagine lethargy kindled!) by the Weisses: they are waiting impatiently in these their last days here like a railroad station for a train long overdue. Paul's hardly anxious to return to Minneapolis; his pride dislikes the thought of being exposed to the scorn of others for having studied so long without any material results, & he's thoroughly disturbed at the thought of any work. Renee, of course, is ebulliently eager to return to her parents & her own camping ground. Naturally their condition, working on the very fallow soil of my own, is bound to prove infectious. Thus I've my hands full just to fight off feverish aimlessness.

To italicize all this, I receive a letter from my Mom this morning, couched in her customary whiny, berating tone. As I told you, she & my Pop are beginning to wonder when your Pop's going to "help" me. Forgive me for reiterating her words; they're too much for me to carry alone:

"The way her family are spending money lately, just got a nice car, fixing the house all the time & other things, so I'm sure they can give you & should give you plenty. I know we can't do any of these things. But Abe doesn't seem to be in a hurry to give you. Just like he gives his own children. He & his wife come first as usual. Oh well what's the use of talking. It doesn't do a bit of good as usual."

The only reason I repeat this twaddle is to show you

that with such an attitude it's totally absurd for us to expect them to soften & to permit me to remain at home during the summer: I suppose I'll have to put up at the Schuberts' till I find a better room.

May 28, 1941

Sweetkins, already the goodbyes are beginning. I've gone through several with fellows who helped me talk & dine the year away—goodbyes, of course, that combined mean goodbye to a whole year of living. I'm hardly (hardly!) a sentimentalist, but as early as now I've felt an occasional twinge of nostalgia: on the whole, though we've been so much apart, the year's been good to us, hasn't it? With its assistance we HAVE come many steps nearer to each other &, I hope, many steps nearer to having each other permanently. I only pray that the next year completes (but soon!) this year's fine work.

I do have the Weisses, but they are not in a position to serve as corrective. In fact, we fatten each other's fatigue & deep uneasiness. The prospect of a summer alone here is quite distressing. Monotonous as my classes were, at least they acted as necessary interruptions to my days, gave them pivots around which I arranged my time, places to go to & to leave. And the lectures, many of them (NOT Van Doren's), by their very limpness, afforded me subject-matter for vehement complaining! In short, they helped to keep me occupied. Now my days flow by unmarked & unmoored, so smoothly & the same they seem non-existent.

Before catching the train back to New York, I had dropt into my Pop's warehouse to say goodbye. Stutzy greeted me like a long-lost brother.

~

T & R
A HANDY MAN

Who is this
sidling in
piecemeal?

A Chaplin gait,
a gap-toothed grin,
  eyes faded
  sky blue
as his overalls,
  through it all
  a dandy.

  It's Stutzy,
the handy man
in your father's
second-hand store!

  As he strips
the elegant legs
  of a battered
  antique chair,
    to your
"It's a beaut,
a work of art,"
his Pennsylvania
  Dutch accent,
  down to earth
but riding high,
  lilts like
the hilly landscape:

"Art?
See dat woman?"
With look lit-up
he elbows you,
  "Walking
all de town aroun
 she adds a shine
 to every thin."
                    His hands shape
                                  air.

"Dat's a work
    of art
    dat works."

 You two gawk
  till Father
 orders Stutzy
to get a move on.

You offer help.
   Father
shakes his head
"That's not for you,
 let Stutzy do it.
   You do
              your homework."

But hasn't Stutzy
 more to teach
than fussy Fritch
                or old maid Schwaninger?

The Public Library's
    another story:
      under cover,
  alluring misfits
        whisper
hothouse fantasies.

    Words become
  a kind of deed,
you made the best
      of them,
    you here,
  not so much
      to do,
as to be, to see,
    to say.

    Yet now,
    once more
    fumbling
  at shoe laces
and shirt buttons,
      you think
of all the things
  you didn't do:

Stutzy cuing you,
    rehearsals
for this latest skit,
  "The Old Guy
Putting on His Pants."

~

June 5, 1941

Now, My Little Coquette, I've another worry! Maybe in my frustrating your "flirtatiousness"—after all, a normal, healthy response to living & the world around you (were I to carry it to its logical extreme, I'd become jealous with you for waxing enthusiastic about a bird, a flower, sunset, morning, or even a song!)—I'm sowing the seeds of future worry: all the days to come you'll be controlling—so collecting—the many little daily flirtations you might otherwise innocently indulge, till the accumulation may grow too huge & overflow into an all-out flirtation!

Woe is me! So, drearily enough, I have to brood over the possibility that maybe I made a mistake in remarking your not too witting coquettishness. And here's an additional paradox (or simply a contradiction?): I expect—nay, require—you to possess the energy & animal spirits that prompt flirtatiousness, whether it be with men, animals, or things; yet I also expect you to curb those spirits, reserve them for home consumption—for me. I seem to be painting "My Last Duchess" all over again!

Amusing, isn't it, that you should conclude your letter with flirtatious words & I should open mine with the same. (I started the above before receiving your letter.) Apparently our thoughts, even apart, are intimates.

This afternoon, just before letter-time, I went over to the English department to find out about the Latin exam. I told the professor in charge of Latin I'd like to take the exam the end of next week (before I return to you; I intended to cram day & night for it). Alas, he's leaving this weekend & shan't return till the summer-school session, July 6. I'll have to postpone taking the exam till then.

I'm finally packed, Phew!—a big wooden book-filled crate & two cartons. Fortunately I prevailed upon the manager to let me store them till the fall. You're right about the graduation exercises: I didn't say anything about them to the

Weisses. After all, what was there to say?

I'm staying with the Schuberts for the remaining time. Please write to me there. Seems my parents (at least my Mom) are resigned, even willing, to have me in Allentown this summer. Thus she writes today, "I miss you even with all the fuss. And wish you could be in Allentown being you hate N.Y. so. Well, maybe the Karols will arrange something so you won't have to be in N.Y." (She doesn't realize I hate it for want of you.)

June 6, 1941

Boy O Boy! My Best Girl, a minute ago, when minutes were mountains to climb, I finally reached the Schuberts'. Since this was my last haul of three I loaded everything remaining into my bulging suitcase. After a while the luggage grew so burdensome I began to LEAN on its pulling!

When I at last reached the 7000th floor the Schuberts' apartment is on, David welcomed me with Herrick. And after all that wretched physicality, a delightful relaxation it was, David's poem-reading. Herrick has that gay, blithe profundity, a laughter that puts all the terribly serious people to shame. His tone—lightness, ease, fun, best of all sweetness—is what one finds at the beating heart of the greatest writing. Shakespeare, even at his most sombre & intense moments, rarely forgets this; for this is the tone of energy, exuberance, & so sublimity. Herrick wears the world—all its tribulations, as well as its happinesses—a rose in his buttonhole.

By being playful he can say anything—even the most distressing—& we gladly accept it. This is because he's shed the human light over all, made it man-&-woman liveable. With his margin of mirth Herrick can be as earnest & penetrating as he will—like a Shakespearean jester reeling off magnificences (wisdom) by cloaking them in motley: the Shakespearean fools are often THE soothsayers,

That's one paramount fleck in poetry today: the humor, the play, the gaiety has gone out of much of it; it takes itself deadly (really deadly for the poem & the reader) serious. The music & the charm have abdicated & now poems, many of them, are essentially dull & longfaced. Forgive me, My Dearest, for running on so headLONGly, especially at a time like this! But what better time for preachments against solemn preachments than one so turmoiled?

June 6, 1941

So, My Dearest, the lonely vigil (five days!) begins again.

Your "Florida-plan"! Wow it IS appealing. After all, you could have a scholarship there, & I could spend the year in study. But, much as your high school year with your grandparents was a very good year, don't you think two would make too much of a good thing for us, for them? Anyway, this WILL be one of the major things to tide me through to Friday—though we mustn't allow the sweetness of the idea to seduce us into too-high hopes. Frankly I'd just as gladly settle for Emmaus, say, or Mauch Chunk. With you these would be Florida as much as I need.

You'll certainly have to practice: you gotta get that Miami U. orchestra scholarship first!

What do you mean "My father told Grandpa there was a surprise in the store for them. And an addition to the family! And he's borrowing a baby when he goes to get them at the train. And he wants me there too?" This sounds very complicated. Is this one of your father's elaborate punny jokes?

So while you prepare, I'll get to work on Virgil, the poet I'm to be examined on, immediately. David tells me he's a good Latin student, so we intend to read Virgil together some hours every day.

June 8, 1941

What a cockeyed world are David & Judy—especially living with them! Casual breakfast words of a sudden bonfire into ripest argument. Judy sides with "practicality;" David, with the "Platonic" (ideals). Swiftly they're at each other. David is walking through the rooms, just having left a long speech he's made; suddenly he stops, lifts his finger to his lips in a loud shush, this though no one's saying a word— as though he's trying to hush the loud voices in his own head. And Judy asks me, "I bet you find it hard to live with us?" I beg her not to ask me embarrassing questions. Then she wants to know if it's easier to be with her or with David! She's in the other room as she asks this, & David whispers-implores me to say him. Living with them is pretty arduous. I hope I can last the week through! They're petulant, paper-tearing, like children. Yet I truly love them, but I'd rather not live with them. And My Strength doesn't even send me the support of a postcard! I'll have to hold them off all by myself.

Do you think you too, disillusioned & fed-up, will eventually hurl at me "You & your ideas! You think you're smarter than everybody: you're too good for this world!" or "You & your poetry, always sitting around, doing nothing. Why don't you get a job like other men?"

Thus David, noticing me write a moment ago, said, "Gee! I just realized how disgusting it is to see a grown man sitting like that, doing nothing but writing!" This out of resentment of course, because at the moment HE wasn't writing. It's fear too that "the one writing may be discovering brilliancies that really belong to ME." My Dearest, though thought-&-spirit is the only wholly unpropertied world, even here ego asserts itself, insists that ideas, images, phrases belong to it.

You're wondering, aren't you, if I'm working? Thus far not too well, though I have done some Latin. The conditions here are not exactly conducive; David's a constant interruption, just by his frenzied presence; he bursts into my thoughts, my work, like some rocket. And when he & Judy let their tongues loose at each other, the very idea of work is absurd. Of course, I'm not forgetting myself—how distractable I am as far as studying is concerned, especially when there's a coquettish poem pulling on one side of me & an aversion for the work I ought to be doing on the other. You WILL have a job on your hands keeping me at my job!

Another discouraging note: this Latin will require much more application than I had anticipated. I've grown frightfully rusty (I've been away from it four years). I had thought, most cavalierly, that I could rid myself of it in a week! I'll need all the time that the professor will be away. By then, however, I'm sure I'll be prepared.

Are you working hard, what with your violin-campaign & the dance recital soon to be? Are you still busy at your Store? Have your Pop & mine had a run-in yet about the way my Pop ran out on the terms of the agreement HE proposed? But if Abe can afford it, it seems to me, we're certain to be together much sooner. Or do you think I'm wrong?

June 9, 1941

And you ask me, "When are you going to come home, Sweetheart? Make it as soon as possible." Why the devil am I here? Why didn't I come home yesterday or the day before? At dinner Judy asked me casually why I'm in New York now that school's over: to study? To their astonishment, & my own!, I couldn't tell them. Finally, it simmered down to the opinion that I'm waiting for the arrival of your grandparents. Do you think they'll agree to your idea that I also live with them, study for my exams, while you're at Miami U.? I know your Grandpop is very fond of you. I know he drove you to high school every morning & waited patiently in the parking lot for you after orchestra. Still, will they want to put up with me too?

It's occurred to me that your Pop wished me to be in Allentown at that time because he hoped your Grandpop's words might influence my Pop into some sanity. My Pop, however, despite the aberration of his graduation-engagement gift to you (what unpredictables, irrationals &, I suppose, loveables these parents are!), I should imagine—only imagine, since he IS an unpredictable—he declared his position irrevocably last time I was home. If this is true what's to be gained by biding time till your Grandpop comes?

Why then am I here, living with these crowded & crowding Schuberts? Jumping telegraph poles, but they're difficult! Talk about hitching your wagon to a star: being with David is like hitching yourself to a falling meteor & volcano combined. Beware, My Lovest, of these hypersensitive, superintellectual, superiorly neurotic people. Yet I'm all of me fond of them, poor, harried dears!

David's more than not a gentling fantastic, sometimes utterly the child. A moment ago, for example, he noticed his name on your envelope (the c/o David Schubert): instantly he was completely possessed: "Gee, I've never seen my name like this before! Usually when letters are written to me I don't even notice my name. But here where it's about me, but not to me, I see myself for the first time." And he carried the envelope around for several minutes, staring at it, as though it were some prodigious charm. "It makes me feel so out of myself, yet here I am all of me." I'm writing as he says this, so I merely nod my head. Suddenly he demands, "Tell me, Ted, do you think I'll be recognized as a great poet some day?" I groan, "He's in again!" & return totally submerged to my letter writing. Of course, much of this is pose, but it's an obvious one, a pose to please & so occasionally most pleasing. Then he suggests, "When you get to Allentown will you have at least three of your friends write my name on an envelope & mail them to me? I want to see how those will affect me." At this he fell on the bed, "I'm exhausted!" I ask if his name has tuckered him out! It's a fantasy world he lives in, & deliberately, half the time.

Yet an hour ago he took me to task for being too "playful," not nearly "serious" enough in my writing. "I want to see you succeed," he said. "When you marry you must have Renee keep at you all the time, not to allow any funny business. That's what I've taught Judy to be with me—hard!"

Yes, Taskmistress Mine, I'm working on my Latin. This Virgil is quite a poet. It's a vast, tender, poignant world he's created.

If I can come! You bet I'll come to your dance concert. Why do you say "It would be nice if you could come"? Why can't I?

June 10, 1941

Again, My Dearest One, you propose, "Come home as early as you possibly can!" For crying out loud (can you hear it?), what do you mean by "can"? What do YOU think's detaining me here? I'm simply (simply! the wild dogs of desire, & unhappiness too, are pulling me apart) awaiting "yes, come" from you. But where will I stay? Your house? I AM getting tired of treading the air of uncertainty.

Not of course that the Schuberts are difficult to me. On the contrary. Judy is as considerate, but not so pesky, as a mother—& fair too. She doesn't favor David, even though of course she naturally and rightly does. And David manfully struggles up from the depths of his depression or quicksand thinking to bring me a smile. Poor torch of a sweet person! But who the hell (& hell it is!) wants to be even in heaven without you? Somehow it seems you are in possession of my senses (at least at their best) & also my faculties for happiness. I'm coming as soon as I can to claim them, My Best Crook.

I'll meet the same talk at home? Of course I will: jobs, money, what will people say! The same old moldy talk, ticking away these last two years, keeping time precisely where it left off. So, in a sense, I've adjusted myself to it—especially if I've the oasis, the dear shadows & coolest for this blistering heat, of you to escape to. Not that I'll ever adjust myself completely to such absurdity, roughedged as it is.

I can't blame your Pop: if there's anything he hates it's being put upon; here certainly he feels he's been taken advantage of by my Pop pulling out of the deal to share the finances. Why do people prefer unhappiness to happiness, you ask? My Dearlingest, don't you know they're willing to do almost anything, destroy any number of other people's happiness & THEMSELVES in the bargain, for their own version of "happiness"? Look how far people will go to establish their pride over others. Killing is mere flattery!

Last night David tried to impress me with the fact of the impossibility of poetry in a time like ours. Apparently he doesn't realize that I've no intention of "cashing in" on my poetry. He insisted that there's nothing worse, more miserable, or lonely than a failure in society (so he considers himself): "Had I realized years ago what I was getting into, I'd have never gone into poetry." He assured me I must work like the devil ("put everything you've got behind it") this coming year so as to secure my position in society. "You're young now, but what if a few years blight your lightness, what then?" I tried to convince him that I in no way regard my poetry as something to lean on financially & that I've every intention of devoting myself to my studies.

My Sweetling, we are aware, I believe, of everything that David & Judy have been trying their deep-friendship best to tell me. It's good, however, for our youth & eagerness to have it repeated & to consider it again. Darling, in nowise will it be easy. Only if I—as you do to me—mean more to you than anything else, dare we undertake it. I'm still confident that our love is arsenal enough to conquer the odds of this world. This is the only war I care to engage in. What say? And WHEN am I to come home?

~

T & R
Toti Del Monte

("The butterfly effect")

Amazing, that opera
singer, Toti del Monte,
able to sound every flutter
of MADAME BUTTERFLY.

But think of a butterfly,
madame or not, winging
    Toti del Monte,
all 300 pounds of her!

Well, even a butterfly
senses mountains, oceans,
cresting through its wings,
    a summer's day.

Each creature, be it
mite or fiery monster, acts
solo center to the world,
like a note in a song,

whirled about itself,
whirled about the others.
So this butterfly, beating
its wings, that set off

tempests at sea, must
find it a breeze to juggle
all those pounds of her,
TOTI DEL MONTE.

~

June 11,1941

It's all very well, My Dainty, to tell me of an ant's activity—& a very dear telling it is—but aside from its intruding in our conversation, I don't intend to allow anything, let alone an ant, to interrupt us. What in heaven's name would you have me do? Plainly, you wait for me to make the move & I wait for you! I'm sorely tempted to pack up, pull out, & home it today to your surprise & our parents' chagrin! I've decided, however, to give us all an additional day of "grace." Waiting another day & another is hardly going to resolve our situation. So, I'm willing & eager, if you are with me, to brave the lions' den; after all, my dearest creature is there among them too! But maybe in my familiar fashion I'm making a mountain out of a MOLEcule! Perhaps all that's necessary is for me to come home. And though our parents may not be too happy to see me, surely YOU'll welcome me?

What a person is this David Schubert! No matter what he does or becomes, I know there is greatness in him. Everything is high intensity with him. You suggest that desire (ambition or spirit) raises us quite beyond ourselves. Then think what it means to be a human being, & a great one! The body's simply a tiny bit of wood in the midst of an infinite fire.

Last evening David & I spent quite a few hours fitting & hanging a bamboo screen between the kitchen & the living room. With what fervent seriousness he threw himself into the doing—as though the lives of millions depended wholly on his every move. With such almost harsh flame he burns away the minutes of each day—a crackling brush fire. You can readily understand how difficult it must be to stay with him. Yet he fills me with a love only YOU've taken me beyond. The pleasure (at least temporarily) of being with him is worth the pain.

A little while ago we returned from a short crisp walk. (We take one every day.) Striding through the Brooklyn streets, more varied & distracting than a three-ring circus, we proceed in quiet, vast desert stretches, for the longest period of time, David wandering lost in some silence of his own. Suddenly one of us drops a word & conversation flares up. Thus today we discussed the isolation & essential loneliness, really a desolation almost, of the greatest greats, the Dantes and the Beethovens, the Cézannes, the Rilkes— how exiled they are by their art. By contrast with the problems this presents, the social scene (making a living, fitting into society, etc.) is nearly a digression & diversion too. Society has always been essentially the same & of little essential importance as an influence on such people who would have expressed themselves precisely no matter what era or locality. By their very flame few people can come near them, can endure them. Theirs is really a bitter victory. For like a Christ they must strip themselves of all foolish "worldly" ideas, those the mass of people live for & with, & must step forth into the nakedness of their hearts. Imagine the strain, the superhuman effort, of such living! These are, I should think, sports of nature & seldom happy or at any rate easygoing for long.

In fact, remembering my conversation with David of several days ago, I appreciate now that this is exactly what David wants to save me from. Once you are in it you've no longer very much to say; you belong to it. Did you ever see wood quarrel with its flame? All it can do is burn! What David was actually prescribing was a nice, easy society life. Society cannot have much regard for those who are hacking away at its very foundations: dullness or dailyness. Society, wishing above all to preserve itself, rejects such artists & so assures its own ruin; for as soon as respect (& love) for life, especially for the great art realizing that life, leaves the world that world dries up, becomes the ashes out of which the next will rise.

Well, My Jonquil, by the time David & I reach home, we are exhausted from our febrile talk. So I sit down to try to write the what-it-is of it to you. Anyway, by the time you hold this letter I—unless you tell me otherwise—will be holding you in my arms, reading the letter with you. Please be ready for the storm of me!

~

T & R
AT LAST - FOR DAVID

You, like a wildflower,
pressed between the thousand
pages of this new anthology,
just arrived.
        Many years,
barely a ghost, sheet-wrapped,
you wandered lost in swirling
streets.

But here, page-wise,
agile—O so wily—you at last
have fixed on your pittance
of a place.
            Settled among
a mob bickering to be heard,
you live still on the breath
you banked,
                on a reader's sighs
gusting through your lines.

~

June 15. 1941: Grandparents arrive and are met at the train station by the family; and Ted, the "surprise in store," is ceremoniously presented from behind a pillar as bridegroom-to-be. Grandparents agree happily to the Florida arrangement.

July 6, 1941: The couple are married.

~

T & R
A WEDDING

Together, like a dance,
arms brandished in its making,
two, as they seek each other out,
establish space in one another.

Away they fly, far as the inner
eye can go, on gusts the stars are
breathing, uttermost galaxies.

These two are celebrating: comet,
chaos, pulsars bursting, omnivorous
black holes.
        For them a sympathy
accommodates extremes:
                the atom,
sped in light-surpassing company,
to that epic happening all at once,
the hippopotamus:
            like planets
intercoupling—
        heavenly husbandry!

Anywhere's a place to stand.
Within the tingling of such hands
the world is nothing more or less
than a whirling mite.
          And still
each beast, each star, each gnat
twirls out inside itself its universe,
a space to sing and dance.

THE NEWS: 1939-1941

15 March 1939 – German troops move to occupy Czechoslovakia.

28 March 1939 – The Spanish Civil War ends; General Franco is in Madrid.

April 1939 – Great Britain and France guarantee armed help to Greece and Romania.

7 April 1939 – Italian troops invade Albania.

22 May 1939 – Germany and Italy sign a formal alliance.

23 August 1939 – Germany and the Soviet Union sign a non-aggression pact.

1 September 1939 – German troops invade Poland.

3 September 1939 – Great Britain and France, followed by India, Australia, South Africa and New Zealand, declare war on Germany.

5 September 1939 – Neutrality is declared by the United States.

17 September 1939 – Russian troops invade eastern Poland.

4 November 1939 – Neutrality Act of 1939 becomes law.

30 November 1939 – Russian troops invade Finland.

8 January 1940 – Food rationing begins in England and France.

12 March 1940 – Finland signs a treaty with Russia.

18 March 1940 – Hitler and Mussolini hold a conference at Brenner Pass; Italy joins the war with Germany.

9 April 1940 – German troops invade Denmark and Norway.

10 May 1940 – German troops invade the Netherlands, Belgium and Luxembourg. British Prime Minister Neville Chamberlain resigns. Winston Churchill leads the new government.

27 May 1940 – Nearly 350,000 British, French, and other allied troops are evacuated from the beaches of Dunkirk.

10 June 1940 – Norway troops surrender. Italy declares war

on England and France.

13 June 1940 – The French head of state broadcasts a final appeal for American intervention. The next day German troops enter Paris.

22 June 1940 - German troops occupy northern and western France. Collaborationist Vichy government is set up in south-eastern France.

10 July 1940 - The Battle of Britain begins.

24 August 1940 - A German plane bombs the center of London. The next day, in reprisal, the RAF attacks Berlin.

7 September 1940 - Beginning of the "Blitzkrieg" air attacks on London.

16 September 1940 - President Roosevelt signs the Selective Service bill, which begins America's first peace-time draft.

27 September 1940 - Germany, Italy, and Japan sign the Tripartite Pact in Berlin.

7 October 1940 - German troops invade Romania

28 October 1940 - Italian troops invade Greece.

5 November 1940 – Roosevelt is elected for a third term as President.

15 December 1940 -British troops begin the defeat of the Italian Army in Egypt.

10 January 1941 - The Lend-Lease bill is introduced in the U.S. Congress.

1 March 1941 - Nazi extermination camps begin full operation.

13 April 1941 - German troops capture Belgrade, Yugoslavia. Japan and the Soviet Union sign a non-aggression pact.

30 April 1941 - Germany occupies Greece.

7 May 1941 - Stalin becomes the head of the Soviet Union.

22 June 1941 - Germany declares war on the Soviet Union.

31 July 1941 –The Final Solution of the Jewish problem throughout Nazi-occupied Europe is signed by Goering.

9 August 1941 - 13 August 1941 - Atlantic Conference: President Roosevelt and British Prime Minister Churchill

meet off the coast of Newfoundland, and sign the Atlantic Charter, a document outlining the Allied war aims.

14 November 1941 – U.S. and Japanese representatives begin talks in Washington, D.C., to try to ease tensions.

7 December 1941 – Japanese aircraft launch a surprise attack on American naval forces at Pearl Harbor, Hawaii. Japan declares war on Britain, Canada, Australia and the United States

8 December 1941 – The United States declares war on Japan. US finds itself at war with both Japan and Germany. Churchill informs the British parliament that Britain is at war with Japan.

11 December 1941 – Germany and Italy declare war on the United States and sign a new military alliance with Japan.

QRL: BIOGRAPHY OF A LITTLE MAGAZINE

With the *Quarterly Review of Literature* celebrating its sixtieth and final anniversary, its editors consider this a moment to ponder *QRL's* past. We did this, roughly midway into *QRL's* life, by producing four anthologies from its earlier issues: the first, devoted to poetry; the second, to fiction; the third, to our special issues, each occupied with one major writer (Ezra Pound, Marianne Moore, Franz Kafka, Friedrich Hölderlin, Eugenio Montale, Paul Valéry, and Giacomo Leopardi), with original work plus articles on it; and the last, to general criticism.

Now, thirty years later, we feel ready to ask: what does it come to, editing a little magazine? Is it more than a paper boat launched among breakers, battleships, oil-laden freighters? Engrossing though the role may be to editors, at times, whatever their convictions, their passion of commitment, they must feel like unlicensed peddlers in a swirling street, furtively urging a cargo of precision glasses on the blind mob rushing by. In a little magazine's tiny world editors can anticipate, a few scattered readers apart, relationships with this writer and that, good will for the hospitality provided, and the indifference of the great majority.

On the other hand, one of the chief gratifying surprises of editing has been the enthusiastic response of others, even some whose work we have rejected but with comment. We have considered it one of our important functions to acknowledge any flickering promise, let alone actual flashes of talent. We soon realized the patience our reading would require: full-fledged writers often need a good number of pages to warm up; younger writers, even very promising, gifted ones, groping in the dark of their not yet explored resources, are likely to be intermittent. Lonely and uncertain as writing is, people are usually grateful for a serious response. Several have been gracious enough to say that

QRL's rejection proved more meaningful to them than some of their anonymous acceptances. Finally, there is the satisfaction of knowing we encouraged neophytes who eventually became writers of substance.

However, most people, including writers who have not experienced the throes of editing, fail to recognize more than the tip of the volcano, editing's underside, all the hidden work, this with little or no assistance: reading and choosing manuscripts; arranging an issue; proofreading; coping with printers and distributors; packing and mailing; attending to subscriptions, inquiries, complaints; and trying to maintain some regularity. Like houseplants and pets, a magazine requires fairly continuous attention. And if, for financial reasons, we had *QRL* printed abroad, first in Belgium, then in England, we had to expect additional large expenditures of time and the risk of *QRL's* going astray. Somehow, miraculously, despite the worst weather, we never lost an issue.

Attempting to awaken interest was a further trial. Of the millions presumably able to read and also the overwhelming thousands that scribble, no matter how one might appeal to them to support writing, only the tiniest percentage would respond. Writers, aside from what one might consider a desire to learn from others, often fail to realize how much their individual fates depend on the larger fate of writing itself. Sometimes one is sorely tempted to conclude that there are more writers than readers and that we have an always increasing host of writers who can write but cannot read. In short, nervous people, ones easily upset by frequent difficulties, had better not take on editing.

Yet, hardships and all, the recent past has had its share of editors who, considerable writers themselves, thought editing important: Ezra Pound, worldwide honey-making bee that he was, flitting from magazine to magazine as from movement to movement; T. S. Eliot with the *Criterion*;

Marianne Moore and her schoolmarmish scissors, snipping away for the *Dial*; William Carlos Williams in several magazines, midwifing the interests that he believed in and felt neglected. John Crowe Ransom, Allen Tate, Robert Penn Warren, and other writers made editing, at least for a time, an intrinsic part of their lives. Of course, in these writers' editing days, with the New Criticism regnant, a poet was expected to prove himself by his powers as a critic and by his command of earlier literature. How else could readers be sure they were dealing with a poet they could trust? Editing a magazine, for its concern with taste and quality, was approved as a worthy critical occupation.

But the times changed and, quite predictably, veered in a kind of vertigo to the reverse. With the Beat Poets loose in the world, celebrating instinct and spontaneity (so Allen Ginsberg urged honoring of first impressions: never revise), they overwhelmed New Criticism, and the younger poets—and not so young—dutifully followed the zigzag course of these new pied pipers, with little improvement in most of their work. A window was broken, and new air burst in, new but little of it fresh. The less a poet knows about earlier poetry and the past the likelier, many thought, he is to be original, uncontaminated by oppressive, antiquated influences.

Ezra Pound, in his total dedication to poetry, could say that great poetry must be written; it does not matter by whom. No doubt editors should strive for such an attitude. Yet sooner or later, they arrive at what are for them the crucial questions. What does editing a little magazine mean to the editors themselves? How does it affect their lives, their thinking, their own work? Usually an unpaid position, little-mag editing has to be carried on in catch-as-catch-can fashion, with other jobs, as well as one's private life, clamoring at one. A certain amount of Spartan conduct is inevitably required.

One might wonder how, in such helter-skelter, anything gets done. Yet actually one irritation, even as it prompts another, often helps. Editing plunges one into the middle of writing itself and encourages a special kind of friendship. The correspondence with many a writer at every stage of his development is exhilarating. Letter friendships, especially those based almost exclusively, at least to begin with, on literary work, can enjoy an intensity, a purity, surpassing that of more personal ones.

In fact, one of our early naivetes was our assumption that a letter intimacy amounted to an actual friendship. Several times we were shaken by the evidence of our mistake. Edith Sitwell, for instance, after an exchange that resulted in our printing a group of her poems, urged us to visit her at her ancestral Renishaw Hall. And when she came to the United States in 1948, we were invited to the reception for her at New York's Gotham Book Mart. When we met, she, her hand momentarily in ours the weight of tissue paper, hardly acknowledged us. In fairness it should be said that the party, crammed into that small, book-crowded shop, was a huge, crushing one. By the time our section of the seemingly endless line reached her she was, like a seeress, hypnotized by the giant, snake-eyed gem flashing on her own brow, clearly befuddled in her vermilion, serpentine turban.

At one point, shortly before confronting her, we experienced the same theme in another key. There, suddenly sprung into sight directly ahead of us, in tricornered hat, protoplasmically white, looking like a child's version of George Washington, stood Marianne Moore. Having recently published an all-Moore issue, we had corresponded with her a good deal. But even as we introduced ourselves, she seemed to dematerialize. Only later would our puzzlement be settled: Wallace Stevens, come to Bard College to receive an honorary degree, explained that she had been annoyed with us for keeping after her for work of her own to strengthen her issue. But Stevens assured us that he had assured her we were good people and, if we erred, it was mainly on the side of well-intended, excessive zeal for what we were doing.

However, some of the correspondence did blossom into abiding friendships and memorable occasions. Most stimulating it has been for us as people and as poets. After all, in one sense, all writing constitutes a letter to the world. What a pleasure when one's letters receive replies that encourage replies in turn. Who would not like to have corresponded with Homer and Shakespeare or Wordsworth and Whitman or, for that matter, Stevens and Williams, especially while they were producing some of their most exciting work, you possibly abetting it? And now and then the man or the woman behind the work emerged to confirm it in his or her own person.

At the University of North Carolina, where I had just begun to teach, we met the writer Warren Carrier who, with our common interests, quickly became a good friend. And when in 1943 he proposed starting a literary magazine I strongly applauded the idea. Though my chief absorption, as far as writing was concerned, was my own poetry, what harm could a nearby, amiable magazine do to that? Warren invited me to join him. I had no particular interest in being an editor, but I agreed to help and to review books of poetry. With two other North Carolinians, I became an "assistant."

For the first issue we sent out announcements, a half-sheet advertisement. In our youthful innocence we assumed that much of the world would rush to our side in gratitude and delight. Nothing quite so ecstatic happened. Yet responses did collect. Almost at once our first subscription arrived with an enthusiastic letter. However, when the first issue appeared, that subscriber, demanding his money back, excoriated us for our deception; how dared we appropriate such a hallowed English magazine's name, then print under it the nonsense we did, frivolous poems and stories, often impenetrable at that. Marianne Moore promptly replied to our modest circular: she wished us well, admired our courage and economies, and returned the announcement. She thought we might, as part of the war effort, wish to reuse it!

Some writers, like little-mag-supporting e.e. cummings, sent work at once; thereafter, contributing regularly to QRL, he helped to keep us alive through editorial doldrums. His work we supplemented with that of writers we knew, some friends, and ourselves. By the second issue, I became an editor; and D. D. Paige, also teaching in the English Department and eventually to edit Pound's letters, became an assistant. Aside from local lights the magazine began to sport names like Henry Miller, Mark Van Doren, Harry Levin, Thomas Merton, Ramon J. Sender.

The third issue featured work by Wallace Stevens. From then on we maintained a relationship with him, at times intermittent but most reassuring to us, till near his death. This relationship involved several meetings, many letters, and poems and essays in QRL. He, like cummings and Williams, rarely turned away a literary magazine's request, no matter how little or obscure. Of course, at that time magazines interested in modernist poetry were not too abundant.

We also ran articles by critics like Edouard Roditi and Edwin Berry Burgum, a considerable range from the aesthetic to the Marxist. But though in its first years QRL was a fairly normal literary magazine, like other college-based periodicals sharing out its space among poetry, fiction, articles, and reviews, it did reserve pride of place for poetry and fiction. As we said in QRL's 30th Anniversary Poetry Retrospective, "Despite its university location it was very much a private enterprise. And unlike its fellow periodicals it was set on stimulation and innovation rather than on consolidation, evaluation, and scholarly taste-making." In part, probably because of their university origin, most magazines stressed the historical and the prevailing tone was academic. Supported in the main by scholarly sources and exposed to the judgment of boards, such magazines could not enjoy our freedom (or the same degree of poverty!).

The second issue included the first half of my two-part article on Yvor Winters and his *The Anatomy of Nonsense*. Meant initially to be a normal review, the article turned into a counterattack; aroused by Winters' highhandedness with Henry Adams, William Butler Yeats, Wallace Stevens, T. S. Eliot, Ezra Pound, and others, I felt called on to pay Winters back in kind. The article prompted a response as vigorous as that for anything I have published since, and not alone from the writers Winters had mauled, but also from many who resented his berserker conduct as a critic.

Shortly after this exchange, Carrier joined the English Ambulance Corps (World War II had begun), and I, quite bewildered, was left holding the little magazine. Renée, innocent of what she was getting into, offered to assist me. I, equally unaware of the vows we were taking, as though entering a strict religious order, fatefully accepted. Alone, I, like a well-behaved little magazine-editor, would have ended *QRL* at once. Renée, on the contrary, through her many unusual skills, ensured our being committed, for much of the rest of our lives, to an imperious issue that would never grow up. Thus the first part of volume two came out under my name as editor and Renée as managing editor (for all the work she did, she soon became a co-editor), with Ernest Morwitz, once a member of the Stefan George circle, as our "Foreign Advisor."

As though to signalize this change, we moved, lock, stock, and mag, to New Haven where I became an instructor in the English Department at Yale University. However, before his departure Warren and I had planned an all-European issue. And volume two, number one, contained translations of San Juan de la Cruz, Rafael Alberti, Friedrich

Hölderlin, Stefan George, Tristan Corbière, Arthur Rimbaud, and Yvan Goll, as well as articles and reviews on Rainer Maria Rilke, Corbière, André Malraux, Saint-John Perse, Thomas Mann, and the Comte de Lautréamont. The issue amply reflected our determination to do what we could to break down parochialism and to make good-literature-at-large available. Despite the valiant efforts of Pound and others, the United States continued to be as provincal as all the other large countries. However, that did not mean much more neglect than that accorded the best domestic products!

With volume two, number two, we formed another relationship most important to us. William Carlos Williams became a frequent contributor and correspondent, writing to us sometimes two or three times in a week. In that issue we featured "The Words Lying Idle," the fifteen poems that constituted Williams' poetic output for the past year. On 23 September 1944 he wrote, "Since you intend to feature me I'll give you everything I've got, to put it that way." Thereafter, Williams became a kind of vibrant, overseeing presence for *QRL*. He could write on 28 September, "I feel very grateful to you for your support, you'd be surprised how isolated one feels at times and how many small irritations one must face to keep writing. I was sixty-one a few days ago, let's hope that in the next twenty years I shall find more ease." We were indeed "surprised." What sentiments could be more heartening to young, unknown writers like ourselves?

Beyond Williams' suite, in that issue I reviewed, among others, Williams' *The Wedge*. I stressed his (like Moore and Stevens) remaining in this country to fight it out for poetry on home ground. More than not, however, they were inward expatriates; working in obscurity, they hardly needed to flee to Europe like Pound, Eliot, and other American writers. For us, as soon for many others, Williams was a shining example. In his life and his work, so passionately carried on, he proved that America, even in its most impoverished and seemingly dehumanized aspects, looked at honestly, lovingly, still could sustain and comprise poetry. Looked at also with legitimate anger.

At this time, and for months after, Williams referred to the finishing of *Paterson I* and complained of delays, printing failures, etc. On 22 August he wrote about *QRL's* new issue with his usual enthusiasm, but as for his own part in it: "I for myself want to go bury my head in a manure heap. It may be the times or it may be something else but I come away from a look at myself as a writer profoundly depressed. . . .Oh well, I'm low and I know I'm low. I waken, like all old men or old shits at around 2 a.m. and lie there and ponder the world and my fly speck of a place in it and there I lie and look up into the dark and it's like the inside of a sewer drain. I see nothing good but only my own weaknesses and unpreparedness. The first light of dawn does cheer me, I get up and go to work, only they [then] do I feel lighthearted but the work is too hard and I cannot always do it to my own satisfaction. Congratulations on your issue—it is human, it is faulty but it's enthusiastic and in spite of that emanation of the pit Winters it is honest, beautifully honest, unpretentious and non-sectional; local."

His depression continued. On 8 September he wrote: "I hate to say this—but I dread the appearance of my Paterson (lst part, of 4) this fall after seeing the galleys. It is just dirty sand when I thought I was building at least a rock shelter. I'm ashamed and yet can't quite bring myself to suppress it. I am not kidding, I am sick over the matter. And yet, bad as it all is, there is something there I want to say. If I quash the whole now I'll never do it again. So I am risking a fiasco for that poor lost thing. And for the sake of common honesty DON'T say what isn't true of the thing if and when it gets into your hands. Don't try to be a friend for if I detect it we're through." Fortunately, *Paterson I's* reception was splendid; and with the help of enthusiastic reviews by Robert Lowell, Randall Jarrell, and others, Williams began to receive the general attention and praise till then stinted him.

With volume two, number three, we inaugurated a project we had long contemplated: the giving over of an entire issue to one writer, usually a foreign one we believed neglected or inadequately understood. We agreed with Pound that one of the primary functions of a literary magazine was the melting of national boundaries, the presenting of first-rate work lost to most of us for the alien country of a foreign language or a distant age. We knew how enriching such transplanting could be. Had we and our generation not benefited tremendously from English translations of Rainer Maria Rilke, Federico García Lorca, the French Symbolists? Thus through our friendship with Angel Flores we conceived an all-Kafka issue, one that would print not only examples of his work never before (or newly) translated, ranging through his life as a writer, but also articles on his work and, wherever possible, on his particular pieces in the issue. Such weaving back and forth gave, we felt, an integrity to the issue and in the interplay made it many times richer.

While the issue developed, my correspondence with Kenneth Rexroth flared like a straw fire. Lusty, formidably learned, flailing out, he often was a happy combination of abuse and warmth. He found some merit in *QRL*, but excoriated our having anything to do with the, as he saw it, altogether decayed world of the academic. We must in no way resemble that world's magazines. He was especially upset at our announcement of the Kafka issue. And when it appeared he wrote, "For God's sake get out of that Kafka-Kierkegaard-Henry James-Rilke-Proust cul de sac full of castrated Phi Beta Kappas—it is not for you."

Our third volume opened with a selection from the unpublished poetry of David Schubert, a writer of great originality much too little known. He had died in April 1946, the year of the issue. We had met in 1938 when we both began graduate work in English at Columbia University. Though he was only a few years older, he was in life as in letters many years ahead of me. And our friendship greatly accelerated my interest and development in poetry. Williams, with his habitual, spontaneous warmth and no doubt recognizing a younger brother-in-arms, responded at once: "Many thanks for the Schubert poems, they are first rate more than that, far more. They are among the few poems I read that belong in the new anthology. . . . There is, you know, a physically new poetry which almost no one as yet has sensed. Schubert is a nova in that sky. I hope I am not using hyperbole to excess. You know how it is when someone opens a window on a stuffy room."

Meantime, in that same issue, I reviewed Randall Jarrell's second volume of poems, *Little Friend, Little Friend,* as well as Ernest Morwitz and Olga Marx's *Poems of Alcman, Sappho, Ibycus.* Jarrell's individual poems, when I read them for the first time in magazines, puzzled me; but in a book they impressed me with a wholeness, a reciprocal strength, I was hardly prepared for. My review emphasized that feeling. And some time after Jarrell wrote: "Would you care to use these poems in your magazine? I've meant to express, in some way, my pleasure at your review of *Little Friend, Little Friend*, and I can't think of any other way except to send some poems. I hope you get to review my new book this winter—I thought your *Little Friend* review extremely accurate about what the poems say, and I was particularly pleased with the remarks mixed in the Sappho part; I don't have the regular modernist-poet attitude toward ordinary people, and am extremely glad to have that said." More letters and poems followed, and several meetings, fiercely argumentative as well as most memorably pleasant. Eventually Bard College awarded him, as it had Williams and Stevens, an honorary degree in literature.

Having moved to Bard College in *QRL's* fifth year, with Bard's strong emphasis on the arts and their practice, we felt it time to change our format accordingly. Disturbed by the growing assumption that this period was a non-creative one, best devoted to criticism, we considered it of prime urgency to do what we could to encourage creative work, especially among young writers. We set out, therefore, to devote our pages to poetry, fiction, and drama. Stevens greeted the change, though he recognized the difficulties it entailed, but several writers demurred. Marianne Moore, for instance, admitted that she often preferred articles to poems, found the former more interesting and useful. But we recognized that she was a writer who looted all kinds of prose to furnish her poems with odd and revelatory details.

The change generated additional excitements in our involvement with the work of new, most promising young writers like James Merrill, John Gardner, James Dickey, Jean Garrigue, Robert Coover, Donald Finkel, Joyce Carol Oates, Denise Levertov, David Galler, Hayden Carruth, Arthur Gregor, Gil Orlovitz, Linda Pastan, George P. Elliott, W. S. Merwin, Roger Hecht, James Wright, Harvey Shapiro, Leonard Nathan, and a host of others. The exchange of letters with many of these and the witnessing of their development were as stimulating as they were pleasurable. If we had been bolstered by older, more experienced, established writers to begin with, now we were grateful for and encouraged by the support of writers just coming on. We felt, happily enough, the labors notwithstanding, indeed like pilots of a paper boat miraculously able to accommodate a full roster of fascinating passengers at their entertaining best and improving as the cruise continued.

We are amused to observe, if somewhat wryly, that soon after, with the bursting forth on the scene of the Beat Poets and outrageous happenings in the world at large, New

Criticism was unseated, in poetry and criticism alike. Eventually, as though in revenge on New Criticism, but on this new, would-be intuitive, if not mindless poetry as well, the criticism that emerged abroad and in this country began to express its impatience with literature altogether and proposed that criticism was at least as valuable as poetry and fiction.

QRL's position seemed more important and precarious than ever. Now the sociologizing, psychologizing, philosophizing, politicizing of literature and culture, certainly the cerebrating, was on full blast. With woeful attempts to find an opaque, ponderous, "professional" jargon, equal to that of science, one might look back wistfully, not to say nostalgically, at the gentler, innocent-seeming days of New Criticism when a poem, however much it might be entered into, even overrun, did not, like Achilles' armor borrowed by Patroclus, disappear altogether in the tug-of-war among furiously rival contenders.

Certainly under the assault of the newer new criticism, the author, too much the text's authority, disappeared also; at least so these new new critics hoped and did their dubious best to bring it about. Now no genuine poet would gainsay the overall importance of language, but poets know it is the extent of their responsive and responsible use of the language, even as it writes much of the poem, and so too what they add of themselves, that determines their merit.

Reasonable midwives are most urgently needed: essays, reviews, magazines that will attend to the poetry and the fiction themselves so that they and their writers be born again strengthened and deepened by the struggle. At this point I am amused to think how much—only partially realized, I admit, by its editors—QRL has been engaged. One emergent occasion may serve to illustrate this involvement. I have mentioned how important to us have been our special issues devoted to a single writer. The more the writer is deeply embedded in his own language, the harder usually it is to reach him or her. So Hölderlin had long tantalized us. We knew his reputation as a great German lyric poet. For our own pleasure and edification as well as for our readers, we decided to undertake a Hölderin issue.

Around that time Mary McCarthy, a former professor at Bard College, wrote to the chairman of its Language and Literature Division to inform him that she had recently met a very charming, formidably learned, young man named Paul DeMan, just right for Bard. She hoped we would consider him for our faculty. We did and hired him to replace a faculty member off on a year's sabbatical. He quickly proved to be a great favorite of the students. But, alas, with the regular member of the faculty returned, there was no opening available. Fairly desperate, DeMan and his new wife, a Bard student, picked fruit in the Hudson Valley until he fell and sustained considerable injuries.

They removed to Boston, his wife's hometown. During that time Renée and I had become close friends of the couple. We visited them in Boston where, to our consternation, we learned that he was making a most meager living by teaching at a Berlitz school. Knowing his passivity in such matters, I suspected his whole life could go by at Berlitz. I urged him as strongly as I could to call on Professor Harry Levin, a friend of ours (after the Winters fracas, Levin invited Renée and me to Harvard University, and we stayed in touch) and an important figure in the humanities at Harvard. I wrote to Harry about my friend. Harry invited him to a meeting that resulted in a fellowship at Harvard and the beginning of a remarkable academic career. Long afterward Renée and I were amused to suggest to ourselves that, in a sense, we had midwived Deconstruction, at least in the United States.

There is a further strand to be traced in this network. When we decided to prepare a Friedrich Hölderin issue, we had some feeling of the richness of our situation. Heinrich Blücher, the husband of Hannah Arendt, was a brilliant, major presence at Bard with whom I taught and with whom I became good friends. Given their intense love of poetry, how could we not call on them for help? They were delighted and made many fruitful suggestions. At this time DeMan was also at Bard. He offered to translate Martin Heidegger's seminal essay on Hölderlin.

Other gifts of time and place also fell to our lot. Having heard a great deal about Eugenio Montale and having at Bard the Dante specialist Irma Brandeis, a dear friend and a friend of Montale years ago, we asked her to commandeer an issue devoted to his work. She was pleased to do so, and she collected a distinguished lot of translators and critics for the project. Only much later did we discover that she did indeed know Montale. She had been his inamorata, the prominent Clizia of his poems.

In 1966 I was invited to be writer-in-residence at Princeton for the year. At the end of the time I was asked to stay as a member of the Writing Program and the English Department. Once again we moved with *QRL* in tow. And the move brought about a basic alteration in our lives, especially as it involved *QRL*. Having been a reader for the Wesleyan University Press's Poetry Series and later, inaugurating and serving as the first editor of the Princeton University's Poetry Series, I was impressed by the large number of good books to be considered, many more than either press felt able to accept. Such meagerness was more or less universal on the part of publishers.

In 1978 Renée and I, brooding over this distressing situation, decided to do what we could to ease it. Renée, a natural recycler, suggested we turn all our pages over to books of poetry, an unusual idea for a magazine. In fact, by establishing an open competition and maintaining our subscription format, once a year we could publish five complete books under one cover and award each poet a prize (it soon became one thousand dollars). This arrangement made it possible to sell each issue for twelve dollars, or by subscription two volumes (usually ten books) for twenty dollars. The volumes were also put out in cloth editions for libraries and interested readers.

Now, with seventy-four books of poetry behind us, and twenty-two years, some observations seem in order. We look back with pleasure and pride at the number of first books we have published that initiated substanial careers: books as good as Brian Swann's *Living Time*; Reginald Gibbon's *Roofs, Voices, Roads*; Mairi MacInnes's *Herring, Oatmeal, Milk and Salt*; Jane Hirshfield's *Alaya*; Christopher Bursk's *Little Harbor*; Anne Carson's *Canicula di Anna*; B. H. Fairchild's *Local Knowledge*. We also published English translations of such distinguished foreign poets as Wislawa Szymborska (Poland), much later a Nobel Prize winner; Lars Gustafsson (Sweden), Rafael Alberti (Spain), Dannie Abse (Wales), Eugénio de Andrade (Portugal), Yves Bonnefoy (France), Fadhil Al-Azzawi (Iraq), Dan Pagis (Israel), and Maria Banus (Romania). We have done our best to erase national linguistic boundaries. As Pound said, we don't study French physics, Romanian mathematics; then why stress American or English poetry? Wherever great poetry breaks out that's where we should strive to be.

In *QRL*'s fiftieth year we decided to celebrate the occasion with an anthology comprising new work, whenever possible, poems in suites by the poets whose books we had published. And, to acknowledge the poets we presented in our first volumes, many of them now permanent figures in our poetry's history, we included a selection from their previously printed *QRL* work. This anthology we hoped would serve to illustrate not only our past poets but also what remarkable productivity our recent poetry has come to and how many impressively accomplished singing birds have somehow, attended to or not, prospered among us.

The recent surge of interest and broadening involvement in poetry in college writing programs, in summer workshops, and even on television, is an exhilarating change, as is the richly expanded poetry book publication mainly by university and small presses. The Internet, with its being everywhere at once, may help to wipe out artificial boundaries and restore something like the powerful presence, precious in its very ephemerality, of the ancient bard.

Finally and most emphatically, we are eager to express our gratitude to our contributors for their generosity. Private venture that *QRL* has been, a barely supportable portable, wherever we have gone it has trundled after. In Wallace Stevens' words, "You carry the QUARTERLY REVIEW around with you the way a Chinaman carries his bird." An itinerant nest for migratory birds, it has enjoyed several very different roosting places. Housed at present in Princeton University's Program in Creative Writing at 185 Nassau Street, *QRL* continues to be an independent publication.

However, it has enjoyed many helpful favors from the University and the Program and has been grateful for choice manuscripts from members of the faculty: Edmund Keeley, Robert Fagles, Clarence Brown, Joyce Carol Oates, and James Richardson are prominent among those who have graced *QRL*'s pages. And we want to thank the host of Princeton University students, volunteers, and work-study undergraduates and graduates. They were, in their persons and their assistance, an absolute necessity and a tremendous pleasure for *QRL* and its editors. And many remain abiding, corresponding relationships. Without them *QRL* would have disappeared long ago. Such relationships alone have more than justified *QRL*'s existence.

ABOUT THE AUTHORS

Theodore Weiss (1916-2003) was the author of: *The Catch* (Twayne, 1951); *Outlanders* (Macmillan, 1960); *The Medium* (Macmillan, 1965); *The Last Day and the First* (Macmillan, 1968); *The World Before Us* (Macmillan, 1970);*The Breath of Clowns and Kings, Shakespeare's Early Comedies and Histories* (Atheneum and Chatto & Windus, 1971); *Fireweeds* (Macmillan, 1976);*Views and Spectacles* (Chatto & Windus, 1978); *Recoveries* (Macmillan, 1982); *The Man from Porlock, Selected Essays* (Princeton University Press, 1982); *A Slow Fuse* (Macmillan, 1984); *From Princeton One Autumn Afternoon* (Macmillan, 1987); *Selected Poems* (Tri-Quarterly Books, 1995); *A Sum of Destructions* (Louisiana State University, 1996). He was also the recipient of a PEN "Lifetime Achievement Award" which he shared with Renée, a Guggenheim Fellowship, a Brandeis award and the Shelley Memorial Award.

Renée Weiss was manager and later co-editor with Ted of *QRL*. She is a violinist who has played with: the Miami University Symphony Orchestra, North Carolina State Symphony, Oxford University Symphony, Hudson Valley Philharmonic, Woodstock String Quartet, and the Princeton Chamber Orchestra. She studied Dance at Connecticut Summer School with Martha Graham and José Limon. She studied violin with Sascha Jacobinoff, Emile Hauser, Boris Koutzen, Ivan Galamian, and taught kindergarten at the Tivoli Public School. She is the author of three children's books—*To Win a Race*, *A Paper Zoo*, and *The Bird from the Sea*—and a biography: *David Schubert: Works & Days*. From 1990-2003, she co-authored the Duo poems and read and taught with Ted.

T&R Poems

POSTSCRIPT
A Last Visit with Theodore Weiss

I went to visit Ted and Renée in early April of 2003. At eighty-six, Ted was one of the very last survivors of his remarkable poetic generation, that included David Schubert and Robert Lowell. He had lived through many years of Parkinsons that he had valiantly resisted, and without losing his mental agility; but on this afternoon I saw that physically he had declined very sharply since I had visited him in December, 2002. He was one of those who had received life-long and profound pleasure from poetry, music, the visual arts, the seasons, and above all human affiliation—he had spoken from time to time, over the many years I have known him, of having been struck and inspired by the relationship between Hannah Arendt and Heinrich Blücher, friends of his early career. In conversation he told of imponderable, tragic or joyous turns in the lives of persons he had known. His own marriage to Renée was perhaps the most strikingly attuned relationship between partners that I have ever seen. Over the years of his writing, editing, reviewing and making a conversation—whether viva voce or in correspondence—with many other extraordinary poets, Ted had had a very rich life of both artistic accomplishment and generosity toward others. He was a master of an existential self-situating that laments with clear eyes the sorry conditions of the world and the miserable behavior of those who become the stewards of power, and he spoke holding no illusions about the national and world history that his lifetime had spanned, but I knew that he would not utter any personal valedictory complaint. Indeed, I expected him to make some characteristically gentle remonstrance against giving way to despair or grief.

On the telephone in February, Ted had said that he had been trying to write but was seeing on the blank page shimmering lines that seemed to him tiny dancing figures. He said this not with sadness but with a somewhat gentle curiosity. Then he told me of having gone outside the day before, after a snowfall, of having seen and heard what seemed "thousands of birds," starlings, he thought, all taking flight at once from bare trees and creating a din of wings and shrieking. I admired the way Ted, thoroughly alive in the present, and without religion or a belief in an afterlife, did not take these birds to be a symbol of his own foreboding, or of death itself. He did not believe in whatever it was that would supposedly supply such a symbol. Instead he freely chose to ponder the snow and the birds in his very charac-teristic mood of what Plato called wonder, and he refrained, also as a matter of preserving his own imaginative freedom, from assigning the birds and snow any meaning. That would take time, but recently he had come to feel that he had stopped writing poems.

Ted had always been one of the great conversational-ists, and on this day in April—perhaps the last day on which, despite being very thin and weak, scarcely able to move at all, he was speaking to visitors—he was still able to say a few words and to make them memorable. The day, although chilly, was sunlit. Renée had put Ted in a hospital bed in the small room that she had used for many years as her home office for The Quarterly Review of Literature, and which had often served as a bedroom for overnight guests. It seemed to me that Ted was now the temporary guest, not the host, of the living household. A hospice aide, assisting Renée in caring for Ted, left the house not long after I arrived. All afternoon, sunlight poured through the large casement win-dows. Ted's room was warm. I sat off and on for a few hours in a chair beside his bed as he slept and woke and slept. Several times Renée came into the room, to see how Ted felt, to ask if he wanted something. He seemed not to want anything, unless it was a little company, and on this afternoon, a little bit to eat. I saw that he especially enjoyed, as he had all his life, chocolate.

I went to Ted's study which I had first seen when I was about twenty, and which I had thought of for most of my life as one of the unmistakable locations of the life of poetry. It had been a place not only of Ted's writing but also of the arriving poems that were (or were not) going to be published in issues of The Quarterly Review of Literature, the poems in other literary magazines sent to Ted and Renée, and the poems that had already been written elsewhere or would be written by the poets who sat talking here, in this comfortable room, with Ted-and-Renée. On this day I remembered a moment in one of Ted's poems: "Have you ever thought that these might be the last days?" a door-to-door Jehovah's Witness asks the poet, and he answers, "Yes, I have."

From the shelves of poetry I took down two old and now fragile paperback collections—Blake and Hopkins, two of Ted's earliest favorites—and I returned to the bedside and read aloud to Ted a few of their short poems. Aloud I mused over them a little, myself, if only to give us both the sense, despite how seldom Ted spoke and how softly, that we were conversing as we had done before. I remembered aloud how it had been Ted who had first set me reading these two poets, when I was a freshman in college at Princeton, in his poetry writing workshop—he had given me the first of the man-made stars by which I would set or correct my own course many times, over the years. Two or three times Ted said a few words softly but intelligibly. I thought: Even in his last days, he is still himself with his almost always surprising way of looking at things. But what he said has disappeared from my memory. What I seem to recall is something about Blake's courage, the extraordinary clarity of his integration of both the psychical and the outward in his images—something about how Hopkins had a touch of Sisyphus in him.

When I had to leave to catch a plane, and I felt that drenching weakness of the moment of a final good-bye, I leaned down to Ted, taking his hands in mine, and said what I could say to him. Ted startled me and Renée, too, for she was on the other side of the bed, whispering, "I need to be like everybody else and admit my defeat, and so be equal to it." I could respond only by saying a loving good-bye. "No grand speeches," he cautioned. Not knowing whether he meant that I should not try to offer such an utterance, or that he did not intend to do so, I said, "No, but you've just said something marvelous, as I should have expected." Renée said, "you're still up to being yourself." So he was, for that moment, but he did not reply.

Reginald Gibbons
Evanston, Illinois, March 2004.